UNVE
JAZE

'Compelling, ambitious, beautifully written
and about so much more than cricket.'
TIM WIGMORE, *THE TELEGRAPH* AND AUTHOR
OF THE MULTIPLE AWARD-WINNING *CRICKET 2.0*

'Profound, poignant and important – this was a story that had to be told.'
LAWRENCE BOOTH, *WISDEN*

'A history of women's cricket in Pakistan is not only long overdue, it is a grand story
in its own right. It is a tale of bravery and audacity, and of giant personalities who
simply refused to maintain the status quo. This is an essential work.'
OSMAN SAMIUDDIN, AUTHOR OF
THE UNQUIET ONES: A HISTORY OF PAKISTAN CRICKET

'Aayush Puthran movingly and eloquently tells the stories of the Pakistani
women who have had to fight to play the sport they love, in the face of
extraordinary societal challenges. Read it, weep for the lost
opportunities and share in hope for the future.'
RAF NICHOLSON, JOURNALIST AND WOMEN'S CRICKET HISTORIAN

'A forensically researched history covering the rollercoaster ride of the Pakistan
women striving to embrace the game they love against all the odds. From
the doom and gloom of the religious fundamentalism of the 1990s to the
administration wrangles of the 21st century, *Unveiling Jazbaa* perfectly
captures the shining stars of their plight. A story that must be told.'
ISABELLE DUNCAN, FORMER MCC CRICKETER AND AUTHOR
OF *SKIRTING THE BOUNDARY: A HISTORY OF WOMEN'S CRICKET*

'A remarkable story, told with empathy and respect, *Unveiling Jazbaa* serves
as a celebration of Pakistan women's cricket – of personal journeys as well
as those of the collective, in the context of society and politics, without
hiding the warts, the stumbling blocks and the petty jealousies.'
KARUNYA KESHAV, JOURNALIST AND AUTHOR OF
THE FIRE BURNS BLUE: A HISTORY OF WOMEN'S CRICKET IN INDIA

'A fascinating re-telling of the highs and lows of Pakistani
women's cricket. A must-read for any lovers of the sport.'
AATIF NAWAZ, BBC TMS CRICKET COMMENTATOR

'What a fantastic insight into the previously uncharted world of women's sport in Pakistan. Aayush has married expressive detail with an engaging storytelling approach to produce this powerful and compelling read . . . For the past 25 years, I have struggled to explain what playing cricket is like for the women of Pakistan. In this book, Aayush not only brings to life the on-field drama of the game but more importantly, he tells the stories of the courage, resilience and drive of the remarkable women who wanted so much to play cricket for their country. A comprehensive and compelling account of the indomitable sisters who would not give up their dreams in the face of political and cultural resistance, personal threats and hardships, carried through to the teams of today who stand on their shoulders and continue their vision. It was a privilege to be there at the start.'

JODIE DAVIS, WOMEN'S NATIONAL COACH
– FIRST PAKISTAN WORLD CUP TEAM, 1997

'From running an obstacle race to worldwide recognition, Aayush traverses a difficult ground in charting the journey. The story of Pakistan women's cricket comes wrapped in a labour of love, from India.'

AFIA SALAM, PAKISTAN'S FIRST FEMALE CRICKET JOURNALIST

'While the history of men's cricket has long been documented, stories of the women's game, especially in the subcontinent, are only starting to be unearthed and examined and this is an important contribution to the archive. Aayush Puthran does an exceptional job of juxtaposing the socio-political situation in Pakistan with the development of women's cricket. He treats the game with the seriousness it deserves, while not losing a lightness of touch.'

FIRDOSE MOONDA, ESPNCRICINFO

'A fascinating collection of incidents and experiences of these women – full of striking events. An in-depth discovery and revelation of the history of Pakistani female cricketers and of the sport in a country where women's sports have just started taking shape . . . hooked on to it from the word go. A must read!'

EBBA QURESHI, FOUNDER FEMGAMES

First Published by Westland Sport, an imprint of Westland Books, a division of Nasadiya Technologies Private Limited, in 2022

No. 269/2B, First Floor, 'Irai Arul', Vimalraj Street, Nethaji Nagar, Allappakkam Main Road, Maduravoyal, Chennai 600095

Westland Sport, the Westland Sport logo, Westland Books and the Westland Books logo are the trademarks of Nasadiya Technologies Private Limited, or its affiliates.

ISBN: 9789395073639

10 9 8 7 6 5 4 3 2 1

Designed and typeset by Polaris Publishing, Edinburgh

Printed at Parksons Graphics Pvt. Ltd,

UNVEILING
JAZBAA

A HISTORY OF PAKISTAN WOMEN'S CRICKET

AAYUSH PUTHRAN

SPORT

CONTENTS

To my family

Jazbaa

Definition: spirit, feeling, passion, desire, sentiment, emotion

ABBREVIATIONS

* Not Out
BBC British Broadcasting Corporation
BCCI Board of Control for Cricket in India
BCCP Board of Control for Cricket in Pakistan
DLS Duckworth–Lewis–Stern method
ICC International Cricket Council
INR Indian rupees (currency)
IWCC International Women's Cricket Council
lbw leg before wicket
MCC Marylebone Cricket Club
MMA Muttahida Majlis–e–Amal
OCA Olympic Council of Asia
ODI One Day International
PCB Pakistan Cricket Board
PIA Pakistan International Airlines
PKR Pakistani rupees (currency)
PML(N) Pakistan Muslim League (Nawaz)
PML(Q) Pakistan Muslim League (Quaid-i-Azam)
PWCA Pakistan Women's Cricket Association
PWCCA Pakistan Women's Cricket Control Association
T20 Twenty20 cricket
T20I Twenty20 International
UAE United Arab Emirates
WBBL Women's Big Bash League
ZTBL Zarai Taraqiati Bank Limited

AUTHOR'S NOTE

❖ The Pakistan women's team played its first-ever international match on 28 January 1997. This book primarily documents their first 25-year journey in international cricket. As a result, all stories, statistics and photos (except that of Bismah Maroof with her daughter, Fatima) in this book only go to 27 January 2022.

❖ Since the documented history of Pakistan women's cricket has been limited, the story has had to rely heavily on oral testimony. Almost all incidents mentioned in the book, except those involving the personal stories of the lives of the cricketers, have been confirmed by multiple individuals before being included. In cases where there are alternate views, all positions regarding those specific incidents have been placed on record or not taken into consideration. All views on the social, political and cricketing state of Pakistan are based on the interviews conducted and on documented evidence.

❖ Ayesha Ashar, Bushra Aitzaz, Najam Sethi, Nazia Nazir, Sabih Azhar, Sajjida Shah, Qanita Jalil, Urooj Mumtaz and Wasim Khan were approached for this input but were unavailable for comment. As a result, any mention of them either does not include their version of events or has been taken from secondary sources (quotes and interviews with various news publications, interviews with other individuals, etc.).

❖ Shahryar Khan was also approached, but on the advice of his wife, Minoo Khan, the version of events during his tenure as

PCB chair was taken from Shamsa Hashmi. Ali Khan, Shahryar's son, was also interviewed for this book.

❖ asiancricket.org, cricbuzz.com, cricketarchive.com, espncricinfo.com and pcb.com.pk have been referred to for scorecards.

❖ There have been multiple instances of conflict between the records and the version of events from the players. For example: Nain Abidi has been credited for picking up the wicket of Britney Cooper in the third T20I against the West Indies in Providence in 2011. However, she claims she has never taken an international wicket. Similarly, Sania Khan has been credited as captain in two matches (against Ireland and South Africa) at the 2010 ICC Women's T20 Cricket Challenge. However, a number of players who were part of the team claim that Sana Mir walked out to do the toss and led the team in those games before adding that Sania has never led Pakistan. Even Sadia Butt has been noted as the captain instead of Shaiza Khan in the 2003 IWCC Trophy match against Scotland. In such cases, where there are undisputed claims by multiple players which do not reflect in the scorecard accordingly, the players' versions have been taken into account considering scope for data entry errors.

❖ In various records and write-ups, the name of the player's father has replaced their surname. For example, Javeria Khan has been referred to as Javeria Wadood, Nida Dar as Nida Rashid, etc. The English spellings have also undergone some changes. For example, Ayesha Ashar and Ayesha Ashhar, Mohtashim Rashid as Mauhtashim Rasheed, etc. have been used interchangeably.

FOREWORD

The story of professional women's cricket in Pakistan opens with a scene that could easily come from fiction: 11 years of dictatorship have ended, a 35-year old woman, Benazir Bhutto, has been elected to power, and a teenaged girl decides that if a nation is ready for a woman Prime Minister it's also ready for a women's cricket team. From there the story spirals into death threats, a stadium filled with spectators who are all on-duty police personnel, and a father who tells his daughter to leave the country and do her cricket-playing in England. At the very centre of this story is the determination and love of the game of the teenaged girl, Shaiza Khan, who goes on to become the founder and captain of the first Pakistan women's cricket team, supported in everything by her sister and teammate Sharmeen, and her vice-captain, the record-breaking (and, to date, record-holding) Test batter, Kiran Baloch. Along the way there are political intrigues, trouble with the board, off-field rivalry with other women, fears of conspiracy within the team. . . there is also a great deal of cricket.

Part of the pleasure of *Unveiling Jazbaa* is its determination to keep cricket at the centre of things — as every Pakistani player from Shaiza to Sana Mir and onward would doubtless want. Aayush Puthran introduces us to many of the extraordinary women who've played for Pakistan, but he does so while weaving their stories through those of cricket series and tournaments — we witness a team that starts off with some players who've never played cricket before turn into a professional unit that learns what winning feels like. There is drama both on field, and off. Many of the problems and intrigues will feel familiar to anyone who follows the men's game (shifts in form, cliques within the team, captaincy crises, Indo-Pak politics disrupting cross-border tournaments), others are particular to the women's game (players whose family members don't want them to play for reasons of honour, pressure to quit the game for marriage and motherhood, a board that isn't interested in supporting the team).

'What do they know of cricket who only cricket know?' C L R James asked. While reading this book you might well ask yourself the question: 'What do they know of cricket who only men's cricket know?'

Kamila Shamsie

INTRODUCTION

FOR A DESIRE as frivolous as wanting to play cricket, Saba Nazir, a 17-year-old from Muridke, decided to commit a 'crime greater than murder' in 2009.

She cut her hair.

The locks on her head represented her family's honour in their small, conservative hometown of Muridke, located less than 50 kilometres from Lahore, the cultural capital of Pakistan. By cutting her hair, Saba defied tradition and put her family's dignity at stake in a place that was a breeding ground for fanatical Islam. Saba, though, was willing to bear the repercussions of her act – two slaps and a thrashing with a shoe. It was her ultimate declaration of love for the game.

Hailing from the conservative Rajput caste, the women of the Nazir house had to observe *purdah* (the wearing of a veil). They weren't allowed to step out of their homes without a male relative accompanying them, and education was limited until the tenth grade, after which it was anticipated that they would get married.

It was a tradition that Saba was expected to follow. But as an 11-year-old, she had watched women in action in the armed forces on the state-run PTV channel; this first exposure to women stepping out of their homes and working amused her. Then she came across a local magazine which had pictures of girls playing sports at Queen Mary College in Lahore. It was a concept which had never occurred to her before. It triggered in her a desire to see the world outside the four walls of her house and a drive to create a sense of identity independent of her family. 'I didn't want to be like the women in my house, who would spend their lives looking after children. I wanted to go to a university.'

When a society's central goal for young girls is to make them marriage-worthy, 'excessive' education is detrimental to those prospects. Even though academia didn't interest Saba, she realised that further education offered her an escape from forced early marriage and she convinced her father to let her study for a couple more years. It was her first step towards emancipation.

The act of playing sports was also seen as unwomanly, and cricket – popularly known as 'the gentleman's game' – even more so. Saba utilised the break periods between college lectures to run around and play cricket, something she wasn't allowed to do at home, where she could only secretly watch her brothers play the game with other boys in the neighbourhood.

Saba reserved her run and shadow-bowl practice for the afternoons when the scorching sun stopped anyone else from coming to the rooftop and she was free to behave in a way that many believed didn't befit a girl. Playing was an escape from her mundane life. 'But then again, when I went back home every evening, I felt suffocated. There was no freedom.'

A four-day, annual, inter-collegiate event in Sheikhupura, a town nearly an hour away from Muridke, offered an opportunity to escape that suppression. Without telling anyone in her family, she sneaked off to Sheikhupura. Surrounded by other girls who were free to run around and play all sorts of different sports, she was almost overwhelmed by the experience of this more liberated world. 'I wished I'd been born in Sheikhupura so that I could also get to play like those girls.'

She participated in a few sprints and badminton competitions, but the joy wasn't to last long. On the final day she returned home late – at 6.00 p.m. – and was caught by her mother. For the first time, she had to share her long-kept secret and confide that she had been playing sports. 'Ammi [Mother] scolded me and warned that my brother would cancel my admission to college if he found out about it. But I was happy that I got a chance to play. For me, it was a risk worth taking.'

It was in Sheikhupura, a year later, that she eventually got the opportunity to bowl in front of the selectors from the Pakistan Cricket Board (PCB) in an inter-division tournament trials. Saba's bowling impressed them, and she was chosen to play in the game the next morning.

But the selection landed her in a quandary because she would have to make her own arrangements for the journey to Sheikhupura rather than travelling with the rest of her university classmates. Not only was her family too poor to afford the extra expenses but she couldn't even let them know she was playing. Moreover, that evening after the selection trials, she returned home late again, leaving her mother furious. 'Ammi banned me from playing cricket again. I cried a lot that day.'

The next day, she quietly escaped to the neighbouring town. With help from her school coach, she worked out a travel route and boarded a bus from Muridke to Batti Chowk, then took a rickshaw to the ground. It was a journey laden with fear. 'I was scared of losing my way. And to compound that was the fear of my brothers or someone from the neighbourhood spotting me boarding a bus by myself. If anybody at my house had found out, *mein nahi bachti* [I wouldn't have survived].'

No one spotted her, but she lost her way a little and was late for the match. It didn't matter. 'When I wore the kit and entered the ground it felt unreal. Even in my dreams, I hadn't imagined that I would actually be able to play cricket.'

Nothing perturbed her that day. Not even the fact that the opposition were tearing them apart. The only exception was when the umpire claimed that she wasn't a fast bowler. The assessment hit her hard. 'I argued that I *was* a fast bowler but, at that time, I didn't know any other type of bowling.'

In fact, she barely knew anything about cricket at all, except swinging the bat and rolling her arms over. Yet, her performance that day earned praise, and the recognition kept her going.

But it wasn't a straight path ahead. Well aware that going home would mean the end of her cricketing ambitions, she pleaded with the coach to help her escape and provide accommodation. Her request was declined, and she had to return home dejected.

However, she did get to keep the jersey she had worn while playing, which had the PCB logo embossed on it. Even though she had no clue what that logo signified when she was flaunting it around in college, her friend's brother noticed it. Impressed by what she had achieved, he suggested she try her luck at Country Club – a gymkhana in Muridke where his grandfather worked as a groundsman.

The club was only three kilometres from where Saba lived, but it was in a secluded region. It wasn't considered safe enough for a girl to travel there alone, and her family's financial constraints didn't make it any easier. Her father, who owned a small provisions store, could barely make ends meet. Her brother, the only other earning member of the family, worked as a labourer in a footwear factory. Saba courageously urged her mother, who was averse to the idea, to come along with her. 'I told her that I just wanted to check if there were any rewards for playing cricket.'

The trip proved to be disastrous. Having spent a valuable portion of their savings on public transport, they were denied entry by the guard, humiliated and told to leave. The whole experience infuriated her mother. 'To appease her, I did all the domestic chores that night: cooked dinner and washed all the dishes.'

But Saba didn't give up on the opportunity. A few days later, on the holy day of Friday, she requested her mother to come again with her to Country Club, offering to pay the transport fare from her own savings. This time, she carried the jersey with the PCB logo, and it was enough to persuade the guard that she was a cricketer.

The coach, Waqar Sarfaraz, who was training a bunch of boys at the club, was also impressed by the jersey. He took her to the nets and asked her to bowl. Wrapping the *dupatta* (traditional shawl) around her waist, she rolled her arms over. Her bowling impressed the coach enough for him to suggest to her mother that she should let Saba train under him. The most impactful of his promises was that, if she excelled, there was potential for significant financial reward. The coach also offered to pick her up and drop her off from training to ensure her safety.

'Ammi was hesitant. She was convinced that Abu [Father] and Bhai [Brother] wouldn't approve.' But despite her initial hesitation, her mother eventually agreed.

'I was so thrilled I couldn't sleep that night.'

The next day, Saba turned up four hours early for the practice session and went out running in the open field, the hot sun beating down. She had been given an opportunity and she was going to make the most of every second of it – even though it remained a close secret between the two women of the house.

In order to keep her safe from outsiders and her family members, one of her teammates would always drop her back in the middle of a crowded market on their scooter, and from there she would walk back home. That arrangement, though, didn't last very long.

A few months later, her coach left the job at Country Club and resumed his training at a local ground, which was close to the factory where Saba's brother worked. 'Whenever the factory workers left for home, I would hide behind the nets.' What she couldn't avoid, though, was the gaze of male strangers who would flock from neighbouring villages to witness the rare sight of a girl playing cricket.

It made Saba uncomfortable, and she would often hide behind a tree. The coach noticed her unease, but within the societal limitations they were dealing with in getting her to play, he only had one piece of stern advice to offer: 'With this attitude, you will never grow. Accept it and play.'

Her mother, meanwhile, wasn't fully convinced by the arrangement, living partly in fear of her husband and son finding out about what Saba was doing. She was happiest when it rained and training sessions were cancelled.

Saba had been given a free hand by her mother because they lived under the false assumption that if she played for a few months, she would be ready to represent the national team. The realisation that a lot more time and hard work would be required prompted her mother to stop giving Saba the transport fare. 'I told the coach that my mother would rather have me sick than play cricket.'

One of the boys at the academy bailed her out briefly by paying for her travel to Lahore's Kinnaird College, where she would play competitive matches. After a while, she realised that arrangement was becoming a burden on him and, as a way out, a teacher at the college suggested that she could take a bus which ferried students free of charge.

As instructed, she took the bus the next day but was asked to get off at the next stop as the conductor said that the service was only for boys. 'I felt so sad and lonely, I wanted to cry. I didn't go for the match that day and returned to my teacher, asking him for some advice. He suggested that I get a haircut. I told him that, in my house, it would be a crime greater than murder; my family would beat me to a pulp.'

Despite knowing the fate that awaited her, Saba's yearning to play cricket had overcome the threat – not just of physical assault, but the possibility of her secret escape routes being shut down. With all her PKR 150 (Pakistani rupees – the equivalent of 64p) saved up, she took her younger brother along with her as they searched out the most affordable haircut they could find in town. The barber, equally uncertain of her decision, would enquire after every snip of the scissors if it was short enough. Saba told her to keep going until it got so short that the barber eventually refused to go any further.

Saba wasn't particularly happy with the length – but it was short enough to leave her family both embarrassed and livid. Her father slapped her across the face and her elder brother grounded her. 'They said I'd brought disgrace to the family. They cursed my mother for letting me get out of hand, and she stopped giving me food.'

It was a punishment that backfired for without food she became enraged rather than compliant. With an opportunity to play an inter-district match, she confronted her brother. 'You can kill me if you want,' she said flatly, 'but I'm not going to stop playing cricket. Even if you cut off my legs, I'll crawl to the ground and play.'

The following morning, with a cold fog shrouding the streets and with her life on the line, Saba left the house in defiance of their orders and climbed on to the rooftop of a bus crowded with men. 'When I sat on the bus, shivering in the cold, I was holding back tears, barely able to comprehend what I was doing.'

She continued to defy her family over the following weeks, but with money running low she had to try to sneak aboard the bus for free or else she wouldn't have had enough to buy herself any food. There was one occasion when she was caught by the bus conductor without a ticket. She refused to pay the fare and was slapped, threatened with the police and thrown off.

The humiliation and the fright were terrible, but the bus had taken her most of the way, and because she had refused to pay for the ticket, she could afford lunch – a naan dipped in water. At times that would suffice her for an entire day; on other days she would go to sleep hungry. 'Students in Kinnaird College were rich and it hurt to see them waste food. How is it that Allah has given some people so much that they can throw food in the bin, and not give me enough to even take the edge off my hunger?'

The match days were especially difficult because she wouldn't arrive home until 9.00 p.m. In an effort to avoid the attention of her parents, she had to quietly sneak in, helped by her younger brother, and pretend that she'd fallen asleep – but in doing so she had to skip dinner.

The poor eating patterns and the quality of water consumed eventually led to Saba falling sick with high fever. Taking her out to the doctor with shortened hair was too embarrassing for her family, so they forced her to rest at home without medical attention. Nearly a month of missed training sessions eventually got her coach curious, and he turned up at the house to check on her. He offered to pay for her medical treatment and took her to a doctor, where she was diagnosed with typhoid.

When she was better, Saba resumed training, and her iron-clad perseverance paid off when she was selected to play in the inaugural edition of the Shaheed Mohtarma Benazir Bhutto Women's Cricket Championship – a domestic competition organised by the PCB – a few months later. This selection changed the fortunes of her household.

Her photo appeared in a newspaper, and neighbours went to greet her family. It was the first time they realised that Saba playing cricket hadn't shamed them; it had, instead, brought them honour.

Their attitudes towards her and her passion shifted overnight. Not only did they allow her to play freely thereafter, but they even agreed to let her stay by herself in Lahore, making her the first woman in the family to be allowed to live an independent life.

Saba lived on campus at the University of Lahore, but had only a meagre PKR 300 to her name. It wasn't enough to survive. Living largely on a diet of porridge or chapati and pickle, she remained undernourished and couldn't afford medicines.

Furthermore, even though there were a number of year-round sports for girls at the university, cricket was only played for two weeks a year. To get further practice, she joined the Aleem Dar Cricket Academy, which was situated nearly ten kilometres from the campus. It was a long walk, but she didn't have enough money for transport. A few months later, however, having earned PKR 2,500 from playing inter-university games, she was able to buy a second-hand bicycle. She travelled 28 kilometres to pick up the bike and was thrilled to take ownership of it. It had the potential to transform her life – the only issue was that she didn't know how to ride it. She set off back to her hostel at the University of Lahore but struggled to maintain any sort of balance and eventually gave up and decided to walk. Finally, too exhausted to continue, she attempted to take a bus – but she wasn't allowed to take the bike on board. Rickshaws were asking for PKR 500, which she couldn't afford. So, she decided she had little option but to try to ride her bike again. The trip back from Nila Gumbad to her hostel was longer and more painful than she had ever expected; it took three hours and was punctuated by falls and numerous near accidents. But she made it.

It took her another week to eventually learn to ride the bike properly, but she hadn't fully appreciated the repercussions of her decision. Her coach had warned her that riding the bike to practice would be a silly decision but she believed, in the absence of any other option, that she could overcome the challenge. During the summer month of Ramadan, with poor nutrition, riding one and a half hours to and from training took a heavy toll on her body.

One evening, without ample food to fuel her through the hours of fasting, she collapsed off her bike and sat in the middle of the road. A random stranger took pity and offered her a meal box. 'He was godsent. I cried while eating.'

The cricket continued for six months before she ran out of money. All that she had saved from playing was burnt through when treating another bout of typhoid, and the financial situation back home was worsening. She tried looking for a job and found an opportunity with the Water and Power Development Authority – a government organisation. But for that, she had to quit cricket and play baseball instead.

Despite the financial support the job offered, baseball wasn't a sport she enjoyed. She worked and scrimped and saved and eventually squirrelled away PKR 35,000, which allowed her to go back to the game she loved by enrolling herself in Kinnaird College – the crème de la crème of women's cricket in Pakistan.

That decision was her way of giving herself one final shot to see if she could achieve her dream of representing Pakistan. The desire to play cricket for her country was what had driven her to rebel against the wishes of her family and to break down the myriad social barriers between her and her goals; it was the reason she had made so many compromises and so many sacrifices over the years. She didn't want to let go of the opportunity, for which she had given away a part of herself, without one final effort.

A year later, when the shortlist of 75 cricketers selected for the national training camp was posted, her name wasn't on it.

It was a devastating blow. But her desire persevered. She would give it one more year to see if her cricketing ambitions, sacrifices and hard work would materialise into something significant.

It was a brave and bold decision. And one that bore fruit.

In 2018, she was selected as a part of the PCB XI for the 2017/18 edition of the Departmental Women's Cricket Championship, played in Karachi. Even though she was again struck down with typhoid ahead of the first match (against the strongest team in the domestic circuit – Zarai Taraqiati Bank Limited [ZTBL]), she refused to give up on the opportunity. 'I was scared that if my teammates found out about my high fever, I wouldn't get a chance to play.' She hid her symptoms and battled through.

Her team was beaten convincingly, but she returned impressive figures of 1 for 7 in four overs. Three games later, against State Bank of Pakistan, she picked up three wickets and was awarded Player of the Match. She finished the tournament as the joint-highest wicket-taker and caught the attention of the press. 'There were cameras in front of me, journalists asking questions. I was so overwhelmed that I could barely understand what I was being asked.'

Also impressed by her performances was Pakistan's head coach, Mark Coles, who selected her for a training camp ahead of the T20 World Cup that year. During the camp, she had her first photo taken in the Pakistan jersey. 'I didn't get to keep the jersey but, as I saw myself in the mirror, I couldn't believe how beautiful it looked. I didn't want to return it; I wanted to go to sleep wearing it. I never wanted to take it off.'

Saba didn't make it to the World Cup that year, but just a few months later she was selected for a squad that would fly to Dubai for a series against the West Indies in early 2019. A girl who found it difficult to afford a rickshaw ride was set to fly in an aeroplane. When she told her father, he became worried. Where would she get the money for the trip?

'I told him, "Allah has heard my plea. I won't have to pay for the travel."'

The national team would cover all expenses for the players; but more importantly, the long-dreamed-of Pakistan jersey was at last in her possession. She wore it all day long at the training camp, while eating lunch, while offering *namaaz* (prayer) and even while sleeping. 'My teammates were laughing at me, but

I didn't know how to explain the feeling of finally having that jersey. To know it was mine.'

The news that a girl from Muridke had become a part of the Pakistan team had reached the ears of local journalists, who all wanted to interview her to find out more about her story. 'I told my father not to tell anyone that we'd become rich. What if thieves found out about it and came to steal from us?'

Fearful of what the press attention might bring, she didn't return home for three days.

But when she did come back, she gave PKR 50,000 to her father. Even though she still held a grudge for everything she had had to go through, she saw the other side of her family's worries. 'I wanted to hand over my first salary to my father, just like my brothers would do. He had struggled so hard all his life to feed us. He was extremely proud of his sons, but they couldn't achieve what he wanted them to – neither did they study, nor did they earn enough.

'He refused to take that money and admitted that he hadn't done anything for me. But I knew, such are the constraints of our society, that had I been in his position I would probably have done the same. He was so proud of me that he said, "What my sons couldn't give me, my daughter has given me."

'I pray to Allah that he gives me so much money that my father won't ever have to work again. He is old and sick and it's difficult for him to work. After getting a central contract, the expenses of my house are being taken care of. I'm even able to look after the expenses of my younger brother and sister.'

Born in 1992, Saba has played only one international match – a T20 International against Bangladesh in Lahore. 'I've played cricket in loneliness all my life. Only my *khuda* [lord] and I know my journey. Whenever I would play my matches, I would see the parents of other girls come to support them. I couldn't even call my parents to tell them that I was playing.

'All I needed from my family was their support; I didn't need any money. My progress was delayed. If only they had supported me earlier . . .' she adds before breaking down in tears.

Saba has endured an extraordinary journey to overcome poverty, hunger and social exclusion unlike anyone else in the team. Not everyone who has played for Pakistan has been poor. Not all parents have been unsupportive. Not everyone had to play in hiding. Not everyone was beaten for playing.

Yet, within her story lies the unifying thread experienced by most of the women who have gone on to play for Pakistan, who at different stages have faced some part of the same struggle. Saba's experiences give a peek into the issues of playing a sport that is highly celebrated in the country yet kept at arm's length from half the population.

Sana Mir, Pakistan's longest-serving captain, is clear where she stands on the issue. 'Whenever stories about a father who was not supportive of his daughter's cricketing ambitions get published, I get really furious.'

She has her reasons – but not necessarily the ones you might at first assume. 'There might be a few girls whose parents have beaten them, to punish them for playing cricket, but when these stories are told, the West always picks up on them and glorifies them. But our parents had to be courageous. The system doesn't provide them, or us, with any sort of security. They are worried about us.

'While our stories are about strong women, they're also about strong men. My father had to have a big heart to send me into a system where he knew I wouldn't be given proper food, where he knew I wouldn't be sleeping on a proper bed. What kind of a heart would a person need to have to let their daughters go through that? Most of them are misunderstood – they aren't trying to control their daughters, they are trying to protect them. Yes, there are a few brothers and fathers who are trying to control. I've gone and tried to convince them about the benefits of women playing cricket – sometimes I've been successful, and in some cases I've failed.

'We have to tell the stories of thousands and thousands of families on whose backs we've stood,' she adds, before referring to the speech she delivered after her team defeated India in the 2016 Twenty20 (T20) World Cup, in which she credited the parents of the players for their support.

As Sana rightly points out, those who made it to the top, despite all the obstacles, at some point found support from their families. Unfortunately, the stories of those who never made it may remain unheard forever.

Was Saba unlucky to play only one match for Pakistan? Or was she fortunate to have had an opportunity that so many others haven't?

From 1997 to 2022, 86 women have represented Pakistan. This is the story of those women who, over the course of 25 years, lived the journey and, in the face of enormous political and social challenges, shaped the identity of their country's cricket team.

PROLOGUE

THE AUDITORIUMS AT the Alhamra Arts Council, in the busy Mall Road of Lahore, have a seating capacity of a few hundred. Yet there is an urban legend that nearly 50,000 packed out a single one for Iqbal Bano's performance at the annual Faiz Mela (Faiz Festival) on 13 February 1986.

The audience numbers may not be accurate but the sound of defiance – a passionate rendition of the protest song 'Hum Dekhenge', accompanied by the rapturous cheers and chants of 'Inqlab Zindabad' ('Long live the revolution') – has reached millions in the years since.

Not only was the ghazal singer presenting banned poetry, termed un-Islamic by Pakistan's then dictator Zia-ul-Haq, but she was also defying the state's diktat by performing a musical in public in a black sari – which was banned attire.

Her act – and the song's lyrics – were seen as an open challenge to Zia's idea of Islam, which he had misused to suppress the people of the country for nearly a decade.

Ali Madeeh Hashmi – the grandson of the original songwriter, Faiz Ahmad Faiz – was present during the performance.

Afterwards, he wrote in his blog that the show's organisers, predicting a government crackdown, smuggled a copy of the performance to Dubai, from where it went to India and then reached the black market in Pakistan, exposing the masses to Faiz's poetry.

That version exists online today, and in the background you can hear the crowd reaching a crescendo at 'Sab taj uchaale jaayenge, sab takht giraye jaayenge' ('Every crown will be flung, each throne will be brought down').

At a time when the social fabric of the country was being altered, it was one of the most prominent acts of defiance in the post-British-colonial era, a call for liberation from the regressive military regime that had misused religion as a tool to subvert the population. Under the iron fist of Zia-ul-Haq, state institutions were controlled, journalists, activists, lawyers and political figures were routinely arrested, and Pakistan was being 'Shariarised'.

The rights of women were especially hard hit, with Hudood Ordinance replacing parts of the Pakistan Penal Code. 'Hudood' meant restrictions to what was deemed acceptable behaviour, the 'Ordinance' coming in the form of laws. Amputations for theft, 100 lashes for sex by unmarried couples and stoning to death for *zina* (extramarital sex). Public floggings were common for theft, consuming alcohol and *zina*. Women were relegated to second-class citizens; their public performances in music, theatre and sport were banned, and their court testimony considered half as worthy as a man's. Hundreds of women were jailed for failing to prove accusations of rape, which required *Hadd* – the testimony of four 'honourable Muslim men'.

Those interviewed for the book believe the first half of the 1980s was possibly the worst period to be a woman in Pakistan. But with great oppression came great resistance, and many – like Iqbal Bano – emerged in defiance.

When the blind 13-year-old Safia Bibi, who had been raped and impregnated by her employers, was found guilty by the court, flogged publicly, jailed for three years and fined, her lawyer Asma Jahangir and other members of the Women's Action Forum took to the streets. They were beaten up, tear-gassed and arrested for protesting.

In Lahore, Madeeha Gauhar's Ajoka Theatre told the stories of people's lives in a dictator-run state despite being ousted from public spaces by the president's men.

Kathak dancer Nahid Siddiqui was forced to live a life of exile in England and was banned from performing in public anywhere in the world. Needless to say, she too defied the orders.

While a certain section of the socio-economic class could get away with the newly defined crimes, the law of the land didn't protect them. The 1980s was an eventful decade of oppression, resistance and the idea of a Naya (new) Pakistan being defined.

In this political climate, two teenage Karachi girls, studying in London, dreamed of returning to Pakistan and forming a cricket team.

THE AUDACITY TO PLAY

THE YEAR 1988 was a watershed for female leaders in politics as much as it was for the Khan siblings Shaiza and Sharmeen, Pakistan expatriates living in London. The year saw Margaret Thatcher become the longest-serving British prime minister of the 20th century. Her act of breaking through what looked like invincible societal and political barriers to reach into the heart of the establishment was being emulated in a different form in the Eastern world as well.

For Shaiza (19) and Sharmeen (16), settled comfortably in their English lives, 1988 proved to be a watershed for another reason – both as women and as Pakistani expatriates. Years of repression had come to an abrupt end in their home country with the demise of dictator Zia-ul-Haq, under whose rule Pakistan had been run by martial law.

There was change in the air in the South Asian nation, carrying the promise of a new dawn, new beginnings, and above all a break from the past. The Harvard and Oxford-educated Benazir Bhutto, who had spent most of the Zia years in prison, exile and raising international awareness of the political crimes from London, became the first female prime minister of Pakistan.

Political affiliations notwithstanding, in Benazir's peaceful revolution, many became *jiyalas* (supporters of the Pakistan Peoples Party), seeing her as the harbinger of a new era. The air of optimism and the sounds of her political campaign – the Lyari disco version of 'Dila Teer Bija' – had travelled all the way to England.

For the Khans, the event was life-altering, and they returned to Karachi, the land of their birth. Even though their ancestral roots were in Punjab, their affinity was towards the life they identified with in the capital of Sindh. Karachi was the most cosmopolitan city in the country, offering space to the most diverse lifestyles and rewarding industrious people. Pakistan's first capital, Karachi, was the prime settlement of the *mujahirs* – Islamic migrants from India who moved to Pakistan during the partition. Till the 1970s, it had been the hub of a buzzing nightlife, of discos and cabarets. Even as alcohol was banned and restrictions were put in place in the 1980s, it remained the most Westernised of Pakistan's cities.

The philosophies of the city shaped the hearts and minds of the Khan sisters as well. Daughters of a wealthy carpet merchant, Saeed Khan, Shaiza and Sharmeen were brought up in a palatial house near the upmarket Civil Lines in Karachi. Saeed was a self-made millionaire, having established a carpet business – United Carpets Limited – with his elder brother at the age of 17. Their mother was a cricket buff, who had postponed her wedding to watch the touring West Indies team in action in 1959. Much of that love for the game, as well as values of independence, were passed on to Shaiza and Sharmeen, who lived life on their own terms.

A little over five feet tall, the big-boned, short-haired Shaiza defied conventional expectations, almost rock-star-like, and relished challenging the status quo. She was a boss – well read and travelled. Her look, speech, walk and even the cigarette she unabashedly smoked contrasted with the social norms for women in Pakistan at that time. A strong-willed individual, she was unyielding when her mind was made up, dwarfing and daunting most people around her with her confidence. Sharmeen wasn't much different, although she had an even more imposing frame. 'When they spoke, it unsettled a lot of people, especially men,' recalls Afia Salam, a journalist who covered cricket in the late 1990s.

With much of their childhood spent in London during Zia's reign, they developed their skills at the Winchmore Hill Cricket Club. Shaiza was only 12 years old when she joined the club during a summer trip from Karachi to London in 1981. It was there that she enjoyed her first moment of glory, hitting the winning runs for Winchmore Hill with her nine-year-old sister at the other end of the crease.

That victory helped forge her identity – that of a cricketer. The game was no longer a recreational sport. It had turned into a burning obsession which would come to shape her life and drive her to desperate and extreme measures.

That night, while she struggled to sleep, she dreamed of what she might achieve in the game, and the focus of every trip to London thereafter was to play cricket.

Playing a match on a proper cricket square wasn't possible in Pakistan, where women were supported neither culturally nor legally to play outside the confines of their home. In Karachi, the Khan sisters had to play on a tennis court, where they would often be joined by three other boys – children of their mother's close friend. In their own dreamy world, they practised signing autographs, with an extended note that read 'from the world's greatest cricketer'.

After a while, playing cricket for just a few months a year wasn't enough for them. In 1986, in order to let his daughters live their dreams, Saeed decided to send them to the UK to study. It was this move that helped Shaiza's cricket career to flourish. After leaving school she went on to captain Leeds University and even played for Middlesex County.

In 1993, when England were preparing to play the World Cup, she was called to practise with the national team. It made the sisters believe that they were good enough to play for England, even though they were ineligible. They loved their life in the UK with all its freedoms and comforts, but they longed for home and had struck upon a new dream: they wanted to start women's cricket in Pakistan and become Test cricketers for their homeland.

They had tried once before as well. In 1988, with Benazir's election victory, they were convinced that if a woman could run the country, women could also play cricket. But it was a naive assumption, and they soon found out that Zia's rule had left lingering after-effects.

〇〇〇

If 1977 witnessed the dawn of greatness for the Pakistan men's team, by the 1980s they had consolidated their position as arguably the second-best team in the world after the West Indies. Live, televised cricket matches had catapulted their two best players – Lahore's Imran Khan and Karachi's Javed Miandad – to superstardom and drove the Lahore vs Karachi battle, a feisty constant in the country's traditional cricket heartlands, to never-before-witnessed heights.

While men's cricket had flourished into mass popularity, becoming the country's uncontested favourite sport to watch and play, there were few signs of women playing it. Even though there are accounts of infrequent matches at schools and even more rarely on the streets in the 1960s, it was never developed further. Pakistan was far behind the rest of the cricketing world in this regard, especially when compared to neighbouring India, whose women's team was playing in World Cups and drawing tens of thousands of spectators to its games.

Women's cricket dates back to at least 1745 in England, when maids of Bramley played against the maids of Hambledon in Gosden Common. In a more modern context, the first Test match was played in 1934 – between England and Australia. Women's cricket was largely played between those two countries and New Zealand until the 1970s. Alongside them, representatives from Jamaica and Trinidad & Tobago had also participated in the inaugural World Cup in 1973 – staged two years before the men's version. India played in the 1978 World Cup, and by 1988 even Ireland and the Netherlands had joined in (two countries which didn't even have a first-class status for their men's teams).

In Pakistan, hockey remained the primary team sport for women, while a number of women in the elite strata of Pakistani society took part in individual pursuits. Afia Salam, one of Pakistan's earliest female cricket journalists, recounts, 'Tennis and badminton were quite popular. Individually, it was easier because women from a certain class of society were able to say, "I don't care what you think, I'm going to do it." But team sports were an issue because there were only a few women able to behave like that.'

The attempts to organise professional women's cricket in Pakistan hit roadblocks very early on. The Pakistan Women's Cricket Association (PWCA), with the patronage of Begum Razia Azam Ali Baig, was initially formed by Tahira Hameed in 1977. A former tennis player who had represented Pakistan at Wimbledon in the 1950s, Tahira was the daughter of Captain S.A. Hameed, the first secretary general of the Pakistan Olympic Association, and sister of Test cricketer Farooq Hameed. She served as the secretary of the association, which was presided over by Dr Iqbal Dar, the principal of Lahore College for Women.

The cricketing activities of women, which during the reign of Zia were restricted to behind closed doors, took place in four colleges in the uptown regions of the city – Lahore College for Women, Kinnaird College for Women, College of Home Economics, and Government Islamia College for Women. These were largely friendly or invitational one-day matches of varying lengths – 20, 35 or 40 overs.

The women in these colleges played among themselves, and even the odd tournament, titled as a 'national championship', took place between women from Lahore, barring the odd exception of a couple of players from Hyderabad and Karachi. Despite the backing of the Lahore oligarchy, women's cricket suffered from a severe shortage of funds.

The PWCA, which had failed to organise a single official cricket match in the first year of its existence, needed support from the Board of Control for Cricket in Pakistan (BCCP) – the former name of the PCB, which was running the affairs of men's cricket in the country.

The PWCA's request for funding to tour India in 1980 was declined. In a letter dated 26 January 1980, Lt Col. (Rtd) Rafi Nasim, secretary of the BCCP, wrote: 'The case of your team's visit to India or the Indian Women Team to Pakistan was considered in the last meeting of the BCCP. The board was of the opinion that Women's Cricket in Pakistan is still in its infancy. It would, therefore, not be appropriate to face India at this moment or in the near future. Your request for exchange of visits with India will be considered some time in 1981.'

Abdul Hafeez Kardar, the first captain of the Pakistan cricket team, donated a set of cricket gear to all four colleges. Aitchison College also provided a few bats and pads for the players. Sponsorship from companies like Bio Amla, Zemrok Fibre Glass and Medora Cosmetics, gathered by Khawaja Parvez Masood, helped them pay for a few lunches and umpires.

On some days, Masood, who was working with Aitchison College, would pay out of his own pocket. Most of the groundwork, however, had to be done by the players themselves. 'After nets, we used to roll our pitch and water it,' recalls Shamsa Hashmi, who was one of the players at that time. 'The prize for the best performer was that she got to sit on the roller while the rest of us would push it.' A few teammates had the task of carrying lunchboxes, which would suffice for the entire team.

Within the financial and social confines, it appeared that cricket was starting to blossom – until the association that had been formed in the elite circles of Lahore split, and two groups claimed the rights to organise matches under the same banner. Much of the PWCA's efforts to develop women's cricket was abruptly halted when Azra Parveen, who was working for Tahira, and was also one of the founding members of the PWCA, shifted allegiance to Shirin Javed. Azra and Bushra Mateen (vice chancellor of Lahore College for Women University) had founded the Universal Cricket Club in 1978 at the Lady Maclagan High School, which later came under the Shirin Javed-led PWCA.

Shirin hailed from an affluent family which owned Servis Industries Limited, a leading shoe manufacturer, who were also one of the bigger sponsors of Pakistan men's cricket and had a team on the domestic circuit. She was also the sister-in-law of former Test cricketer Ijaz Butt, who later went on to become chair of the PCB. By 1984, he was already its secretary.

As the years went on, more people with political clout joined her. Bushra Aitzaz, the wife of eminent lawyer Aitzaz Ahsan, was the most significant addition to the group in 1988. Bushra, who had fought against the tyrannical rule of Zia and was even famously photographed getting roughed up on the streets by the police, was now on the other side of the political system – with her husband becoming a Cabinet minister in Benazir Bhutto's regime.

Despite two politically strong sections willing to run the affairs of the game in the country, it never got a lift, largely due to Zia's insistence on not letting the women of the country display their sporting skills to the world outside. Women playing in public was viewed as un-Islamic. And power struggles weren't the only bane impeding their progress. Shamsa Hashmi, also a former international hockey player, recalls her team not being allowed to participate in the 1982 Delhi Asian Games due to the president's order.

That women's sports couldn't flourish in the 1980s was a reflection of Pakistani politics during the martial rule of Zia, who presided over the country from 1978 to 1988 as a dictator. His insistence on keeping Western culture at bay resulted in Pakistan becoming a more conservative society. Female actors in films and on television were portrayed wearing only traditional outfits. The norm for girls in schools and colleges was also to cover their heads. Sport wasn't immune to these demands.

'A lot changed when Zia came to power,' Afia states. 'In the 1960s and '70s, women were playing tennis in shorts, but that was never going to be allowed under his rule.' When the PWCA organised its first cricket tournament, at the Gaddafi Stadium, the players turned up in unusual cricket attire – collared kurtas and pyjamas matched with sweaters – and the matches were played with no male spectators allowed entry, except for the players' family members.

Abdul Hafeez Kardar was one of only a few male cricketers who lent their support, and on the whole, prominent figures steered away from women's cricket and – says Munizae Jahangir, a journalist and daughter of prominent human rights activist Asma Jahangir – from women's issues. This included Imran Khan, the then superstar of Pakistan cricket and future prime minister of the country. 'Once, when he passed by one of the protests, a woman asked him, "Why don't you join us?"' recalls

Jahangir. 'He replied, "Main iss tarah ki cheezeh nahi karta" ("I don't get involved in such things"). He just wound up the window and drove away. He wasn't at all political or interested in taking on any of the powers that be at that time. That was his reaction to the women's movement as well.'

The impact on cricket was insignificant compared to elsewhere in society. To fight the tyranny of Zia, several women rose to the fore. Benazir Bhutto became the face of the golden age of resistance, led by women across different cultural spheres.

When the winds of change began to blow, Shaiza and Sharmeen were swept up in the wave of optimism moving through the country. At the time, they were unaware of the existence of women's cricket in Lahore, which paved the way for a 'Karachi vs Lahore' battle of a different kind, and which would have a significant impact on the swings and roundabouts of women's cricket in the future. But they would come to know it well.

Benazir Bhutto's seven-hour caravan ride along the crowded 25-kilometre road from Lahore airport to Minar-e-Pakistan, echoing with the chants of 'Dartay hain bandooqon walay ek nehatti larki say . . . Mulla, tajir, general jiyalay, ek nehatti larki say' ('The gunmen are afraid of an unarmed girl') while women flung their dupattas in the air, was a symbol of democracy's victory. But the electoral triumph of a woman in politics didn't necessarily mean emancipation for the rest of the women in the country; it was a fact that Shaiza and Sharmeen, now in Karachi, were among the earliest to realise.

Zia may have gone but his warped contribution to society hadn't. His rule had empowered extreme religious outfits in the country, which were rarely voted to power by the people. 'Every time a dictator comes to power, and democracy is threatened, women's rights are impacted,' Munizae Jahangir notes. 'For dictators to remain in power in Pakistan, they need the support of religious groups. And every time these religious groups get support from the government, women's rights are the first affected.'

Shaiza and Sharmeen experienced this first-hand when their plans to play a friendly game against a men's veteran team, which included the legendary Zaheer Abbas, were abruptly cancelled.

Shaiza had returned to Pakistan in late 1988 and formed the Karachi Ladies Cricket Club, assembling a group of women who were playing an assortment of sports – hockey, netball and javelin – into a new cricket team. In the metropolitan pockets of Karachi that wanted desperately to break away from the recent past, they were widely encouraged. Karachi Gymkhana offered the women their ground to practise, and a few former cricketers agreed to help their ambitions take off. However, the conservative political parties railed against the idea.

Some members of the Jamaat-e-Islami, a right-wing political party, threatened to stone their houses and even issued death threats. When the news of their threat broke, Shaiza attempted to hide the newspaper from her father, but it was in vain. Saeed received a call from the police commissioner of the city, who suggested that they call off the match – but Shaiza refused to be cowed. She was adamant that a way forward could be found. She approached Jamaat-e-Islami and began a negotiation process which ended in compromise: her team could play, but only against another group of women.

With the death threats out in the open, it was an uncomfortable deal. Parents naturally feared sending their daughters to play in such an environment, but Shaiza bargained with them as well. 'Now when I think about it, I was crazy to guarantee those parents that I could keep their daughters safe,' she admits. 'I was willing to sign any form, anywhere, without thinking or consulting anyone just to make that match happen.'

All 24 of the girls stayed with Shaiza and Sharmeen and travelled with them to the stadium on match day. No spectators were allowed in the stadium but Shaiza claims that there were nearly 8,000 policemen offering them protection in case members of Jamaat-e-Islami reneged on their word.

The risk was clearly huge, but to Shaiza it wasn't a big sacrifice – which in itself was a testimony to the enormity of what they achieved: a chance to play cricket in the open in Pakistan.

Throughout that period, Saeed had remained in the background – conflicted about wanting his daughters to be independent and worrying for their safety. Once the match was over, he asked them to return to England to complete their education and pursue their dreams in a safer environment. 'Leave this country and come back when it is ready,' he said, understanding that despite the landmark achievement of staging that match, his daughters were pushing boundaries which the rest of the new 'democratic Pakistan' wasn't yet prepared to fully adopt.

During their stay back in England, Pakistan became politically volatile again. Benazir Bhutto's Pakistan Peoples Party was thrown out after just 20 months in power, and Nawaz Sharif, who had taken over as prime minister after the conservative Pakistan Muslim League (PML[N]) won the fresh election, and later had his government dissolved by the president in July 1993. Sharif challenged the decision in the Supreme Court and resigned, but not before agreeing on a settlement which forced the president out of his post as well.

Despite the continuing political chaos and the threats they had endured, Shaiza and Sharmeen tenaciously held on to their belief that the time for assembling the first-ever women's team from Pakistan was on the horizon. A key trigger in that belief was the 1993 Women's World Cup, which was taking place in England. In late July that year, they were watching the games from the stands – but wanted to be out on the field playing in the tournament themselves.

Their first attempt to assemble a Pakistan national team had come about during a period of hope for political and societal change. Their second attempt had no such hopes to bank on. But experience is the greatest teacher, and they now appreciated that they would need more tact than bravado to navigate their way through the challenges of setting up a new team. This time they operated in a more organised manner and went through official channels.

During their stay in England, they had understood how the structure of international women's cricket functioned, and duly wrote a letter to the governing body, the International Women's Cricket Council (IWCC). They submitted it with newspaper clippings of their 1988 match along with a souvenir magazine they had published. On 21 July, during a match between England and New Zealand at the Lloyds Bank Sports Ground in Beckenham, they went searching for the IWCC officials in attendance.

After a nearly two-hour-long conversation with Mary Brito – the IWCC chair – Shaiza was invited to join them for the final, scheduled to be played at Lord's, and to attend (as an observer) a full council meeting of the committee at Guildford University in Surrey.

At the meeting, Shaiza moved for an application to become a full member, writing on an A4 piece of paper: 'I would like to be a part of IWCC and propose that we be accepted.' Her proposal, made verbally at a post-dinner speech at the Rose Garden in Lord's following the final, was met with applause and an unofficial acceptance. Unfortunately, though, the event was covered by the BBC and the news reached Saeed in Karachi.

'He called me up and asked, "What the hell are you guys doing?"' Shaiza recalls. '"You're there to study, not to start a national team. You wanted to play cricket, we sent you to England. I don't want to hear about this again."

'Our parents thought we just wanted to play cricket, and we were getting to play. They didn't understand that we wanted to play cricket at an international level. We wanted to be a part of history. So, whatever had to be done thereafter had to be done behind closed doors.'

The applause and support of the IWCC members notwithstanding, Shaiza still had to fulfil several formalities to be a part of the set-up. To be eligible to play as 'Pakistan', she had to reside in the country for at least a year, form an association and draft a constitution, get approval from the PCB and Pakistan Sports Board, form a provisional team and district teams, host a tournament, and then have the other members of the IWCC nominate them and be accepted. A lot had changed in Pakistan since the last time they had been in the country. Imran Khan's men had led Pakistan to their maiden World Cup win and propelled the popularity of cricket to heights never witnessed before. But there was still no place in the streets for women to play. In the light of this, the IWCC's demands were steep. And it had to begin with Shaiza abandoning her PhD studies and heading back to the country where she'd received death threats.

On reading the approval letter from Mary Brito, her professor at Leeds University made Shaiza's passage back to Pakistan easier. He offered her a ten-year window to complete her PhD. She returned to Pakistan to join her father's carpet business, while Sharmeen stayed in the UK to complete her undergraduate degree.

Back at the carpet factory, she went to work – not so much for her father's business, but rather secretly preparing a cricket team. She wrote to the cricket boards of India, England, New Zealand and Australia to request copies of their constitutions and worked on creating one of her own. That was the easy part. Attempts to have the final version registered met with severe objection at the registrar's office. It was, after all, an attempt by a bunch of non-political individuals to take over the affairs of running a sport which had massive public interest. Fortunately, they had individuals willing to aid them with the official documentation at key posts in the offices.

Arif Ali Abbasi, then director of the PCB, was not only a rock of support for Shaiza but had also encouraged other women in sports. He aided them in setting up the board and even secured the required permissions. Support also came from former fast bowler Sarfraz Nawaz, who was at the helm of affairs in the Pakistan Sports Board. Sarfraz, who hailed from Lahore, was probably aware that women's cricket was unlikely to get interest from elsewhere, so there wasn't a lot to lose if he helped Shaiza with the required approvals.

With the Pakistan Women's Cricket Control Association (PWCCA) formed in September 1996, the final task at hand for Shaiza was to get several more women interested in playing cricket and to organise a tournament. As a quick fix, championships were organised in various schools and colleges, from where players were picked for a divisional tournament. A call was also made in the newspapers for players to turn up, and women who were playing sports of any kind were invited to join in. Sharmeen also returned to Pakistan for the inaugural championship. 'We'd managed to assemble a bunch of girls, but they weren't really cricketers,' says Shaiza. 'They could barely throw the ball – but we'd managed to organise a tournament.'

Details and newspaper clippings of the tournament were sent to the IWCC, and their proposal to be associated with the international body was accepted on 30 September 1996.

To play in the World Cup though, the final requirement was to feature in three international matches. Before that, Shaiza and Sharmeen needed at least nine other women to form a proper team.

October 1996 was an unsettling time in Pakistan, and even more so in Karachi. 'The city of two summers' was boiling in every sense. The Sufi rock song of passion – 'Jazba-e-Junoon' – was occupying radio and television airwaves but it had little impact on the spirit in the country, which was downbeat both in cricket and political terms. The song had risen to mass popularity through its association with the Pakistan men's cricket team, but they had then crashed out of the World Cup quarter-final against arch-rivals India and the pain hadn't fully subsided. After the loss, violent incidents were reported across the country. Some viewers shot their television sets; some shot themselves. Meanwhile, Benazir Bhutto, who was serving her second term as prime minister, was once again in the midst of a political upheaval.

Her brother was assassinated, her relations with President Farooq Leghari soured, and her government was on the verge of being dismissed on charges of corruption.

For Shaiza though, it was Pakistan's time to rise. To qualify for the Women's World Cup, which was to take place in India a year later, her team was required to play three international matches. She was confident of playing that series against a familiar English side, but with snow predicted in December that year, the English cricket board refused to host them. Given that only winter months remained for most of the cricket-playing nations before the global showpiece, the options to tour were limited to the countries in the southern hemisphere, and they zeroed in on Australia and New Zealand.

To find a team, they made another national call for aspiring cricketers.

The advertisement caught the attention of 18-year-old Kiran Baluch in Karachi. Kiran, whose father Maqsood had played first-class cricket, believed she could be one of the players the PWCCA was looking for. It was the first time she had heard of a women's cricket team.

Growing up, cricket had been only a recreational sport for her, played with her two younger sisters and brother. Her father's love for the game, along with some basic skills, were passed on to his children. Not surprisingly, the excitement of the trials which were set to take place on 26 October at the National Stadium was shared by the rest of the family. Her mother, sisters and house-help squeezed into a tiny car – an 800cc Suzuki Alto – to take her to the stadium.

As well as Kiran, around 60 other women had turned up for the trials that day. Sixteen-year-old Aisha Jalil was one of them. However, her journey to the National Stadium was quite different. After coming across the advertisement, she needed to pass several levels of patriarchal permission before her family joined in support.

'Women who were sporty in the 1990s were frowned upon. It was not acceptable,' Aisha remembers. She had lost her father when she was four, and all the decisions in the family were taken by her uncle and grandfather. 'It was my paternal uncle who stood up for me and said, "She will play cricket and I'm responsible for her."' As it turned out, she became the youngest player to be selected for Pakistan, when the team got ready to fly to New Zealand and Australia for their first-ever tour.

Once the squad was announced, it underwent basic training under the guidance of Shabbir Hussain, a former first-class cricketer, and even engaged in a few friendly matches with local men's teams. Eventually, Najmunnissa Ismail, Aisha Jalil, Maliha Hussain, Kiran Baluch, Shahnaz Sohail, Shabana Kausar, Sultana Yousaf, Abida Khan, Meher Minwalla and Nazli Istiaq were selected for the tour, alongside Shaiza and Sharmeen.

Much of the training had taken place at the Karachi Gymkhana and Shaiza and Sharmeen's magnificent house in Karachi. The turnaround time to get the team together was limited, and within that there were complex challenges to deal with. Shaiza was racing against the clock to get passports and kits arranged for the players and to calm the nerves of parents who weren't completely sure what was happening in the frenzy. For Kiran's parents, the apprehension about sending their daughter to play a sport which had no professional future at the cost of her education preyed on their minds. It needed Arif Ali Abbasi's reassurance for them to let her go on tour.

The most arduous challenge was to get the official documents they needed to travel abroad. With Benazir's government dismantled and the affairs of the country being run by a provincial caretaker government, the notoriously slow-moving offices were operating at an even more glacial pace than usual. With less than a day remaining, the former Pakistan men's captain Hanif Mohammad suggested they reach out to Anita Ghulam Ali, an erstwhile teacher, broadcaster and journalist who was Minister of Education.

Shaiza, unaware of what role Anita could possibly play, made a call around 11.30 at night. Anita heard her desperate plea for a few minutes and called her to the office the next morning, where a letter of approval for the team to fly out had been made ready. That letter, however, held little official significance. Shaiza knew that, historic as that tour was going to be, with the limited documentation they were carrying, the team still had to maintain a low profile before leaving the country.

According to Shaiza, it was the first time a Pakistani women's sports team – outside the Olympics – had travelled abroad to play. Past experiences had left scars and lessons suggesting that, irrespective of those in power, there was a serious threat to their safety from extremist political groups which might act to stop them travelling.

They boarded the flight in small groups and with their cricket kits packed and sealed in cartons.

'We were worried that we might attract a lot of attention and the tour could be stopped,' Kiran recalls. 'When we were leaving Karachi, we didn't wear our official kit because we knew they would attract too much attention.' They had left in casual wear, planning to change into their official uniforms (which they carried in their hand luggage) when they reached the stopover at Singapore. But despite their disguises, they were caught by the customs officials at the airport.

One of the cartons was opened and they found a cricket kit with 'Pakistan' inscribed on it. Shaiza and Sharmeen were summoned to the customs office and, in the absence of the required documents, were warned that they were leaving the country illegally. All Shaiza could show in response was the invitation to play by the New Zealand and Australian cricket boards, a letter from Anita Ghulam Ali and the money they were carrying. She made another plea: 'You will not even remember who you stopped but we will live with this memory for the rest of our lives.'

The cartons were sealed, so were the lips of the customs officials, and the team was allowed to fly out – albeit under a cloud of uncertainty. Even though the first match of the tour was scheduled to be played in New Zealand, they were travelling to Australia. The delayed confirmation of the series had left them with little time to get through to the officials in New Zealand, who were on Christmas leave, to secure visas. Without these, they had to make a stop on the other side of the Tasman Sea.

'We were constantly in touch with the New Zealand officials, and, once we landed in Australia, they promised us that we would get our visas on arrival,' Kiran recalls. 'Once we landed in Christchurch, everyone else got off. But the Pakistan team were left sitting in the plane. Our passports were taken, they stamped our visas, and only after that were we allowed to get off. But the wait to see if we would be allowed off that plane seemed to last forever.'

Unlike Kiran, Aisha doesn't recall any of the panic. For much of the tour she remained silent, a defence mechanism she had developed during her teen years. 'I was a shy person. I didn't have the courage to interact with people. In my school, we were supposed to speak in English or else we were fined. Since I was afraid to speak incorrect English and get fined, I became very reluctant to speak at all.'

For the Khan sisters, to fulfil their dream to play for Pakistan had meant that apart from facing death threats, running around government offices and dealing with seemingly endless logistical hurdles, they also had to take on the financial burden of the entire team. Even though there were no match payments and daily allowances, their expenses included airfares and internal travelling, boarding in lodges, a cook on the move to serve fresh food at all times, cricket kits, official uniforms and even trips to Mount Cook and other recreational activities the team was involved in – from kiwi sighting to sheep shearing. They even bought off-field clothing for some of their less well-off teammates, and occasionally gave them money to shop for their families. Additionally, they were paying nearly NZ $3,000 to the hosts to play each game against the national side and shared the costs of cricket balls and umpires for the tour matches with local clubs. Even though Shaiza refused to divulge the expense she had to bear, a rough estimate for the tour lands at nearly PKR 2 million.

The Khan family had single-handedly played the roles of administrator, sponsor and selector for the maiden tour, simply to fulfil the desire of representing 'Pakistan' in international cricket. They made it a tour filled with cricket. Kiran claims close to 25 tour games against local club sides were organised in New Zealand and Australia, apart from three internationals. Aisha recalls crowds of as many as 5,000 in Canterbury gathering to watch some of those games: 'They had a good national campaign run around that time about how it was the first time that a Pakistan team was there,' she recollects.

For Kiran, it was a cricketing paradise. 'For someone coming from Pakistan, where we'd never seen women play cricket, to suddenly land in New Zealand where it seemed like every neighbourhood had a women's cricket team, it was quite a change.'

Pakistan's reputation as a strong cricket team was largely due to the history and exploits of their men, and the hosts expected the women's team to turn up with as talented a bunch. 'In the first tour game, they had several national players. We lost badly.'

That remained the trend for as long as they were in New Zealand. Nonetheless, in one of the games against Canterbury Timaru, Pakistan found their ideal opening combination. With back-to-back games organised against the club side, most of the players were tired by the end of the morning session. Aisha, who was picked in the team for her slow left-arm bowling and batting lower down the order, realised that there was an opportunity to bat longer. For that, she would have to break from her shell and speak up. She mustered the courage and asked the captain.

Shaiza agreed to her request and let Shabana Kausar pair up with her at the top. The young duo put on a 50-run partnership for the opening wicket the next day, and even though they lost the match, their partnership was a positive development.

On 28 January 1997, the day of their first-ever international cricket match, Kausar was shifted back to the lower middle order, while Aisha was at the crease when the first ball was bowled – Najmunnissa Ismail taking the strike. Aisha was yet again unaware – this time of the enormity of the occasion. 'I really didn't know that this was the first-ever match for Pakistan women's team,' she says. 'It's only over the years that I've come to realise what a historic moment it was.'

Najmunnissa played out the first over without scoring and, in the second, Jalil was adjudged lbw off the second ball she faced, by Julie Harris, for a duck. Najmunnissa, Shahnaz Sohail, Abida Khan and Meher Minwalla were also dismissed without a score against their name as Pakistan folded on 56, in only 33.3 overs. Kiran spent the most minutes (44) and scored the most runs (19). Shaiza Khan, who faced the most balls (42), was the only other to register a double-digit score in the innings (13). In a 50-over game, New Zealand wrapped up the chase in only 8.1 overs, without losing a wicket. It was a harsh welcome to international cricket for Shaiza's team.

More than 13,000 kilometres away from their home town, without the chaos and pace of Pakistan, New Zealand was quite a lonely country to be in. Losing games only made it lonelier. In Christchurch, a city which sleeps early, even more so. 'It was a dead town,' Kiran recalls. 'The only entertainment we had after dinner was going to a gas station nearby, where we'd sit looking at the cars coming in – if they ever came in.' There were the occasional phone calls from home, or messages sent through fax to let the families know that their daughters were safe and well. The warmth of victory was hard to come by, though.

The second international, also played at the Hagley Oval in Christchurch the next day, wasn't any sweeter. They won the toss again, but this time they decided to bowl. New Zealand skipper Maia Lewis registered her only international century – a 72-ball 105. Debbie Hockley (with a 68-ball 88), Trudy Anderson (with a 65-ball 85) and Clare Nicholson (with a 53-ball 73*) also feasted on the inexperienced bowling as New Zealand amassed a score of 455 for 5 – the then record for the highest score in One Day Internationals (ODIs), which has been surpassed only once since by a women's team.

Even in all the gloom, there were some reasons to be cheerful. Kausar became the first Pakistani woman to bag an international wicket when she bowled Hockley, denying her what looked like a comfortable century. Sharmeen picked up two wickets with her medium pace and was the highest scorer with the bat. However, the general disappointment with the batting continued, as yet again, only two players managed to reach the ten-run mark and three were dismissed without scoring – including Shaiza and Kiran. Pakistan were bowled out for 47, in 23 overs, handing New Zealand a 408-run win: a record which still stands.

Shaiza and Sharmeen were very similar in many ways, although Sharmeen was slightly more rebellious and enjoyed playing pranks and would sometimes break the team's undefined code of conduct. Neither of the sisters was particularly good at keeping their emotions in check, and would often display flashes of love and anger in equally dramatic ways. In good times, they would go out of their way to make everyone in the squad feel at ease and taken care of as if they were family. However, in more stressful times, especially on the cricket field, both sisters could fly off the handle – particularly Shaiza. Even though Pakistan was essentially an amateur side taking on professional and much better-equipped international cricket teams, Shaiza could erupt in fury if she felt her teammates weren't stepping up to the challenge. She had put so much effort into bringing the team together and dreaming of glory for her country that she had no time for any lapses of concentration on the field. Very few of her teammates fully understood or grew close to her; those who did, however, have maintained a lifelong relationship of trust.

Kiran is one of them. 'I've been told off by her so many times, but that's what a captain does,' she argues. 'If I'm faltering, the team is suffering because of that. The captain needs to be strict.' She was, however, in the minority in feeling this way. Being so far from home and in such an alien – and testing – environment was extremely difficult for each of the players, and they would have preferred an encouraging arm around the shoulder to a roaring and intimidating leader.

A harsher time awaited the team in Australia. On 7 February, at the Wesley Cricket Ground in Melbourne, the hosts secured a 374-run win, the second-biggest-ever margin of victory behind New Zealand's efforts in the first ODI a few days earlier. Electing to bat, Australian skipper Belinda Clark and Lisa Keightley registered centuries, putting on a 219-run partnership for the opening wicket. The latter's 147-ball 156* remains her highest score in international cricket.

Several records tumbled as Australia posted 397 for 4. Zoe Goss, the No 3, missed out on a century when she was dismissed by Sultana Yousuf for a 55-ball 94. Shaiza conceded 111 runs from her ten-over spell, making it the most expensive return in ODIs, a record which had until then been held by Sharmeen.

In response, Pakistan were bundled out for 23, the lowest score at that time, 'bettered' only by the Netherlands in 2008. Defying the Australian bowlers for more than 24 overs for the paltry score, Shabana Kausar top-scored with six.

By the end of the tour, the relationship between Shaiza and several other players had become bitter, and when they returned home they left the set-up. Some shifted allegiance to another cricketing group which soon rose to prominence, trying to seize the title of the Pakistan cricket team from the PWCCA; some left the game forever. Aisha also left after falling out with Shaiza, but she was grateful for what the tour had offered her. 'That tour in Australia and New Zealand instilled confidence in me and changed me as a person. I remember, while leaving the airport in Sydney, I closed my eyes and prayed to Allah, promising him that one day I would return to this country.'

In fact, she did return to Australia a few years later to study, and almost two decades after that, she was back with the Pakistan women's team – this time as their manager.

Despite three heavy defeats, and despite losing a large chunk of their team in the aftermath, the larger cricketing purpose of the tour had been served. Pakistan had officially qualified for the World Cup and were set to go to India for the tournament scheduled at the end of the year. At least, that's what they thought.

SHAIZA AND THE 16 FUGITIVES

'PAKISTAN HAVE WON the World Cup just by turning up here.'

It was a bizarre announcement by Brijmohan Lall Munjal, the founder of Hero MotoCorp – principal sponsors of the 1997 World Cup – while welcoming the neighbouring country during the tournament's opening ceremony in New Delhi. For a team which had only just entered the world of international cricket and had the most unpromising of results, the description bemused many. But those who were aware of what had transpired en route to their arrival in India's political capital weren't surprised. Shaiza and her team had, despite everything, escaped Pakistan after being put on the Exit Control List – a tool used by the government to restrict criminals charged with grave crimes.

Shaiza's team might have returned from their first cricket tour with massive defeats, but their act of touring abroad and playing cricket under the banner of 'Pakistan' had gained them a great deal of media coverage. It flustered the two groups in Lahore – headed by Tahira Hameed and Shirin Javed, respectively – who had aspired to achieve what Shaiza eventually did by taking her team for an international tour to New Zealand in a relatively short span of time. Both groups, which had been fighting each other over the last two decades for the title of PWCA, had now turned their sights on Shaiza, giving the Lahore vs Karachi tussle in Pakistani cricket a different turn.

Together, the three groups could have mustered ample financial and political clout to advance women's cricket in Pakistan. Instead, it turned into a battle of egos with all three using their respective resources against each other.

'In Lahore, it was only a specific class of women who played cricket,' Afia notes. 'Shaiza and Sharmeen weren't playing with their own class of women in Karachi. They were playing with women who didn't have the opportunities elsewhere, who wouldn't have been able to play cricket on their own. That's the difference.'

With Shirin Javed having family links to influential people in the PCB, many of the resources from the Pakistan board were not coming to the PWCCA's aid. As a result, the tussle had also seen the latter unable to gain easy access to established coaches. Even those who supported them in spirit refused to help them in an official capacity due to the fear of missing out on opportunities which would come along with the PCB.

One of the solutions Shaiza came up with was to look outside Pakistan. Having witnessed first-hand the quality of cricket being played by the women in Australia and New Zealand, she was convinced that a female coach from one of these two countries would be invaluable for the team. So, they called the Australian Cricket Board (now called Cricket Australia).

Jodie Davis, a 30-year-old Canberra cricketer, who had captained her club side against the touring Pakistan team earlier in the year, was approached for the role by the Australian Sports Commission in July 1997. Jodie had coaching experience with the Australian Institute of Sport, and it had been nearly a decade since she had played for the country. It was an enticing offer to make the step up to coach a national team. 'I agreed straight away without understanding what I was getting into,' she says.

It didn't take much time for her to realise that Australia and Pakistan were not just geographically far apart, but culturally distant as well. It had taken her three months from giving her verbal agreement to landing in Pakistan, largely due to the financial constraints. Barring her airfares, food and accommodation, there weren't any financial perks to the job. 'They wanted me to come over immediately. That was something I couldn't do because there was no pay involved and I had a job here which was paying for the house,' she explains.

However, she began her preparation for the new assignment long before she received any payment, sending day-to-day plans for each week. She prepared cards, laminated them and sent photographs to help the players understand her drills and training methods. The routine was structured – start easy and get harder. Since at that time she was also serving as batting coach for her housemate, Australian cricketer Bronwyn Calver, she knew that the challenge with the Pakistan team was going to be much different. 'The programme that I sent over was basic. There was no point trying to jump down the track and getting them to prepare similarly to the Australians.'

When she eventually arrived in Pakistan, in October 1997, just over two months before the World Cup, she came with a bag full of cricketing goods donated by the Australian team. Christina Matthews, the Australian wicketkeeper, provided the slip catch cradle while others chipped in with balls and other training gear.

Davis was serious about cricket and so were the Khan sisters, who picked her up at the airport and drove straight to the training ground at the army ground barracks in Lahore. On a flat piece of land, with no grass or nets, Jodie couldn't spot a cricket field, but that was only a brief shock in the early hours of her stay in the new country. With most of the grounds either not available for the team to use or with the prices quadrupled to discourage them, that was the only place where they could practise.

From the assembly of nearly 40 girls, Jodie's first task was to play the selector and identify the best squad for the World Cup. Which was a struggle, to say the least. Several players had turned up in 'traditional outfits and sandals' for practice. 'It turned out, they hadn't even been training before I arrived,' she notes in disappointment. 'I found my programme in the corner of the lounge room. They hadn't even opened it.'

The welcome wasn't what she had expected, but it offered her a peek into the more dramatic events that were to follow. It also gave her an idea of why training for the World Cup wasn't the only challenge they were up against. During a selection trial which the PWCCA had planned to organise in Kinnaird College, members of the PWCA got into a physical altercation with them.

'There was some push and shove and stuff thrown at us from the outside,' Jodie recalls. 'I was taller and more imposing than most of the players, so Sharmeen and I tended to be the "muscle" when these sorts of events occurred. Both groups were quite fiery.'

With the possibility of playing a World Cup in sight, the battle to hold the rights of 'Pakistan women's cricket team' stepped up a level between the groups from Karachi and Lahore. The two groups from Lahore, which were already infighting over the title of PWCA, now had to contest another rival in the form of Shaiza Khan in Karachi. With the aid of the PCB, the PWCA started to rope in sponsors and announced in the media that the team assembled by them would represent Pakistan at the World Cup.

'There were times when we would book training sessions and they would turn up there instead,' Jodie reveals. 'There would be a confrontation. At one point, the PWCA even tried to steal our uniforms. Shaiza was constantly paranoid that they were spying or stealing or trying to undermine the team.

'The PWCA were constantly emailing the IWCC to say they were the official team and wanted details of the World Cup travel and team arrangements. The poor World Cup organisers were very confused, and Shaiza spent lots of time trying to ensure the PWCA didn't succeed. The PWCA had photos of their "team" and boasted to the media that they were going to the World Cup.'

They didn't just boast, they prepared a team, named a squad and booked the tickets for India. More importantly, they had even got hold of the squad that Shaiza was going to take to the World Cup and resorted to despicably underhand tactics to prevent them from leaving the country.

Three days before Shaiza and her team were to leave from Lahore to New Delhi for the tournament, she was informed by people close to her at the airport that the members of her team had been put on an Exit Control List. However, poor governmental administration meant the list had only reached the airport in Lahore. Shaiza was certain that an escape route from Karachi was still possible. Fearing that the visas from the Indian High Commission office in Islamabad wouldn't reach them in time, she left for the national capital while the rest of the team made a quick dash to Karachi.

Jodie Davis, though, didn't have permission to travel to Karachi. Following the murder of two US consular officials in 1995 – communications technician Gary Durrell and secretary Jackie Van Landingham, who were killed in their car by unidentified gunmen – the city was identified as unsafe by the Australian Department of Foreign Affairs and Trade. 'I was a bit nervous about that,' she explains, but left with no option, she joined the team.

'In Karachi, since it was also the weekend, we knew that they wouldn't be able to get us on Exit Control,' Kiran recalls. But then another obstacle confronted them. When they reached Karachi airport and tried to book their flights, they discovered that the only available one leaving for India was a small aircraft, which had room for just 33 passengers running at full capacity.

Sharmeen, Kiran and Maliha Hussain began another mad dash – to the control tower, to the head office and back to the airport, using the World Cup invitation from India in a desperate plea with Pakistan International Airlines (PIA) to replace the aircraft. 'They eventually changed to a bigger plane and issued us the tickets,' says Kiran. 'Once we were on board, the captain announced that we were going for the World Cup and everyone on the flight cheered for us and wished us well.'

As they soon found out, though, they weren't the only ones to reach India. Tahira Hameed had turned up with Khawaja Parvez Masood. So did the PWCA's Shirin Javed, Azra Parveen and Bushra Aitzaz. All trying to make a case for being the rightful representatives of 'Team Pakistan'.

Brijmohan Lall Munjal was flanked on the dais by Anuradha Dutta, secretary of the Women's Cricket Association of India, when all 11 participating teams lined up in symmetrical rows for the inauguration of the tournament. Since the PWCCA was the only body affiliated with the IWCC, Shaiza's team stood in the row reserved for 'Pakistan', dressed in green blazers and white shirts.

It was the first time the cricketing world, outside Australia and New Zealand, had caught a glimpse of the Pakistan team. Even Indians, who have been closely related to their culture, were awestruck by what they saw from their neighbours.

Chander Shekhar Luthra, a journalist with *Asian Age* who covered the team extensively during the tournament, recalls, 'We didn't know what the Pakistan women's team would be like. We assumed they would be coming from orthodox families, some of them possibly even wearing burkhas. We were so wrong. They were well spoken, well exposed, liberal and knowledgeable women. Their lifestyles were ahead of their time. Beyond their lives and cricket, we even ended up discussing the works of Salman Rushdie.'

Nooshin Al Khadeer, who had played against the team as a 14-year-old in a warm-up match before the World Cup, was awestruck when she came across Shaiza during a dinner party at the Capitol Hotel in Bangalore. 'That was the first time I had seen a woman smoke. When all the players were introduced to the team, we learned that she was the captain of Pakistan. It was quite fascinating, I thought she was pretty cool.'

Purnima Rao, the Indian cricketer playing in the World Cup, who was equally ignorant about their backgrounds, added, 'They looked extremely confident.' That confidence was palpable to her because Shaiza genuinely assumed the team was good enough to make a mark, if not to beat a couple of teams and qualify for the knockouts.

Pakistan were scheduled in Group A, alongside Australia, England, South Africa, Denmark and Ireland – of which the top four would qualify. She assumed her team had enough skill to outdo Denmark, and possibly give a tough fight to Ireland and South Africa. Her optimism wasn't quite in sync with that of her coach, though.

'Shaiza had probably talked it up,' Jodie believes. 'When she was speaking to the media, her father and the PCB, she said, "We'll win games, and our aim is to make the quarter-finals." Her expectations were high and she voiced it.'

A harsh reality check came before the tournament opener, however, when they lost a practice match against Karnataka, a domestic team, in Mandya. Attended by a crowd of almost

27,000, Pakistan was humbled by the state side, on a matting pitch. 'It was all too foreign for them,' Jodie notes. There wasn't a lot of quality at her disposal. Kiran and Shaiza had the technique to stay, and Sharmeen was a powerful hitter. Maliha Hussain could contribute too – with both bat and ball. But that's all there was in the batting department. Sharmeen was the chief medium-pacer, while Shaiza and Kiran provided spin options. Nazia Nazir and Sadia Bano were the other players who, in Jodie's words, 'could bowl on the pitch'.

She would go on to add, 'Nazia wasn't bad, Sadia wasn't too good.' Most others were making up the numbers. Sixteen-year-old Asma Farzand was handling the wicketkeeping duties since she had the strongest legs, most coordinated movements and wasn't one of the seven bowling options in the team. The limitations were soon exposed.

Their campaign began against Denmark, the team against which they believed they had their best chance of winning. However, when they were put in to bat, they were rolled over for 65 after little more than two hours of play. Shaiza, who had walked out to bat at the fall of the second wicket, remained unbeaten but only on 11, as the last six batters were dismissed without scoring. Denmark's attack was largely filled with medium-pacers. The batters had to make up the pace for their shots. Past the top four, there weren't many who could do that. Even as the new-ball pair was played out safely, Susanne Nielsen and Janni Jonsson combined to pick up seven wickets. To add to Pakistan's woes, Sharmeen, Nazia and Asma were run out.

Denmark took nearly as much time to chase down the small total, but lost just two wickets in the process, both picked up by Kiran. Shaiza conceded only 18 runs from her ten-over spell, nine of which were wides, making up the majority of the 14 bowled in the innings. The defeat might have punctured a few holes in Shaiza's inflated hopes but it gave a more realistic idea of where the team stood. Six players from her side were making their debuts, while there were no international newcomers for Denmark.

Regardless of the fact that Denmark were a low-ranked team, they had been a part of international cricket since 1989.

With a tame surrender against the weakest opposition, Pakistan stood no chance against the next opponent: England, the defending champions, the favourites, and the joint-powerhouse of women's cricket. With only a day's break between the two games, the players had to travel for three hours to Bangalore before catching a flight to Hyderabad, then take an eight-hour bus ride to Vijayawada. It was already a hectic travel day which was only made worse by an eight-hour delay of the flight. Having landed late at night, the players had sleep to catch up on, but also a near 300-kilometre bus ride before they reached their destination. To make matters worse, the driver tried to make up time by speeding across the rough roads, and the journey was so hair-raising that few managed to rest. Not surprisingly, even the view of the lush, picturesque Indira Gandhi Stadium framed by rolling hills didn't do much to stimulate their exhausted minds and bodies the next day.

That they were not match-prepared was ultimately immaterial as the contest was always going to be heavily one-sided. One of the Pakistan players overheard the English cricketers telling their bus driver to arrive at lunchtime, so confident were they that the contest would be wrapped up by then. It was probably a fair assessment, but it riled the Pakistan team and when Shaiza won the toss, she elected to field.

The English batters thrived against Pakistan's inexperienced bowling attack. Janette Brittin and Barbara Daniels scored centuries, sharing a 203-run stand for the second wicket as England amassed 376 for 2 – the second highest in history after New Zealand's efforts against Pakistan earlier that year. Fatigue from the hectic travel and low fitness levels meant that several Pakistan players suffered injuries during the course of their 50-over stay on the field. It got so bad that they eventually ran out of substitutes and Jodie had to take the field.

Even though victory was impossible, they did achieve one objective – England were kept in the game beyond lunch. Sharmeen and Maliha Hussain, who had bowled 19 overs between them earlier in the day, put up strong resistance with the bat, stitching together a slow 67-run stand. At one point, Sharmeen even tonked Melissa Reynard and Karen Smithies for three sixes. The duo fell in quick succession to Reynard, but Kiran and Shaiza continued the defiance. Pakistan managed to score 146, losing by 230 runs. But more importantly, they had shown the steel to bat out their entire quota of overs.

'That game was our highlight of the World Cup,' Jodie admits. 'For a team that's out on the field after only three or four hours of sleep, having lost to Denmark and then conceding 376 runs, running around . . . to bat out 50 overs and lose only three wickets against a team like England was quite an achievement. On top of that, we hit their fast bowlers for sixes. That was the pinnacle.'

The confidence gained from that showing wasn't to last long, though, as two days later in Hyderabad they came up against the other tournament favourite, Australia. Shaiza had the luck of the toss again. However, this time, she chose to bat. Three out of the top four batters registered ducks. Sharmeen, who was the only one to get off the mark, added one run. Kiran Ahtazaz, who was making her debut, was the only player to register a double-digit score, top-scoring with an unbeaten 11. Pakistan folded for 27 in less than 14 overs – the lowest ever in women's ODIs at that stage, and still the second lowest today. Australia chased down the total in 37 balls, losing only Zoe Goss in the process, run out for a duck.

With ample time remaining after the game, the Pakistan players took advantage of the net facilities available at the stadium for training. Any access to quality net training was gold dust, especially since they needed to beat South Africa in their next encounter to keep any hopes alive of securing a place in the quarter-finals. With a day's rest, they headed off for another long journey to Baroda, more than 1,000 kilometres away in the western part of India.

The extra practice didn't help much, though. They produced a more disciplined bowling performance, reducing South Africa to 100 for 4 at one stage, but a counter-attacking 63-ball 74* by Ally Kuylaars lower down the order propelled South Africa to 258 for 7, a total way beyond what Pakistan had managed till then. Much of South Africa's score was also helped by a generous offering of wide deliveries – 46 in total, with all six bowlers contributing to it.

However, Sharmeen and Maliha put on an 84-run stand for the opening wicket, helping Pakistan to a strong start. While the latter had crawled to 16 in 76 balls, Sharmeen had blazed away to 48. Once the duo was separated, the rest of the order crumbled. The remaining nine batters added only seven runs as Pakistan folded for 109.

The defeat dashed Pakistan's hopes of going any further in the tournament, but given all the promises Shaiza had made in Pakistan, a victory against Ireland was much needed when they headed north to the wintry climes of Gurgaon's Karnail Singh Stadium for their last match of the competition.

The desire to win, however, struggled to fuel their energy levels. They were a tired bunch by then. 'We had 16 flights in 22 days,' says Jodie. 'A lot of these girls had never been away from home, never flown. They were missing their families. They were carrying sores, niggles and injuries. They weren't used to playing every day, and we were training every day. There was no recovery facility. We didn't have a physio or a masseur. Against England, they were on the field as they scored 360. That's a long time chasing the ball. They didn't have any previous experience of that sort of pain, and it was difficult to work out whether some of them had a serious injury or were just experiencing extreme muscle soreness.'

Ireland were equally determined to secure a crucial victory against what was, by then, its easiest opposition, in order to qualify for the quarter-finals ahead of Denmark. Put in to bat, skipper Miriam Grealey scored a half-century, while Catherine O'Neill and Clare O'Leary made handy contributions, scoring 45 and 48*, respectively, as Ireland posted 242 for 7. Barring Maliha Hussain, who batted on for nearly an hour and a half for a 69-ball 11, none of the Pakistan batters provided resistance. O'Neill returned figures of 4 for 10 to cap off an excellent all-round display as Ireland won by 182 runs.

'To go home with no wins was disappointing,' the Pakistan coach admits. 'If they had played the way they played against England against the other teams, then we would've had a chance. But it didn't happen.'

Shaiza, Sharmeen, Kiran, Maliha and Meher stayed in India till the end of the tournament, while the rest of the players flew back home after the Ireland match. In a meeting between the three Pakistani groups and the IWCC on 26 December, it was noted that since Shaiza Khan's group had an affiliation with the international body, only it could represent Pakistan going forward. Jodie's tenure with the team came to an end and she tagged along with the Australian side through the Christmas period before flying home with them.

'The Pakistan team looked, for all practical purposes, like a real cricket team,' Jodie says with hindsight. 'They had the whites, the cricket gear, even though it was all borrowed from Shaiza and Sharmeen. To get anywhere close to looking like a cricket team was where it started for them. Five or six girls, who were pulled out of the countryside, had to get permission from their fathers to play. The parents thought that there was no point in sending their daughters to play cricket. For those girls, getting trips in the country, flying overseas and staying in hotels – they would've never experienced that in their lives before. Every week that we would train, more girls kept turning up, wanting to train with us, wanting to be a part of the team, right up until we left for the World Cup. There were proud fathers bringing them along, wanting them to play for Pakistan.

'For the girls who had a bit more life experience, that World Cup was a highlight of their cricket career. But for those other girls, those who would've otherwise only married and had kids, to travel to India and play for their country, it probably changed their lives. It was more than just cricket. It doesn't matter what happens to them for the rest of their lives, they have all worn the Pakistan cap, the uniforms, and have memories of playing cricket against the likes of Belinda Clark and Cathryn Fitzpatrick. You can't take these things away from them. Pakistan now have a very competitive team, good athletes, and more players have come in as the game has progressed. The class of 1997 laid it out for them.

'If they'd waited for 11 good players to start a team, they would have never got there. They just had to get it going and it all started with two sisters.'

IN TIMES OF *JUGAAD*

IN KARACHI LINGO, Shaiza was a *jugaadu* – a person who possessed the ability to find solutions with limited resources. She was inspired by the Hollywood movie *A League of Their Own* – a fictionalised account of the real-life All-American Girls Professional Baseball League – which saw two sisters get the opportunity to play baseball professionally during the Second World War and go on to become Hall of Famers.

The 1992 movie offered hope to Shaiza. The League, started in 1943 as a makeshift tournament to cover for the absence of men from the Major League who were serving in the armed forces, grew in popularity and existed for a decade longer than intended.

The support hadn't come easy. Amidst apprehension about women playing baseball, the owners attempted to glamorise the sport and the players to draw crowds. Over the opening months of the first season, they gained a growing swell of media coverage and with it came the crowds, which began to fill the stadiums.

Shaiza's team too made a mark. Whether for the cricket, the great escape or the infighting between the three groups vying for control of the team, Pakistan's presence in the tournament didn't go unnoticed. Shaiza trusted that over time even those mocking her team – as a bunch of individuals who were travelling just because they had the money – would have to change their opinion. To make that happen, though, they would have to win games. And to win, they would have to play – which was proving to be a challenging task.

Despite having taken the team to a World Cup, Shaiza was left to consolidate her position as the guardian of women's cricket in the country. The failure to win a single match at the tournament had already led to a wave of criticism. Moreover, the group led by Bushra Aitzaz and Shirin Javed had bargained aggressively with the IWCC officials and members in Kolkata to have the PWCCA removed from representing Pakistan. Shaiza knew that she had to strengthen her position in international cricket to retain the PWCCA's right to continue.

However, Majid Khan, chief of the PCB and a former national captain, was openly unsupportive of women's cricket. Furthermore, he had a major firefight on his hands with the Pakistan men's team, which was reeling after controversies ranging from match-fixing allegations and infighting to disciplinary issues. With the PWCA also lobbying against the Khan sisters, Majid claimed in *Wounded Tiger*, a book by Peter Oborne, that he was too busy with the issues surrounding the men's team to embroil himself in the business of the women's team as well.

'I didn't want to get involved,' he told Oborne. 'I was having trouble handling my own cricket people.'

It was obvious that if Shaiza was to further her ambitions, she would have to do it without any institutional support. Given Pakistan's performances at the World Cup, and the limited budgets which other cricket boards were operating with, it was difficult for the PWCCA to find an ally in its time of need.

The Sri Lankan board, which had ventured into international cricket around the same time as Pakistan, had favours to repay, however. When it was desperately pushing for a place in the 1997 World Cup, Sharmeen had offered support by agreeing to nominate it as a member to the council. Shaiza now needed Sri Lanka not only to host Pakistan for a tour but also to play a Test match against them. Even though interest in multi-day cricket was waning in the women's game, Shaiza believed that playing the oldest form of international cricket was the best way for her to establish a strong position from which she could run the game.

However, Pakistan and Sri Lanka, by virtue of being associate members of IWCC, were ineligible to play a Test match. According to the rules at the time, they would have to wait a further four years before they could have full membership. With the pressure mounting, this was too long for Shaiza to wait. So, she chose to bargain with the IWCC officials instead.

Her pitch, she reveals, was simple: 'For cricket to flourish, we need role models and we need more and more Test cricket to happen. What's the point of waiting?' Whether it was emotional or pragmatic, it worked. Both Sri Lanka and Pakistan were recognised as full members and they played their first-ever Test match at the Colts Cricket Club in Colombo, starting on 17 April 1998.

Even though Sri Lanka had only played their maiden international game a year and a half earlier, much like Pakistan, the gulf between the two sides was massive. Sri Lanka had had a fairly strong local women's cricket circuit in schools and colleges for nearly a decade. More significantly, it had access to some of the premier venues in the country and its best available players weren't divided across three warring groups as they were in Pakistan.

In the 1997 World Cup itself, Sri Lanka had made a significant impact by beating the West Indies and qualifying for the quarter-finals. Not surprisingly, in this maiden Test, Shaiza's team was humbled.

Having elected to bat, Sri Lanka piled on 305 for 9 before declaring. Vanessa Bowen's 78 had made up for an otherwise underwhelming performance by the top order. There was a point in the match when Pakistan's players had their noses ahead, with the hosts reduced to 183 for 6. However, they let their grip on the game loosen and allowed Sri Lanka's lower order to stretch ahead.

In response, Pakistan provided a derisory fightback. Amidst a batting collapse to the medium pace duo of Rasanjali Silva and Chamani Seneviratna, who combined to take nine wickets, only Kiran Baluch stood tall. Her innings of 76 – the first half-century by a Pakistan Test cricketer – helped her side muster a fairly reasonable 171. But there was no way back thereafter.

Riding a 134-run lead, Sri Lanka piled on further agony in the second innings. Seneviratna, who had picked up five wickets in the first innings, cracked a century in the second. Sri Lanka amassed 275 for 8 before declaring for the second time in the Test.

Chasing 410 was a bit too steep a climb. With just more than a day's play remaining, a draw was an easier escape for the visitors. But by then their stamina had been tested. Efforts to block their way out didn't help much as they were cleaned up for 100 in fewer than 50 overs.

The differing standards at which the two teams were playing was obvious even in the one-dayers. Preceding the iconic Test – which remains the only international four-dayer Sri Lanka have played to date – the teams competed in three ODIs. Pakistan were hosted in Sri Lanka's premier venue – the Sinhalese Sports Club in Colombo – for the first one, but the welcome on the field wasn't particularly warm. The tourists were handed a seven-wicket defeat after being bowled out for 135.

Pakistan improved on that performance in the next match, scoring 157, but yet again Sri Lanka had little difficulty in chasing down the target. The team lost six wickets in the process but overhauled Pakistan's score with more than 14 overs to spare.

In the third match, a rain-hit 31-over-a-side encounter, wicketkeeper Asma Farzand's 60 helped Pakistan register 120 for 6. But, yet again, Sri Lanka were up to the task, winning with almost ten overs to spare.

Even though it was a fairly unsuccessful tour from a cricketing perspective for Pakistan, the fact that Shaiza Khan had been able to take a group of Pakistani women to a fourth country in a period of 18 months was a powerful proclamation in her fight to play under the banner of 'Pakistan'. That a bunch of women was representing Pakistan abroad not only made headlines at home but was also quickly gathering the attention of the international cricket community.

In 1998, the Marylebone Cricket Club (MCC) – the game's traditional gatekeeper – had opened its membership to women for the first time in its 211-year history, with Queen Elizabeth II being the only woman previously associated (as club patron) during that period. On 11 May 1999, when the MCC fielded its first-ever women's team, against Surrey Under-21s at the Bank of England ground in Roehampton, Shaiza was at the crease.

The following season, Kiran and Sharmeen joined her and in 2003 they became the first three Asian women cricketers to receive membership of the prestigious club.

When all of Shaiza's favours had been repaid, a new ray of hope appeared in late 1999. It came when General Pervez Musharraf, an army officer who had been promoted out of turn to a four-star general by Prime Minister Nawaz Sharif in 1998, staged a military coup against the government and usurped power to become president following the Kargil War against India.

Politically, there was probably never a more opportune time for women in Pakistan to flourish than the turn of the millennium. Musharraf, in his early days, was unlike previous military dictators in Pakistan. A whisky-drinking, moderate liberal, he was driven to build the economy and reduce religious extremism. In order to present an acceptable face to the Western world, he realised that he had to release his country from its regressive bonds. The fashion industry witnessed a boom, female pop stars emerged and the country's cultural vibrancy was showcased to the world. The economy prospered and the crime rate witnessed a sharp decline.

Shaiza's troubles with the PCB also promised to come to an end with Lt Gen. Tauqir Zia, a close aide of Musharraf, elected as chair of the PCB. He gave the Khan sisters free access to the board's grounds and facilities and agreed to sponsor the team's tour to Ireland in 2000. All they had to do was get the payments processed through an employee in the board's marketing team.

For all this promise of progress, however, a shift in government from the conservative Nawaz Sharif to the fairly liberal Musharraf didn't change everyone's outlook, and not everyone approved of women playing cricket.

When Shaiza and Kiran went to the PCB office to have the tour payments processed, they returned empty-handed, much to the surprise of Afia Salam, who was waiting outside. Afia claims that the employee had agreed to process the payments only if the girls performed in front of him and he deemed them worthy enough to play in the team.

Shaiza and Kiran didn't accept his terms and felt there was more to the demands than he had suggested. It should also be noted that the individual concerned was photographed attending an event organised by the PWCA later that year, where he was the guest of honour.

'If Imtiaz Ahmed or Javed Zaman [former cricketers who were involved with the PCB] had said that they wanted to test the players, it would have been fine,' Afia states. 'They were cricketers, who were handling the cricketing aspects for the board. But if a marketing guy says that he was going to assess them, that was just trouble in the making.'

Shaiza, for all her bravado, had felt exploited at the meeting and she left the PCB office never wanting to return. 'Back then, I didn't want this story to come out,' she explains. 'I didn't want it to be published because the girls would've got scared of being in that environment. We ignored it totally and let it go. There was no point fighting it. As my father said, "You didn't have money before 12, you don't have money after 12 (you didn't really lose anything)." We could deal without the PCB money.'

Afia expands on the episode, adding, 'Their reputation was on the line because these girls from small towns had been able to join the team because of the assurance made by Shaiza and Sharmeen – with parents believing that their daughters would be safe with them and there would be no harassment.

'There was also no way to prove what he said and what he had meant by it; but it was understood. These girls were responsible for the rest of their teammates, so they couldn't risk exposing them.

'In the early 2000s, there was no route to justice or complaint. If they had told the story to someone who wasn't sensitive, they may have said, "Oh! You overreacted." It would have been their word against his word. You have to place yourself in 2000, when women were not believed at all, especially when they say, "I had this gut feeling." What the hell is a gut feeling? There were people coming up with evidence of assault and they were asked, "Can you prove it?" So, the idea of having a gut feeling would have been totally dismissed. People wouldn't have taken it seriously. Shaiza and Sharmeen were well-travelled, worldly women. They understood these men and they were not going to expose the girls to dangers like that. They had to leave the opportunity and fund the tour themselves.'

They left for the tour to Ireland with Saeed yet again bearing the expense of the tour, while Shaiza began to obsess about ways the team could create more history. During an intense chat one evening with Kiran Baluch, they chalked out two possible ways to do that – by playing the first women's Test of the millennium and playing against the MCC side.

But Ireland weren't too keen on playing Pakistan. The Irish cricket board had received limited funds from its government, which it wanted to use for its travel to New Zealand for the World Cup that year rather than a pointless bilateral series. As so often, Shaiza had to be wily and pushy to achieve her goals. Ireland were ultimately persuaded to play a Test by the prospect of having its name appear in the *Wisden Cricketers' Almanack* – the world's oldest-running sports publication and cricket's most prestigious annual.

'I guess they [the Irish cricket board] probably pitied us because we had so many problems all the time,' reflects Shaiza. 'I think they sympathised with us because they were well aware that there were so many people trying to stop us from playing. It seemed as if all the members of IWCC were fascinated by our stories, because it felt like they all had it easier than us.'

It wasn't just off the field that Shaiza's team continued to have a torrid time. In the solitary Test match, Pakistan were cleaned up for 53 and 86. Ireland, in response, had to bat for only 47 overs and declared on 193 for 3 to register victory by an innings and 54 runs.

Not used to the pace of the contest, Ireland's Isobel Joyce, the player of the match, recalled to Raf Nicholson in an interview with ESPNcricinfo, 'I just remember thinking, "God, this is really boring." They blocked for most of their first innings. It felt like forever!'

Siobhan McBennett, former manager of the Ireland women's team, also added, 'Pakistan were trying to make a name for themselves. They were very keen to play a Test, so that they could go to the PCB and say, "We've played a Test!" It was a little bit of a tick-box exercise. And for Ireland, too, we were trying to get the men to take some responsibility for women's cricket, and they had little interest. We felt it was a tick-box as well, so that we could say, "Of course we've done that!"'

It has remained the only Test that the Ireland women's team has ever played. In the ODIs, which sandwiched the Test, Ireland swatted away Pakistan just as effortlessly – winning by a massive margin of nine wickets when they chased and by a difference of 117, 150, 54 and 138 runs, respectively, in the last four ODIs when they batted first.

Ten ODIs and two Tests down, Pakistan had yet to register a victory in international cricket. But Shaiza, Sharmeen and Kiran had greater cricketing ambitions to fulfil. Despite the losses, the team returned to Pakistan in joyful spirits – courtesy of an impressive showing in the stopover in England, where they faced an MCC side.

In a 40-over-a-side match, played at Charterhouse School in Surrey on 8 August 2000, Pakistan registered a seven-wicket win. Led by Kiran Baluch's 66-ball 65, Pakistan chased down the target of 144 without much fuss. For the achievement, the team received a congratulatory note from the Queen as well as from the president of Pakistan.

Shaiza had achieved both the records she had desired, but her aspirations knew no limit. Along with Sharmeen and Kiran, she toured the UK, playing games for various clubs. Isabelle Duncan, who was a part of the inaugural MCC side, captained them for Kent's Blackheath Cricket Club. The side included seven men and played against a men's team at Surrey's Old Woking Cricket Club.

Duncan vividly recalls their desperation to compete. 'They were so keen to play as much cricket as possible and played so well. Kiran was very natural. She had such a flair for batting; it was in her blood. What stood out for me, though, was Shaiza's leg breaks, which helped us win the game. She could really fizz it. It bamboozled quite a few men and took them by surprise.

'They were in love with the game and determined to make it work. Shaiza was a natural leader and wanted to fight the fight. She put a lot of time and energy into just making cricket happen.'

Shaiza's Karachi house had always served as a reliable training camp for the players. Those making the squad were given accommodation there, with all their expenses taken care of. The Khans had covered their tennis court with AstroTurf, and the players would practise there with a bowling machine ordered from South Africa. The facilities provided by the sisters were ahead of their time, with the players not only being videoed during practice but also viewing footage of their opposition. This they studied in the garage, which had been converted into a meeting room. For match practice, they would head to the factory complex on the outskirts of the city, where a ground with three cricket pitches (the soil sourced from Multan) was created in 2001 by Aziz Sahib, curator of the National Stadium.

But there were several hats Shaiza had to don before pulling on her whites for the field, one of them being that of team sponsor. Having funded the initial tours, Saeed passed on the onus of generating the revenue to his daughters. Shaiza claims there were many who showed interest but backed out at the last moment. In the absence of a sponsor, the only other way in which she could tour with the team was by meeting her sales target as an employee in her father's company.

Despite the team's recognition nationally and internationally, they weren't able to attract sponsors easily. By then, Shaiza's focus had also shifted from touring abroad to attracting teams to visit Pakistan. A spate of defeats in international cricket up to that point meant that Pakistan couldn't be a part of the World Cup in 2000, for which only the top eight teams in the world had qualified. However, Shaiza and Sharmeen did travel to New Zealand in December to watch the tournament, and it was there that they met the Dutch official Betty Timmer, who harboured hopes of becoming the next vice-president of the IWCC. In the interests of both parties, an unofficial agreement was made. The PWCCA voted for Timmer in the elections, and, in turn, she visited Pakistan to have a look at the facilities.

According to Shaiza, Timmer had returned home so impressed that she promised her Netherlands team would travel to Pakistan for a seven-match series in April 2001. With a quick turnaround needed, Shaiza and marketing manager Shaiza Shabbir hustled to make arrangements for the series. PIA, the national airline, offered subsidised tickets and the army provided the garrison grounds for practice.

It was building up to be the most seamless staging of a series the Khans had yet encountered. The PWCCA found support from administrators at the PCB as well as those holding political offices – Anita Ghulam Ali and Muhammad Mian Soomro, the Governor of Sindh province. But events took an unexpected turn when Timmer tried to back out of the tour at the last moment. On the day Tauqir Zia approved the use of the National Stadium in Karachi to host the games, Shaiza received correspondence from Timmer telling her that the team wouldn't be able to travel to Pakistan. A long negotiation took place between Shaiza, Timmer and Christine Brierley, the president of IWCC, to save the situation. Shaiza made an emotional appeal that 'women's cricket will die its own death' if the Netherlands didn't turn up for the series. Even as there was panic in the PWCCA office, Shaiza ensured that none of that was noticed by the media, pretending everything was in order.

As a way of increasing pressure on the Netherlands to keep their word, Shaiza also used newspaper clippings to suggest that enthusiasm for the series was high in the country and that several dignitaries were turning up for the event. Thankfully, she eventually succeeded in convincing them to play in Pakistan but promises elsewhere were failing.

All the assurances of sponsorship, which hinged on television coverage, were withdrawn. Afia Salam has written in *Women's Cricket International* that officials who had promised television coverage backed out at the last moment. Yet again, in the absence of a title sponsor, United Carpets Limited came to the team's rescue.

9 April 2001 was a historic day for Pakistan cricket for more than one reason. It was not only the first time they hosted an international women's match, but it was also the first time the women's team registered an international victory.

Unlike in Pakistan, cricket has never been a prominent sport in the Netherlands, with a wide gulf between the two countries in terms of the men's teams' quality and fan following. In women's cricket, though, the Netherlands had a massive edge over Pakistan. In 1958, the Netherlands was one of the founding members of the IWCC – along with England, Australia, New Zealand and South Africa. Even though their stock had fallen somewhat over the years, they had still qualified for the eight-team World Cup in 2000.

Pakistan, although in familiar conditions as the home team, had a stiff task facing them. In the first one-dayer, Pauline te Beest, the Netherlands skipper, won the toss and elected to bat.

All their batters managed to get starts but couldn't kick on. Shaiza Khan and left-arm spinner Khursheed Jabeen took three wickets each to restrict them to 156 for 8.

Pakistan, despite the team's batting limitations, knew it was a target within reach. But they wobbled. Sajjida Shah, a 13-year-old, was the top scorer with an unbeaten 28 off 112 balls. Sajjida had been spotted a year earlier by Shaiza in the remote town of Kotri, in Hyderabad. Even though she was extremely young, Shaiza could see shades of herself in Sajjida when she batted, and soon drafted her into the national team when Pakistan toured Ireland. Beyond her ability as a batter and an off-break bowler, Shaiza's idea that a cricketer is never too young to play had a critical role in Sajjida getting the early break. Shaiza had to wait her turn, making her international debut as a 28-year-old, with several years lost in trying to forge the team. She didn't want another aspiring cricketer to lose time. With a limited talent pool, there was also ample space for Sajjida in the 11.

Sajjida wasn't a stroke-maker. Her batting was simple, uncomplicated stonewalling. Its effectiveness was reflected that day when her long stay at the crease allowed Pakistan to take advantage of the wayward bowling by the visitors, who conceded 45 runs in wides. Sajjida's innings played a critical role as Pakistan just managed to cross the line with one wicket and four balls to spare.

A similar trend continued over the next two matches. In the second ODI, Shaiza Khan's five wickets restricted the tourists to 160 for 9, before Pakistan became beneficiaries of 67 runs in wides. Kiran Baluch's 29 was the highest individual score as Pakistan secured their second win on the trot – this time with nine balls to spare.

In the third match, led by Shaiza's four wickets and 28 runs, Pakistan chased down 161 with only a ball to spare. Some 59 runs in wides was their biggest assist.

Pakistan gained an unassailable lead in the series with a fourth successive victory when Shaiza's five wickets rendered Carolien Salomons's 89 insufficient as the hosts raced to victory with five wickets in hand. Unlike the first three wins, Pakistan finally had a decent batting performance, courtesy of Mahewish Khan's 72-ball 69, which helped them chase down the Netherlands' 204.

With the series lost, the Netherlands' captaincy shifted from te Beest to Salomons. It brought immediate rewards as they hammered the hosts in the remaining three games, winning by fairly comfortable margins of 57 runs, six wickets and 19 runs, respectively – the last of which was played under lights. Ironically, it was te Beest who led them to victories with scores of 80 and 90 in the fifth and sixth ODIs.

Pakistan won their maiden international series but that didn't guarantee any more cricket. The next opportunity that came their way was the result of a team's miraculous withdrawal from its tour to Sri Lanka. As a backup to save on the financial resources invested, Gwen Herat, president of the Sri Lankan cricket board, requested Shaiza tour with Pakistan instead.

'It took me two minutes to agree to their request,' confesses Shaiza.

In late January, she hopped on the plane for a short ride south with her team to play a six-match ODI series. There had been a significant turnover in Pakistan players over the three and a half years since the two teams last played, while Sri Lanka had maintained a strong core to their squad. They clean-swept the visitors again – by margins of 123 runs, 104 runs, 129 runs, 155 runs, 42 runs and seven wickets, respectively. To put Pakistan's batting woes into perspective, Sajjida Shah, the highest run-getter for the team, scored only 36 across six games. The burden of bowling fell primarily on the Khan sisters, who combined to pick up 15 of the 30 wickets the Pakistan bowlers scalped in the series.

✧✧✧

Despite all the losses, Shaiza had an opportunity to redeem herself by qualifying for the 2005 World Cup – for which, unlike in 1997, participation wasn't on the basis of mere membership or invitation. Her team would have to win games against a host of competitive rivals vying for the same position.

In the inaugural IWCC Trophy, which also served as a qualifier for the 2005 World Cup, set to be played in South Africa, six teams were pitted against each other. Ireland and the Netherlands made an appearance in the tournament after finishing bottom in the 2000 World Cup. They were joined by the West Indies, Pakistan, Scotland and Japan.

With only two teams eligible to qualify and join the top six teams for the next edition of the tournament, the task for Pakistan was hard, but it was also an opportunity for Shaiza's team to prove an emphatic point at a time when doubts were being raised back home.

Played in the Netherlands in July 2003, Pakistan began their IWCC Trophy campaign well, beating Japan – in its first-ever ODI – by 153 runs. Even against an inexperienced attack, Pakistan's batting struggled to flourish. However, Sajjida Shah returned figures of 8-5-4-7 – the best ever in women's ODIs – to bowl them out for 28 in 34 overs.

Pakistan followed this up with another win over Scotland, which had joined the IWCC only a few months earlier, courtesy of its participation in the 2001 European Championship. Put in to bat, Pakistan scored just 164 for 9 before bowling out Scotland for 126 – with four batters getting run out.

However, the campaign went downhill from the next day, with Ireland cruising to an eight-wicket win. Against the West Indies and the Netherlands in the remaining matches, Pakistan couldn't do any better – losing by seven wickets and 72 runs, respectively. Sajjida Shah finished as the highest wicket-taker in the tournament with 12 scalps, but Pakistan had missed qualifying for another World Cup.

The opportunity to make a mark was lost, but more significant was the failure to appear at the World Cup – which, as events transpired, could have been Shaiza's biggest card in retaining control of Pakistan women's cricket.

KARACHI 2004 – THE WORLD AT THEIR FEET

THE SUMMER OF 2004 was as friendly a time for an Indian to be in Pakistan as it has ever been since the two countries announced their respective independence in 1947. Atal Bihari Vajpayee, the Indian prime minister, had sent across the Sourav Ganguly-led Indian men's cricket team for their first Test tour to Pakistan in 15 years as political doves with a solitary message: 'Khel bhi jeetiye, dil bhi jeetiye' ('Win games as well as hearts'). The tour went ahead despite bombings and threats by fringe forces in the country, and cricket paved the way to improve relations, which had gone sour following the 1999 Kargil War and the 2001 attack on the Indian parliament. With the media also overdosing on the rare opportunity to fuel peace messaging between the two countries, the high-profile cricket and political movement overshadowed one of the finest moments in Pakistan women's cricket.

Shaiza Khan's PWCCA was set to host the West Indies for a fully fledged international series, which consisted of seven one-dayers and Pakistan's first-ever home Test match, all to be played in Karachi. It was a late call on the West Indian team, who had originally been scheduled to fly back following their tour to India.

Relations between Shaiza and the PCB had nosedived by then, and Ramiz Raja, the former Pakistan men's captain, who had been appointed as the chief executive of the PCB, attempted to sabotage the series. Ramiz wrote a letter to his West Indian counterpart, Roger Brathwaite, requesting that he cancel his team's tour of Pakistan. In a press release on 11 February 2004 – just a month before the scheduled series – the PWCCA stated, 'It is surprising for the executive committee of PWCCA to learn of this move of PCB's CEO as Ramiz had personally approached the PWCCA at the PCB seminar held in Karachi last month and had extended his full support, saying the grounds are yours and we will definitely give them to you for the said series.

'It was at Ramiz's suggestion that PWCCA wrote a letter of request to the PCB for the use of the National Stadium to which the PCB, instead of replying to the PWCCA, wrote to the West Indies to cancel the tour.'

The Lahore-educated Ramiz doesn't deny the claims. 'You have to understand that in those days women's cricket was an emerging format run by different independent bodies,' he states in defence. 'The PCB wanted to streamline women's cricket affairs and bring women's cricket under its wing to give it an official, credible status. The Shaiza Khan group, a family of sisters interested in the game, with money and contacts, were controlling the women's game and were making independent arbitrary decisions, introducing themselves as a recognised body to the world, inviting teams and also, with it, inviting criticism of frustrated cricketers from other areas and regions who were being ignored in the selection and administrative process. The PCB had to therefore step in.'

Irrespective of Ramiz's reasons, the extraordinary effort to halt the cricket organised by the PWCCA didn't stand to directly benefit anyone – neither the PCB nor any group of women anywhere.

But there was a larger power play in the equation. The PCB wanted to transfer the power of running the affairs of women's cricket out of Shaiza's hands. Shaiza's primary position of strength was the PWCCA's membership of the IWCC, which was also working to assimilate with the International Cricket Council (ICC), the international governing body of men's cricket. A good performance by her team, as achieved against the Netherlands, could severely derail the PCB's efforts.

Despite Ramiz's attempt to halt the series, the West Indies turned up and all the matches took place as scheduled. Ramiz was possibly only following the orders of Shahryar Khan, the suave former Pakistani diplomat who had been elected as chair of the board in December 2003. Hailing from the royal family of Bhopal, and first cousin of Mansoor Ali Khan Pataudi, Shahryar didn't think too highly of Shaiza's cricket team and dubbed the contest a 'Sindh vs West Indies' affair. He had his reasons for the assessment; at least six players in the 11 for the first Test were from Sindh province.

However, Mehmood Rashid, a former domestic cricketer, was optimistic that the team – despite its failings in international cricket – was a promising project. He had taken over as coach in 2003, during the IWCC Trophy campaign, when he had travelled with the team to the Netherlands.

It wasn't a full-time professional contract for Rashid, who was an employee of United Bank Limited. 'I had told Shaiza that I wouldn't be able to give a lot of time to the team,' he explains. 'Yet she agreed and said that she would ask the girls to come for training at a time that was convenient for me. I said, "Early morning, 5.00 a.m.," and she agreed. She even sent a car to pick me up and take me to the ground. It was only later that I realised that she had agreed to my demands only to check if I was really serious about it.'

Mehmood had little clue about the West Indies team. He had never seen them play. But before Shaiza could hand over tapes of their matches, she sent him the scorecards of the two teams. It was in these that he discovered the most obvious quick fix to Pakistan's problems.

'Our bowlers were bowling a lot of wide deliveries,' he notes. 'That was making a massive difference. Otherwise, there wasn't much separating the two teams.'

In 33 ODI games up to that point, Pakistan had delivered 515 wides: 40 in three matches in New Zealand and Australia; 111 in the five matches at the 1997 World Cup; 16 in the three matches of the 2000 Sri Lanka tour; 40 in the four-match series in Ireland; 165 in the seven-match home series against the Netherlands; 63 in five matches in the 2002 Sri Lanka tour; and 86 in the IWCC Trophy. The average of more than 15 wides per game was high even by normal standards. For Pakistan it assumed even greater significance as their opposition were often chasing low totals.

With Uzma Gondal leaving the PWCCA set-up, another of Mehmood's key responsibilities was to find and train a player for wicketkeeping duties. The early experiment with Mariam Butt failed before he cast his eyes on 21-year-old Batool Fatima. A tall and lanky batter, she – along with left-arm spinner Khursheed Jabeen – was one of Shaiza's most promising finds from the trials at the Sir Syed Government Girls College in Karachi, ahead of the 2001 home series against the Netherlands.

Even though she was slightly tall for a wicketkeeper, her natural hand movement in collecting the ball impressed Mehmood. 'Initially, she had a tendency to get up too early; it was difficult to make her stay low,' the coach noted in his assessment. 'So, I would keep my hand above her head and tell her not to touch it while the ball was in play. By the fourth day, she was extremely comfortable with her keeping.'

Despite the off-field tussles with the board and other bodies, Shaiza was serious about the game. Leading a winning team was going to be her greatest currency and the best bargaining tool to continue running the affairs of women's cricket in the country.

'She would say, "Mein ne jeetna hai" ("I want to win"),' Rashid recalls.

'I had to explain to her that I needed to watch the West Indies team play in order to understand them and devise any possible strategy. We barely had four players who could bat, and our team depended heavily on Kiran.

'When I told Shaiza, "Kaptaanji, pehle do match hum haar rahe hai" ("Captain, there's no chance we're winning the first two games"),' she scowled and responded, "Aap aise bolte ho to mujhe gussa aata hai" ("It makes me furious to hear that").'

When her anger was under control, Shaiza was wonderful to have around – she was both supportive and selfless. In 2003, when she had travelled to Australia with Kiran Baluch for an IWCC meeting, she took Kiran to the Kings Sports Group in Cheltenham, a suburb in Melbourne. The store had a vast collection of cricket gear for women, which was unavailable in Pakistan and most other cricket-playing countries. While picking some equipment for the team, Shaiza also helped Kiran with a personal purchase – a bat.

After trying out a few willows in the indoor nets at the store, Shaiza handed Kiran a Slazenger V100 and told her, 'May you have a world record with this bat.' Whether it was her optimism or simply an obsession with breaking records, it sounded like a pipe dream.

'I laughed at her at the time,' recalls Kiran. 'It seemed like one of those good wishes that you don't really mean. I thanked her, shrugged my shoulders and took the bat.'

They, along with the rest of the team, soon realised that maybe Shaiza's wishes weren't all that fanciful after all. On 15 March 2004 – the first day of Pakistan's home Test against the West Indies – Kiran and Sajjida Shah batted almost the entire day on a flat track. Only four days earlier, the Indian men's team had posted 349 in a 50-over game at the same venue, and the Pakistanis had almost threatened to chase it down before losing off the last ball – making it a record-scoring encounter. A surface that looked ready for a timeless Test was being used for a four-dayer. Not surprisingly, Shaiza elected to bat on winning the toss, and Kiran and Sajjida put on a contrasting display of batting en route to a record opening stand of 241 runs to tire out the West Indians in the Karachi summer heat.

Kiran was elegant with her stroke play, most productive with her sweeps and cover drives, while Sajjida was stodgy but effective through her 286-ball stay. Four overs before the end of the first day's play, the latter fell two short of a century to Candacy Atkins. Kiran returned unbeaten on 138 – becoming the first Test centurion for Pakistan.

'Before going into the match, I thought that our team would lose in three days,' Rashid confesses. 'The West Indies players were huge, with massive hands. Our players looked like kids beside them.'

For the coach, the plan was to stretch the game to the fourth day: which would have been an achievement in itself. 'Our batting depended heavily on Kiran,' he says. 'I told her before the game that unless she scored a century, we wouldn't be able to post 120–150. And if she managed to score a hundred, maybe the team could go past the 200-run mark. For Sajjida, the message was simple: just hang in as long as possible.'

However, with the first goal reached, the team's ambitions increased. Kiran's record ton proved to be a huge motivator for the team. Before Kiran could relax after returning to the pavilion at the end of the day's play, Shaiza asserted: 'You must try for 215.' That total in an innings would have allowed her to go past the highest individual score in women's Test cricket, which had been set by India's Mithali Raj only two years earlier.

'I told the captain and the coach that I wasn't thinking about the record, but I was nervous all night,' admits Kiran. 'I was constantly thinking about it and even when I wanted to dismiss those thoughts, they kept coming back to me.'

The next day, after Khursheed Jabeen – who was promoted to No 3 to see off the end of the first day's play in fading light – was cleaned up by Envis Williams's medium pace after adding 11 runs, a collapse was triggered. Batool Fatima, Urooj Mumtaz and Nazia Nazir fell without scoring in the same over to Felicia Cummings's left-arm spin. In the space of a few minutes, Pakistan were reduced from 269 for 1 to 273 for 5.

'I was standing at the non-striker's end as the wickets kept falling, and I was like, "Please! No!"' says Kiran, recalling those nerve-wracking moments. When Shaiza walked out to bat after the fall of the fifth wicket, Kiran pleaded, 'Tujhe dosti ki kasam hai, tune out nahin hona hai' ('For the sake of our friendship, please don't get out'). Shaiza assured her, 'Tum meri fikar mat karo, you bat' ('You don't worry about me, you bat on').

Despite having batted for more than a day on a flat pitch, Kiran was on edge after the fall of so many wickets at the other end. Nervous, yet steady, she marched on in the company of her most reliable mate. Shaiza took an unconventionally safe approach to her batting while Kiran picked up boundaries quickly after a brief period of cautious play. 'I had started seeing the cherry like it was a football,' Kiran recalls. Every time she erred or got carried away and played a cross-batted shot, Shaiza was quick with her warnings.

The nervousness mounted when she reached the 190s. It was a long battle before crossing the rare 200-run mark, an eternity in Kiran's head. But 200 wasn't even a mark that she was entirely concentrating on, because once she eventually reached it and Shaiza asked her to do the *sajda* (bow down to Allah), Kiran responded, saying, 'I'll do the *sajda* when I overtake the world record.'

With each run closer to the 214 mark, the pressure piled on – on her as well as Shaiza. When she eventually equalled Mithali's record, Shaiza told her, 'You just hit the ball and run.' She followed the instruction, nudging the ball towards the off side and sprinting to the other end.

'It was the happiest moment of my life – firstly because I broke the world record and secondly because Shaiza was there to share the experience with me,' says Kiran.

Shaiza was dismissed soon after by Verena Felicien. However, before leaving the field, she told Kiran, 'Take your score as far away from the world as you can. I will not declare. As a captain, you have my complete support.'

With the Indian and Pakistani men's teams playing out a gripping series elsewhere, there weren't many to notice Kiran's record innings. The day after she had completed her century, her name and picture found space in the newspapers but those weren't enough to draw crowds to the stadium. Hanif Mohammad, the legendary Pakistan batsman who had been supportive of the team for many years, was at the National Stadium though. And at the end of the day's play, when Kiran finished her 584-minute stay at the crease – during which she cracked 38 boundaries – on 242, Hanif congratulated her and handed her PKR 1,000 as a reward.

'I still have that note with me,' Kiran says.

More significantly, having piled on 426 for 7 before declaring the first innings, defeat was almost out of the question, and the task for Pakistan was to push for a win. Even though the pitch was still alive for the batters, the West Indies players had been worn out fielding for nearly two days in the sultry weather. It showed in their efforts with the bat as they folded in 56 overs.

Shaiza was the chief wrecker, picking up seven scalps with her leg breaks, including a hat-trick on the morning of the third day's play. Felicien, who was the highest scorer for the West Indies in the innings, was caught by Nazia Nazir at deep mid-wicket on 47 before Shaiza dismissed Doris Francis for a duck. On the first ball of her next over, skipper Stephanie Power was caught off an outside edge by Sadia Butt as Shaiza became only the second player after Betty Wilson to register a hat-trick in women's Test cricket.

In 16 overs, Shaiza returned figures of 7 for 59 – the tenth best ever in international cricket. After two steady partnerships, the West Indies slid from 140 for 6 to 140 for 9 before eventually folding for 147. With almost two days left, and a 279-run lead to play with, Pakistan sniffed a massive opportunity to register their maiden Test win, and duly imposed a follow-on.

But the West Indies returned a more stubborn lot in their next innings, and Pakistan had limited bowling options. Sharmeen Khan was ruled out of the entire series due to a stress fracture, while two players – Mariam Anwar and Shabana Latif – curiously neither batted, bowled nor were they responsible for any dismissals on the field. In fact, throughout their combined 13 international appearances, they scored only three runs and never bowled. It was, in a way, a reflection of the limited pool of talent Shaiza had at her disposal.

Nadine George, the wicketkeeper-batter, was promoted to No 3 after the West Indies lost opener Indomatie Goordial-John early. Nadine had put on a fluent display with the bat even in the first innings before being dismissed for 22. However, despite having endured a heavy workload in the match till then, the 36-year-old took to the opportunity at hand. Instead of looking to play out time, she and Felicien went on the counter-attack and compiled a 97-run partnership for the fourth wicket before the latter fell lbw to Nazia Nazir. Although Pakistan still had the lead in the match at that point, the quick flurry of boundaries had unsettled them. Especially irked was Shaiza Khan, who had induced an edge off Nadine when she was batting in the 20s, which was put down. The left-hander went on to score 118 – the first century by a West Indies woman. Even as she battled through cramps, and retired hurt soon after reaching her century, her innings – one of the finest in Test cricket – helped her side wrestle the momentum away from Pakistan. She returned to bat and was eventually dismissed lbw by Shaiza on 118.

Pakistan had several appeals turned down by the umpire. As victory seemed to drift away from the hosts, Shaiza's displeasure escalated.

Shaiza, along with several other members of the Pakistan team, was furious that the umpiring decisions hadn't gone their way. According to her, it was a part of foul play from the PCB to deny them victory, even though four batters were adjudged lbw. Ironically, both the umpires – Riazuddin and Arif Ali – were appointed by the PWCCA. While Arif never officiated in an international match outside that Test, Riazuddin was a veteran who had served as an international umpire for 12 years.

'Shaiza would threaten to boycott a match if she felt the umpiring was biased,' Batool recalls. 'That's what she did then as well, taking the team almost to the boundary. Back then, there were no rules to stop the captain from walking off the field with their team in anger.'

Power and Jacqueline Robinson, taking advantage of the now tired Pakistan bowlers and fielders, stroked their respective 50s, further aided by Doris Francis's unbeaten 46, to steer the hosts to 440. Shaiza, who had bowled 55 of the 146 overs, had bagged six of those wickets to return match figures of 13 for 226 – the best in women's Test cricket at the time. However, Pakistan, sensing a win for most of the game, were left to chase a stiff 162 in 23 overs.

Pakistan crawled their way to 58 for 2 on the final day. It was a bitter-sweet end to a contest which had promised happier results for Shaiza's team. For many, not winning that contest makes it a sour memory, but in retrospect it was a match to remember for a lifetime, with two world records set that still stand.

Unfortunately, that Test in Karachi happened to be the last played by Pakistan.

As blatant as the hate between Shaiza and the PCB was, the former couldn't do without the powerful board. To host the West Indies, Shaiza wanted the matches to be played at the National Stadium in Karachi, which was under PCB control.

She could have chosen to host the matches elsewhere, but instead sought permission from the office that not long before had tried to stop her team from playing. After her initial request was denied, she met Shahryar four days ahead of the West Indian team's arrival.

'Initially, Shahryar was willing to give us the stadium just outside the National Stadium in Karachi,' reveals Shaiza. 'He later agreed to let us use the main ground on the condition that we didn't play the Test match. When we went to the Karachi stadium, a gentleman working there wouldn't believe us and asked me to call up Shahryar, who was on his way to New Zealand. We got into a conference call where he verbally gave us permission to use the stadium.'

Maybe there was confusion, with Shaiza ensuring the key details of that authorisation were never communicated by Shahryar (who was on his way to the airport) to the manager at the National Stadium. As a result, a letter was handed to the PWCCA granting permission to use the stadium for a week.

By the time Shahryar realised what had transpired, he chose not to dub that contest as a 'Test' match. Such was the confusion over the validity of the affair that several cricketers outside Pakistan believed it was indeed an unofficial Test match, which was granted official status only later.

In that time, the PWCCA also managed to squeeze in another contest – the first ODI between the two sides – at the National Stadium. The remaining matches had to be shifted to other grounds in the city, three each at Karachi Gymkhana and Asghar Ali Shah Stadium (two of which were played under lights).

The West Indies, riding high after fighting back in difficult conditions, carried that momentum into the one-dayers. They began the campaign with an uncomplicated seven-wicket win in the first match, led by opener Nelly Williams's half-century and Felicien's all-round performance (a 41-ball 31* and 10-1-20-0). Despite losing, there were two stand-out gains for Pakistan. First, the players had managed to bat out all the overs, even though they were limited to only 142 for 8. Second, they didn't bowl a single wide delivery in the 37 overs sent down.

They fell off soon from that improvement though. In the second one-dayer, the West Indies elected to bat and put on a 73-run stand for the opening wicket. They looked strong midway through their innings at 145 for 3 when Debbie-Ann Lewis was stumped by Batool Fatima off Urooj Mumtaz's leg break. Urooj, who had made her debut in the previous game, triggered a collapse and returned a five-wicket haul. Batool too had a memorable outing, claiming six dismissals – joining Sarah Illingworth and Venkatacher Kalpana for the most in an ODI innings by a wicketkeeper.

However, even though the West Indies team had been shot out before playing their full quota of overs, 195 was a steep target for Pakistan. They made a steady start but were bundled out for 60 less than the West Indies' total.

Despite the twin losses, Rashid could gauge an ideal target for batters to aim for. He felt 160 could be a fighting total as well as an achievable score for the team. He pushed for it. And in the third one-dayer, led by Kiran Baluch's 23, Zehmarad Afzal's 21, Nazia Nazir's 26 and Shaiza Khan's unbeaten 30, the team managed to hit just the right number.

Even as opener Nadine George sped away to 34, Pakistan kept chipping in with wickets at the other end. The rest of the top order fell cheaply. And although Stephanie Power, Debbie-Ann Lewis and Candacy Atkins scored useful runs, Shaiza's 4-fer limited them to 140.

The captain's all-round show had finally aided her team to their first win in three matches against the tourists.

With the victory, Pakistan also seemed to have found the winning formula: win the toss, bat and score 160. They went ahead and reached 163 in the fourth one-dayer, led by an 82-run stand from openers Kiran Baluch and Sajjida Shah, and followed up by a 52-run partnership for the fifth wicket by Shaiza Khan and Zehmarad Afzal.

In response, the West Indies top order underperformed yet again and they were reduced to 87 for 8 before the lower order offered a fight. They stretched the contest to the last over before No 10 batter Atkins was bowled by Shaiza. Pakistan won the thriller by four runs and levelled the series.

However, playing games on alternate days had worn out the Pakistanis, who were unable to keep up with the fitness levels of their opponents. Explaining their limitations, Rashid said, 'Kiran Baluch had some real calibre in batting. The others could just block. They didn't have the power or physical fitness to score the runs.'

This allowed the West Indies to return to winning ways. Realising their mistake in allowing Pakistan to bat first in the third game, they didn't repeat the call in the fifth one-dayer, and instead asked the hosts to field. Even as four run-outs restricted the visitors' innings, the score of 186 they had posted, courtesy of Felicien's 49, took the target far beyond Pakistan's reach.

However, another slow but assured half-century stand by Sajjida Shah and Kiran Baluch helped Pakistan to a strong start, further aided by Zehmarad Afzal's 32, but Felicien returned to trouble Pakistan again; this time, with the ball. She ran through the lower order with four wickets and bowled them out for 140 off the last ball of the innings.

By then, the energy levels of the Pakistani players had dropped significantly. Even with the series on the line, they couldn't sustain their performances. None of the in-form batters managed to produce the goods. Batool Fatima's 101-ball stay for 27 could only help them to 100 as they were bowled out in 45.1 overs.

Shaiza opened the bowling and picked up three early wickets. But the West Indies were in no hurry to chase down the target. Felicien fought her way to a 111-ball 30 and helped her side cross the line comfortably with five wickets in hand.

The series was lost, and Shaiza needed to figure out ways to help her team convert all their promise into victories. She wasn't happy with the results and she let everyone around her know it. Close to the National Stadium, where the matches were being held, a coaching course was also being organised by the PCB. Shaiza chose to reach out to those coaches, and that didn't please Rashid one bit.

'She called me up at night and asked me to come over,' Rashid recalls. 'When I went there, I saw three or four people, who had come for the coaching course, offering advice to the players on how to play. There was also a photo journalist, who was giving examples of Imran Khan's 1992 team to them. All sorts of irrelevant information was being forced upon them. I had told Shaiza to stay away from them but she didn't listen to me.

Instead, she questioned me about why I didn't tell the players anything after the loss. I quietly heard everyone out.

'After everyone left, I asked her, if she wanted to take their advice, why did she call me over?'

With only pride left to play for in the last match of the series, Pakistan elected to bat again. Kiran Baluch led the way with 61 but none of the other batters made a significant contribution as Pakistan lasted 50 overs but scored only 139 for 8.

The West Indies gave a strong response with openers Nelly Williams and Jacqueline Robinson putting on a 61-run partnership. Despite a brief wobble and stingy bowling by Shaiza, Sajjida and Kiran, the West Indies eased past the total with four wickets still in hand.

Pakistan had lost the series 5–2, but there was no doubt that their performances in both Test and ODIs had improved. But what should have been the start of a promising future eventually turned out to be the end of the road.

The events which followed this historic series ensured that the trailblazers (Shaiza and Sharmeen Khan) and Pakistan's first world-class cricketer (Kiran Baluch) never represented their country again.

5

THE BATTLE FOR THE THRONE

SHAHRYAR KHAN BELONGED to a part of the royal family from Bhopal that had moved to Pakistan during the country's formation in 1947, following the end of British rule. Educated at Cambridge and the Fletcher School at Tufts University, he went on to forge a career as a diplomat and served as the foreign secretary of Pakistan from 1990 to 1994 before working with the United Nations. The highly educated, well-travelled Shahryar might have been suave and forward-thinking, but he struggled to use his diplomatic skills with Shaiza Khan.

By 2002, the wranglings of the different parties claiming to hold the rights of women's cricket had got beyond the PCB's control. Several petitions were filed in court to settle the matter. In response, the Lahore High Court passed an order on 30 June 2002 which directed the PCB to hear the demands of the three groups and settle the dispute in accordance with the law.

Unwilling as the Pakistan men's board was to involve itself in the issues of women's cricket, the order put it in a position to end the chaos. As per the direction of the court, on 2 July, the PCB chair Lt Gen. Tauqir Zia appointed a three-member advisory committee, chaired by former domestic cricketer Javed Zaman, to hear the demands of the three groups. The committee also included former international cricketer Ijaz Faqih and advocate Ahmad Shahzad Farooq Rana.

In the first meeting of the committee, held at the Gaddafi Stadium in Lahore on 18 July, a plan was mapped out and they decided to meet the representatives of the three factions – the PWCA and Tahira Hameed group in Lahore on 24 July and the PWCCA in Karachi on 29 July.

Although the Lahore High Court had demanded the scrutiny be completed within ten weeks, it took them almost three months to finish their inspection of the claims and more than six months for the PCB to release its findings. Through all that, more mud-slinging continued between the groups.

On 2 October, Shaiza publicly claimed that Azra Parveen, with the help of a male guard and 15–20 colleagues, had verbally and physically abused two members of the PWCCA – Miriam Butt and Ambreen Nawaz.

Shaiza was probably aware that the findings of the report would not be in her favour. To begin with, she hadn't made enough friends within the PCB. Yet, on 11 January 2003, when the report was released, the committee had noted that the facilities, training and infrastructure provided by her group were superior to those of the other groups, while the PWCA had no legal status.

However, what worked against the Khan sisters, as per the report, was that they had the character of a single club instead of an association and as a result could not be the authority for women's cricket in Pakistan.

In a bizarre turn of events, instead of choosing one group from the three, the report concluded with the recommendation that the PCB should take over the affairs of women's cricket and establish a women's wing under 'a well-reputed lady'.

Predictably, neither the PWCCA nor the PWCA took the report too well.

Soon enough, in a letter dated 29 January 2003, the PCB's director of cricket Zakir Khan wrote to the IWCC president Christine Brierley stating, 'This is to inform you and reiterate that no women's cricket association including the PWCCA, the current member of IWCC, will be able to participate in the IWCC Trophy scheduled in July 2003. The PWCCA will not be able to represent Pakistan as we will be preparing a true national team to be known as the Pakistan Women's Cricket Team (PCB).'

In another letter, sent on the same day (as reported by Pakistan-based newspaper *The Dawn*), Zakir Khan wrote, 'Concerned authorities, including the foreign office, ASF [Airport Security Force] immigration, and other departments be informed that no women's cricket team be allowed to go abroad to represent Pakistan except the Pakistan Women's Cricket Team (PCB).'

But Shaiza didn't care much for the PCB's warnings or threats. She and her team left for the ICC World Cup qualifiers held in the Netherlands. As it turned out, the squad assembled by the PCB was the one stopped. Its members were denied visas as they weren't affiliated with the IWCC.

The PCB was miffed by Shaiza's stubborn ways, and in order to regain control of an issue which they felt was getting out of hand, they filed a petition against the PWCCA, requesting the court to decide if Shaiza Khan's team could legally play under the banner of 'Pakistan'.

Shahryar Khan had taken office as chair of the PCB in December 2003, in the middle of this heated battle. Ali Khan, Shahryar's son, recalls his father's initial struggles in the set-up. 'He inherited an organisation which was lacking in many different areas. He was coming from a background in foreign service to an organisation which had a lot of structural issues.

There weren't even people who could take notes properly and very few could communicate well.'

While crediting Shaiza and her sister for starting the team, Ali Khan puts forward the other perspective. 'Shaiza has a big role in the history of Pakistan women's cricket, because there was no women's cricket without her. Girls just didn't play cricket. For these two women to do what they did was a massive achievement. They played a lot of their cricket in England, where they could play. And when your father has the resources to make you your own nets, they could make things happen. It happened early on with men's cricket as well – with those who would set aside grounds, facilities and give money. They do have a big role to play, but it leads to a kind of polarisation that "Since I've done it, I'll run it." That's not how institutions and organisations work.'

Shaiza's trip with the team to the Netherlands was the tipping point which especially irked the PCB. Whether self-motivated or on account of the legal push, unlike his predecessors, Shahryar was more proactive in clearing up the mess – which began with an attempt at reconciliation between the three bodies. Its eventual failure led him to form a women's wing under the PCB in late 2004.

Surprisingly, it was chaired by Mira Phailbus, the long-serving principal of Kinnaird College. During her 27-year stint as head of the college, Phailbus had established the strongest infrastructure for women to play cricket in an educational institute in Pakistan. Her work as an educationalist had also earned her the Sitara-i-Imtiaz, the third-highest civilian award in Pakistan. She fitted the Lahore High Court's directive of having a 'well-reputed lady' heading women's cricket, but she had never shown an interest in the power struggle. As an outsider, she bypassed those who had spent their energies and resources trying to take control of the game.

Appointed to assist her as the secretary of the women's wing was Shamsa Hashmi. A former international hockey player, Shamsa had also harboured hopes of playing cricket for Pakistan. A member of the Tahira Hameed group, she had attended the trials organised by Shaiza Khan in 1997. One of the better finds, Shamsa got through, stayed with the team and even trained with the Khan sisters in their Karachi house. But heated arguments between the two eventually led to her leaving the set-up. The reason for their fall-out couldn't be established as both tell differing stories. Nonetheless, Shamsa joined the PCB's women's wing along with Javed Zaman and former wicketkeeper Imtiaz Ahmed – two highly regarded figures in Pakistan cricket.

Neither the PWCA nor the PWCCA was happy with the appointments made by the PCB. Members of the PWCA organised a protest at the Lahore Press Club on 21 December. Holding placards accusing Shahryar Khan of 'favouritism', they demanded his removal as chair of the board.

The PWCCA, on the other hand, served a legal notice on the PCB, reminding it that, as per the Court's order, its only job was to recognise one of the three bodies as the 'real representatives of Pakistan cricket' and not to form one of its own. However, in doing so, the PWCCA also hoped to 'amicably resolve' the issue with the PCB.

One of the key reasons for the PWCCA softening its stand at that point was that it was evident that their biggest card – the IWCC affiliation – would not hold good much longer.

The rumours that had been circulating for a few years regarding the merger of the ICC, the global governing body of men's cricket, and the IWCC were becoming a reality in mid-2004, with the latter unable to inject enough funds for the running of women's cricket. The final nail in the coffin was when the 2005 IWCC World Cup, scheduled for February that year, had to be postponed when the hosts South Africa failed to attract sufficient sponsorship.

The merger meant that women's cricket would have to be run by bodies affiliated to the ICC. In Pakistan's case, this was the PCB.

For the PWCCA, though, the sometimes warm, sometimes cold relationship didn't work out. Way too much bad blood had passed between the two parties by then for them to forget the past and reconcile. The PCB was wary that Shaiza wouldn't accept the situation easily.

With the Tahira Hameed group agreeing on the reconciliation and having Shamsa – one of its members – as secretary, the seat for the vice-president's position was left open for a member of the PWCA in the newly formed women's wing. But the PWCA didn't agree to the offer and instead decided to fight the situation. Unfortunately, Shahryar wasn't patient with this body either.

On 3 April 2005, after ten months of deliberation and legal processes, the merger between the ICC and the IWCC was signed, and the members of the IWCC were offered positions on the ICC's advisory board.

The PCB didn't follow suit. Shaiza, having organised women's cricket with limited resources for more than eight years, had ample administrative know-how to take the game forward. But the legal and non-legal battles which preceded the formation of the women's wing had soured relations beyond repair, and merit was no longer a criterion for selections.

Even though Shaiza didn't gain a position on the board, she chose to continue as a player under the PCB. However, not all rivalries were put to rest.

On 22 November, following selection trials in Lahore and Karachi, the PCB announced a 26-member squad for a training camp ahead of the 2005 Asia Cup, which was to be played in Karachi from December, and was set to be Pakistan's first series under the PCB.

The peace pact between Shaiza and the PCB seemed to have worked as she and several other cricketers who had played under her were selected for the camp. Shaiza was even given the position of honorary advisor with the PCB women's wing for international cricket affairs.

But the calm didn't last very long.

The PCB had sent out a press release naming the 26-member squad without any logic or order to the sequencing of names. When the list was published in the newspapers, the names of Shaiza, Sharmeen and Kiran didn't feature at the top, which infuriated them, according to Shamsa.

'They protested, saying their names should be at the start since they were the senior players,' states Shamsa. 'That was immature of them. They demanded Shaiza should be announced as captain of the team, Kiran Baluch as vice-captain and Mehmood Rashid as coach. Only then would they join the camp. At that time, the PCB wasn't in a state to take such a decision and said, "Let all the players get selected and then we can decide who should captain the side."'

The three players left the camp, and as a result weren't selected for the tournament.

Nonetheless, they tried to mend the relationship again. 'We came to terms with it even though it was very bitter and a bad stab in the back by Shahryar Khan,' Baluch points out. 'But we still agreed, thinking, "Let's look on the bright side – we don't have any administrative headaches, we can just take our kitbags and enjoy our cricket."'

They sensed an opportunity to prove their cricketing worth in the March 2006 national women's championship. But in trying to find a resolution to the bigger issues, they were picking fights they could have avoided.

'Our domestic tournament was called the Fatima Jinnah Trophy. But they announced a new tournament called "Quaid e Azam Trophy for Women". We argued, but they went ahead with their plan and held trials at the National Stadium,' Baluch says.

'Sajjida Shah, Batool Fatima, Shaiza Khan and the rest of us went to the trials because we wanted to get in on merit. However, when we were standing outside the stadium, amid a massive crowd of women, they were asking us, "Who are you?" Like they didn't even know how to honour their national players.

'That was demoralising, but we still stood in the line, got selected, and then Shahryar Khan announced that the captain of the team that wins the national championship would be the captain of the women's national team. We told him that Shaiza, who had captained the side for so many years, was still around, so she should be the captain of Pakistan.

'But we still agreed to his terms.'

The reason they did this was because they were confident that Karachi, the team with the most international players, would steamroll past their opponents.

However, by then, insecurities were rife in all corners. Shaiza was aware that the Lahore clique wanted her to fail – and, as a result, she trusted very few people. That lack of trust reached boiling point during the match against Lahore on 8 March.

The day before the game, held in Lahore, some of the Karachi players were seen mingling with the opposition. Shaiza didn't like this, and it led to a heated argument between her and the 18-year-old Sana Mir, one of her latest young finds.

'Before Shaiza came back to the PCB set-up, we had developed friendships with some of the players from Lahore in the national camps,' explains Sana. 'We hadn't heard good things about them from Shaiza, but when we met them they were unlike anything that was told to us about them. I don't play cricket to develop enemies off the field. Even when we went out to eat ice cream with them, we had to get the manager's permission. But Shaiza was very angry that we were mingling with them.'

On the day of the match, led by Kiran Baluch's 71, Karachi posted a mammoth 255 for 4 in 50 overs. It included a strong

93-run stand for the opening wicket between Baluch and Urooj Mumtaz, who scored 44. However, Lahore were up to the task. Sana Javed, who had captained Pakistan in the inaugural Asia Cup, led the way with a 131-ball 108. Shaiza, who had scored an unbeaten 37, triggered Lahore's collapse with the ball, picking up three wickets. Urooj also contributed with a brace as the hosts were eventually bowled out for 242 in 48 overs, losing by 13 runs.

With the match threatening to get close, Shaiza lost control of her temper. She had no patience for any lapses on the field and was especially critical of the efforts of Sana and Urooj – the best fielders in the team. Unsure where their loyalties lay, she sent them to field deep.

Shamsa, who was playing for Lahore in that match, took notice of the unpleasant words yelled at the Karachi youngsters. Soon after the game, she asked Sana and Urooj to report Shaiza's behaviour to the PCB.

'However, by then, Shaiza had already apologised for getting angry,' says Sana. 'She was very happy after the match. But we did complain at the PCB office the next day. We mentioned that she abused us but also apologised for it later.'

As it turned out, the duo had left for the PCB office under the pretext of meeting their relatives in the city. However, Karachi's coach, who had gone to collect his daily allowance from the office, spotted them along with Shamsa Hashmi, talking to Mira Phailbus. He informed Shaiza about it, and it didn't take much time for her to join the dots and suspect that they were up to foul play.

'Everything turned ugly after that,' admits Mir.

Local news channels carried reports on the basis of that suspicion. 'Urooj Mumtaz, one of the best fielders we had, underperformed that day,' Kiran suggests. 'We didn't understand the reason for that. We assumed she must've been under pressure. But when the coach told us the next day what they were up to at the PCB office, we clearly understood that these two girls had been tampered with.'

The turn of events that day was Rashomonic in nature. Batool Fatima, who was a part of the Karachi team, notes, 'Shaiza completely misunderstood the situation. It was the festival month of Basant, and some of our friends from the Lahore team had invited us to celebrate with them [a day ahead of the match]. There was nothing more to it.'

Giving her version of events, Sana contends, 'We as youngsters were caught in the middle of the mistrust between Shaiza and Shamsa. Shamsa saw Shaiza abusing us and encouraged us to file a complaint. What Shaiza did that day was wrong, but back then, as young players, we didn't understand what she was going through or what kind of pressure Shamsa was putting her under.

'Shaiza had captained Pakistan for ten years. The captaincy of the national team shouldn't have been decided on the basis of a domestic competition. That's how I saw it then, and that's how I see it now. She should have been the first-choice captain. Even then, I didn't think otherwise. I was just playing for Karachi and wanted my team to win, and we did.'

The fact that Urooj and Sana went on to become the next two captains of the Pakistan national team – instead of Sana Javed, who had led Lahore to victory in that tournament and also captained Pakistan in the previous tournament – only served to strengthen Shaiza's theory, that they were 'criminally ambitious'.

Sana looks back at the incident with a broader understanding. 'It was a really tough time for her,' she points out. 'She was just weak at that moment and couldn't judge who were the people who were sincere to her and who weren't. It happens to all of us. I don't have harsh feelings towards her. I respect what she has done for Pakistan cricket.'

'Even though she said some really horrible things, I do understand her position. She had invested a lot of money and time in bringing up women's cricket. The way she was dealt with wasn't right. That anger was passed on to us. She expected us not to play for the PCB and stick with her. Being young, I just wanted to play for Pakistan, I didn't want to be a part of any group.'

Dejected by what had happened, Shaiza, Sharmeen and Kiran left Pakistan cricket forever. Legal battles with the PCB continued until 2009, but without anything concrete emerging from it.

NAYA PAKISTAN

GENERAL PERVEZ MUSHARRAF'S liberal outlook may have had a role in reviving Pakistan society, but by 2005 he wasn't just a military dictator. He had turned into a full-blooded politician. *Time* magazine had realised this in 2002 as its July edition ran a cover story on him with the title: 'The World's Toughest Job'.

In trying to maintain a balance between US friendship, his liberal views and domestic politics fuelled by conservatives and extremists, Musharraf had become a leader of a country in chaos. His decision to align with the Americans in the 'war against terror' and fight the Afghanistan mujahideen following the 9/11 attacks in the USA led to several religious, extremist groups within the country rising up in arms. To retain his position as president, which was under severe threat, in 2002 he started following the policy of several other dictators who had preceded him and allied with fringe religious groups.

Most controversially, in Khyber Pakhtunkhwa, a province bordering Afghanistan and heavily affected by violence,

Musharraf's party, the Pakistan Muslim League (PML[Q]), allied with Muttahida Majlis-e-Amal (MMA), an alliance of far-right Islamist conservative political groups. Theatres were shut, performances were restricted and cultural norms were made stricter as the province was pushed back to the Dark Ages.

As the violence escalated and voices demanding Musharraf's ouster rose, he used his powers to subvert the growing opposition. In 2002, Mukhtar Mai (also known as Mukhtaran Bibi) – a woman from the lower-caste Gujjar community, who was a victim of honour-revenge gang rape which had been sanctioned by the village council in Meerwala – was barred from leaving Pakistan to attend an event by Amnesty International. Musharraf's view was that she would tarnish the image of the country abroad.

While Musharraf's outlook was forever opposed by the conservatives, his contradictory politics had lost him liberal friends and supporters as well. His allies the MMA, however, were in overdrive to force their ideals of radical Islam on the rest of the country. In January 2005, women were beaten up and had their clothes torn for running in public in the inaugural Lahore Marathon. According to the MMA, a mixed-gender race was un-Islamic.

A protest run by the civil rights community in April met a similar fate, disrupted by a mob of reportedly 500 people belonging to the MMA and Baazbaan-e-Pakistan, the students' wing of Jamaat-e-Islami.

It wasn't the safest of times for women to be running on the streets, let alone playing cricket. For parents, there were understandable concerns about letting their daughters pursue sports. The power to run women's cricket hadn't fallen into the PCB's hands at the best of times.

Whether a section of the board was genuinely intent on pushing the women's game forward or was simply under pressure to prove its worth to the numerous detractors, the women's wing continued to maintain a busy cricket calendar.

Despite the political and social tensions, the strength of the institution, with its resources and infrastructure, meant that the PCB could push the game into the deeper regions of the country. This began with the initiation of an inter-district competition. The maiden tournament (which was played between several clubs and colleges) was won by Crescent Club, courtesy of Sana Javed's quick-fire 83, on 28 February 2006 at the Government College Ground in Lahore. Garrison College, led by Marina Iqbal, were beaten by 93 runs in the 25-overs-a-side contest.

By February 2007, a national schools Under-17 championship was also organised, which included representation from 11 regions. Islamabad Schools beat Peshawar Schools by 32 runs in the final, held at the Niaz Stadium in Hyderabad.

This was still a period when cricket boards across the world weren't in favour of spending much on women's cricket. International affairs were limited to World Cups and the occasional bilateral tournament, which was often little more than a token gesture. Pakistan, still in its nascent stage, suffered as much as any country due to this situation.

Although other political relations were falling apart, Musharraf did manage to improve ties with neighbouring India – despite long-standing rifts. While cricket between the men's teams of India and Pakistan had resumed in 2004 and flourished, the first team from outside the country that the PCB hosted since officially taking over the women's game was the Under-21 team from India – in October 2005. Its arrival was part of a larger agreement to host the Asia Cup, which Pakistan had reached with the Women's Cricket Association of India (the body that ran women's cricket before the Board of Control for Cricket in India [BCCI] took over) and Gwen Herat of Sri Lanka. In this inaugural edition of the tournament, the PCB-represented team was eventually unable to participate, making it a bilateral contest.

The rationale of the three boards was to strengthen their respective teams, which were far behind the likes of England, Australia and New Zealand – who preferred to play against each other rather than their Asian counterparts.

Phailbus was aware that Pakistan lacked exposure to the international teams, with several of its players never having played even domestic cricket. Pakistan had the financial resources to host a tournament, and the intent to get cricket up and running. To give them game time before the big tournament, India sent an Under-21 team, along with two players – Karuna Jain and Rumeli Dhar – who had played in the 2005 50-over World Cup, where India had reached the final.

Even though it was a shadow tour, India didn't want to be outplayed by Pakistan. But as the series panned out, the visitors realised their junior players were strong enough.

Playing across three different venues in Lahore – Aitchison Ground, Bagh-e-Jinnah and Gaddafi Stadium – the visitors eased through the four-match, 40-over-a-side contests. It was a non-challenge for India's domestically hardened youngsters against an inexperienced team. The Indian players weren't aware of what had transpired in Pakistan in the last few years.

'When Kiran Baluch scored the record double century, I got to know that Pakistan had a women's team,' recalls Snehal Pradhan, the Indian pace bowler on that tour. 'When I went there, I remember thinking, "Where are those players?"'

For many in the Indian team, it was their first time on a plane, let alone flying internationally for a cricket series. To mitigate the fears of the Indian players and their families, heavy security was provided for the team wherever they went. The PCB didn't hold back on the hospitality either.

Snehal recalls a rather grand welcome by the hosts. 'It was the best treatment we have ever received on a tour,' she concludes. 'They took us out for a few dinners – one of which was at a rooftop restaurant. The meat spreads were especially delicious, and back then, since I enjoyed eating meat, I would often get a few stares from my teammates. In our dressing room, we had fruit bowls and snacks. All of this was unheard of back then, blow-your-mind kind of facilities.'

Since Pakistan was able to pool the money, and India and Sri Lanka were excited to get game time, there was little hesitation in the subcontinent trio agreeing for the Asia Cup. Seven cricketers, including captain Sana Javed, were making their ODI debuts for Pakistan when they faced off against Sri Lanka at the National Stadium at Karachi in the tournament opener on 28 December 2005.

While the results went as expected, the Pakistan players did have their moments, beginning with their first match where they ran Sri Lanka close. Urooj Mumtaz's triple strike limited the opposition to 178 for 9. At one point, with Sana Mir and Asmavia Iqbal's late resistance, Pakistan looked strong contenders for a win, but the lower order fell apart and they ended their innings on 164.

Against India, though, in the next game, they were pounded. The left-handed duo of Jaya Sharma and Anjum Chopra compiled an unbeaten 223-run stand for the third wicket to help India to 289 for 2. This included a century for Jaya and 86 for Anjum.

There were a few obvious concerns for Pakistan beyond the fact that the opposition batted and bowled better. Much as in the game against India, where they conceded 35 wides, against Sri Lanka there was a generous offering of 24 extra runs.

The players improved on that in their third match of the

tournament, against Sri Lanka, but were undone by Shashikala Siriwardene's off breaks. The upcoming spinner, who had already climbed the ladder to claim the captaincy, picked up four wickets to halt Pakistan on 93 in a small 124-run chase.

With that loss, Pakistan's chances of qualifying for the final were dashed, and the last match against India was only a formality. Yet again, they were outclassed by the eventual champions. Electing to bat, Pakistan's innings wrapped up on 94 – a total India chased down without losing a wicket.

Even though Pakistan didn't secure a win in the tournament, they made sure they were good hosts. Nooshin Al Khadeer, the Indian off-spinner who travelled with the team, had previously experienced the Pakistan team that toured India for the 1997 World Cup. None of those players was a part of the 2005 Asia Cup, but it took little time for the current hosts to make their neighbours feel at home.

'With the entire hype of playing an India–Pakistan game, we as youngsters were quite excited to travel, but our parents were apprehensive [because of the rising terror attacks in the country]. But the security officers never left our side and we never felt unsafe in the country. They also ensured that we never had to remain stuck inside our hotels.'

Markets were cleared for two hours to let them shop, and roads were cleared to make way for their travel. Two parties were organised – one of them by the board, where the players danced, and one in a lavish resort where they intermingled.

Within its limitations, efforts were made to deck up the event. Even though Pakistan didn't qualify for the final, a crowd of close to 2,000 people, including school and college students, turned up for the match. Wasim Akram, the legendary Pakistan cricketer, was also invited to watch the final.

It happened to be the only tour to the country by the senior Indian women's team, and it allowed Nooshin to meet her relatives – her father's elder sister – who had migrated to Karachi from Hyderabad during the partition.

Amita Sharma, who was a part of that team, had her moments of connecting with family roots a few months later, when the Delhi team was invited to play in Lahore. It was the city where Amita's grandfather had spent his childhood days, and he often told stories of eating jalebis at Anarkali Bazaar. Quite unexpectedly, beyond the cricket, Amita got a chance to walk through the lanes there.

Shamsa had arranged for the series in late March 2006 following correspondence with Delhi Women's Cricket Association secretary Hardeep Dua. The arrangements weren't as fancy as those for the national team, but to be able to cross the border on foot was a unique experience for a bunch of domestic Indian cricketers.

Five matches were organised across four venues in Lahore – Bagh-e-Jinnah, Lahore City Cricket Association Ground, Government College University Ground and Aitchison College Ground. Although the visitors yet again eased past Pakistan – sweeping the five-match, 50-over series without much trouble – the surge in competitive matches against varied opposition proved extremely useful.

The domestic structure was also beefed up. In the only tournament held that season for women, ten regional teams were pitted across three zones – the Karachi Zone (Karachi, Hyderabad and Quetta), the Lahore Zone (Lahore, Sialkot, Faisalabad and Multan) and the Rawalpindi Zone (Rawalpindi, Islamabad and Peshawar). The table-toppers from each zone – Karachi, Lahore and Peshawar – qualified for the final stage, where they played against each other once. Lahore and Karachi, who were without Shaiza and Kiran in the final, played at the Gaddafi Stadium, with the hosts winning by 40 runs.

Lahore's off-spinner Sabahat Rasheed picked up seven wickets, humbling a weak Karachi side. Another three-match tournament was added in the following season. Despite attempts to get more matches in, international cricket with the top nations was restricted to only one or two series a year.

With limited international cricket, it also became difficult to retain players who had had to struggle their way up, overcoming numerous social, financial and logistical challenges. In any case, with negligible returns for all their compromises and sacrifices, the potential rewards were never great enough for many parents to send their daughters to play.

Qanita Jalil, one of Pakistan's finest pace bowlers, who hailed from the Pashtun tribe in Abbottabad where MMA's rule had confined women within the walls of their houses, had told Reuters in March 2009 ahead of the World Cup, 'I am 27 and my mother is now pressurising me to get married. It might be my last tournament.'

To be able to play cricket was challenging enough; beating top international sides was an afterthought.

Shamsa had led Pakistan when they played against India Under-21s. However, her conflicting dual role as a player and administrator meant that she had to give up on one. At the age of 36, following Lahore's win in the domestic championship in 2006, she quit playing cricket. It was the last List A match for her as well as five other cricketers who were part of that final.

One of the terms of that championship was that the captain of the winning team would lead Pakistan. Fittingly, the departure of Shaiza Khan and Kiran Baluch one match before the final allowed Sana Javed to lead Lahore to victory. A former hockey player who was born in the remote town of Toba Tek Singh in Punjab, Sana Javed had already captained Pakistan in the preceding Asia Cup and was the third-highest run-getter in the domestic competition.

Bizarrely, though, for the next assignment against a touring Hong Kong side, Urooj Mumtaz was chosen to lead.

Urooj was a find of Shaiza's. A black belt in karate, she was also a national-level swimmer who recreationally played golf and tennis. In a piece on ESPNcricinfo, Kamila Shamsie wrote, 'One day Shaiza and Sharmeen turned up at the [Karachi] Gymkhana ground, looking for somewhere to stage a match. They were told to speak to the club secretary – Urooj's father. He said the club's regulations meant he couldn't offer them the ground, but he could suggest a player they might want to consider for their team. There were trials under way in Karachi not long after. Urooj went along and was picked for the 2003/04 West Indies series.'

Although Urooj had done fairly well for Pakistan in her brief career up to that point, her promotion to the captaincy was thanks to more than just her notable contributions with bat, ball and on the field. She came from a privileged background – wealthy and educated. For teams touring Pakistan, she was the host-in-chief when communicating with visiting players and making them feel comfortable. Although still only 19 and studying dentistry in college, her social exposure and ability to articulate her thoughts well in the English language made her a prime candidate for captaincy. Unpopular as it was, such a decision wasn't new in Pakistan cricket.

As an offshoot of the gora complex, for decades the PCB had had a tendency to gravitate towards Oxford-educated and English-speaking cricketers for the role of captain in men's cricket. It took them several decades to dump that belief system, but by the mid-2000s, with Inzamam-ul-Haq appointed as captain, it seemed they had moved on from their colonial hang-up.

In women's cricket, that wasn't yet the case, as cricketing credentials were overlooked for other personality traits deemed necessary for the leadership role. At a young age, already having to juggle cricket with her university studies, it was a challenging job handed to Urooj.

Her maiden assignment was a fairly simple challenge against a touring Hong Kong team. In the three unofficial ODIs played in Lahore, Pakistan thumped the visitors. Sana Javed cracked an unbeaten 117 in the opening game, followed by Urooj's 100* in the second and Tasqeen Qadeer's 106* in the third.

The lowest victory margin in the three matches was 172, reflecting how weak a challenge Hong Kong presented. It was nothing like the competition they would have to face three months later, at the 2006 Asia Cup in Jaipur.

Even as Pakistan put up an improved show in the opening encounter of the Asia Cup, courtesy of pace bowler Qanita Jalil's 5-fer, they never threatened to chase down India's 239-run total. Despite Sajjida Shah's 53-ball 44, they were limited to 159 for 6.

A day later, Sri Lanka also steamrolled them, chasing down the 148-run target with seven wickets in hand. In the third match of the tournament, yet again against Sri Lanka, Pakistan put up a better performance with the bat – reaching 166 for 7 – but provided too little a challenge for the opposition in the run chase.

By the time Pakistan went up against India, qualification chances for the final were already blown. In the inconsequential match, the players' morale was further dented by a 103-run loss.

Not only was there a lack of competitive cricket, but the players who would make it to the national team lacked formal coaching and skills training – often being picked through selection trials. Their limitations would be exposed against better teams.

In a rare bilateral tour in January 2007, they played South Africa in a five-match, one-day series (in which the last match was abandoned due to a storm). Not surprisingly, they were outclassed.

Johmari Logtenberg's unbeaten 79 had led the hosts to a 98-run win in the first ODI in Pretoria's Laudium Oval. In the second match, Pakistan marginally improved on the bowling performance, courtesy of Urooj Mumtaz's 5-fer, but there was never a hope of victory – they lost by 84 runs at Harlequins.

In the third match, at Sinovich Park, Pakistan elected to bat, but there was no change in fortune. The players made 156 for 9 – an improved performance, bettering the previous efforts of 127 and 142 –but the hosts chased it down with six wickets in hand and more than 14 overs to spare.

Pakistan did improve as the series wore on, but in the fourth ODI – which eventually proved to be the last match of the series – Logtenberg's century didn't leave them with much joy as they were ultimately thrashed by 101 runs. None of the batters stood out. Of the bowlers, Qanita returned three wickets twice but, much like Urooj, her spells were expensive.

The team, which was still in its burgeoning stages, desperately needed more competitive matches to level up. Playing the Asia Cup and touring South Africa back-to-back had shown the signs of impovement. But with no international cricket to follow in the next year, all the early developments came undone.

The nature of cricket played in the early days of the women's team was experimental. With international cricket so spaced out, some players left the system and many new ones joined each year. In the months without cricket, form and fitness changed, and so did personal relations among the players. In the time spent on the field, the players wanted to be fully involved – both batting and bowling. Fielding, for most, was an afterthought. The concept of specialisation hadn't fully kicked in at this stage, and, as a result, there was little scope even to maintain a defined batting order.

With all the challenging shifts and changes, victories were difficult yet essential to keep the morale of the players high.

Losses were damning to the spirit, and Pakistan were reeling from a losing streak of 12 international matches.

Some relatively unchallenged contests helped the players move ahead, starting with the ICC World Cup qualifiers, held in Stellenbosch in February 2008. Placed in Pool B alongside Scotland, Zimbabwe and Ireland, with the top two teams scheduled to qualify for the finals, Pakistan brushed aside the challenge with ease. In fairly windy conditions for bowling and softer grounds to dive on, it was an experience that the players had rarely enjoyed before, having mostly played on hard and dusty fields at home.

Ireland were crushed by 57 runs, Zimbabwe were downed by nine wickets in a game which was headlined by Urooj Mumtaz's hat-trick, and Scotland were hammered by a margin of 252 runs. The last two games weren't counted as official ODIs though. Pakistan maintained their dominance against the Netherlands in the semi-finals as well, registering a massive 94-run win.

However, concerns were obvious even in victory. The batting struggled against quality attacks. Running between the wickets was often appalling: against Ireland, six of their batters were run out – five of them by Isobel Joyce.

Pakistan's batting was eventually exposed by South Africa in the final, as the side were bowled out for 61. Asmavia Iqbal struck twice to put the hosts in a spot of bother early, but South Africa cruised to the target with eight wickets in hand. The defeat, though, was of little consequence as Pakistan had cemented a place in the 2009 World Cup by reaching the final of the qualifiers.

It helped that, over the next 12 months, Pakistan played a fair amount of cricket against Bangladesh, whose players were also taking their early strides in international cricket. The face-off hadn't started on a pleasant note, as Bangladesh had crushed Pakistan in the first engagement at the 2008 Asia Cup. Led by off-spinner Tithy Sarkar's four wickets and captain Salma Khatun's unbeaten half-century, the team registered its maiden win against an ODI side.

Nonetheless, over the next three games played between the two sides, Pakistan emerged triumphant – in the Asia Cup as well as a tri-national series held in Bangladesh in February 2009, also involving Sri Lanka. Against India and Sri Lanka, though, Pakistan continued to be distant challengers.

Even as Pakistan were improving marginally as a team, Urooj Mumtaz was losing favour as the captain. For two domestic seasons in a row, she had skipped the tournament to pursue her studies. Her absence from several training camps also meant that when she did turn up to captain the side, she wasn't entirely sure of how the players had shaped up. The control of the team had started to transfer elsewhere.

So commanding was Shaiza's presence in Pakistan cricket, let alone her influence in the Karachi set-up, that the domestic team hadn't ever considered another leader for as long as she was available. When Shaiza walked out of the 2005/06 national women's cricket championship before the final, along with her deputy Kiran Baluch, Karachi were left without a captain. As a makeshift arrangement, the 38-year-old Humera Masroor was appointed to lead against Lahore.

The following season, however, Karachi needed to find a long-term solution – a young but experienced candidate to fill the void. With Urooj away from domestic cricket, Batool Fatima, the 24-year-old wicketkeeper who had played six years of international cricket, was an obvious choice. However, she decided to give it a pass and recommended Sana Mir for the role instead.

Even though Sana was only 20, she was a natural leader – and it was a position she aspired to hold. Daughter of an army officer,

Colonel Mir Moatazid, she hailed from a Kashmiri family. Even though she was brought up in the progressive lifestyle of the army cantonments, where children were encouraged to play sports, cricket remained a game mostly indulged in by the boys on the streets. Even she was initially faced with apprehension and odd stares when she tagged along with her brother Humayun to play in the Taxila and Gujranwala cantonments, before familiarity kicked in and the boys ceased to find her presence strange.

Inspired by Waqar Younis as a child, Sana wanted to be a fast bowler, and ensured she was no different in her head as she steamed in to bowl. 'I could feel my hair flying and the gush of wind blowing on my face while I ran in to bowl,' she recalls. The only difference was that she wasn't as fast and menacing as she had imagined herself to be.

Even though she was first picked by Shaiza Khan, through the PWCCA's selection trials, she made her maiden international appearance under the PCB – during the 2005 Asia Cup. It was quite a forgettable start for her. Not only did she return wicketless but she also ran out her captain Sana Javed in the match against Sri Lanka. It didn't disappoint her terribly, however, because a bigger target lay in front of her in the next contest against India – the wicket of Mithali Raj. She had a score to settle.

When Kiran Baluch had scored the double century against the West Indies in 2004, she had surpassed the record which was held by Mithali. 'Shaiza had told me that Mithali hadn't congratulated Kiran after the world record was broken,' Sana reveals. 'So, I was really angry at Mithali about that. In my mind, I felt she should've congratulated her, it was a sporting gesture. Being from an army background, the India–Pakistan rivalry was quite a big deal for me. From that moment, I was determined to dismiss Mithali Raj.'

Her pursuit, in which she had no stake, drove her – and brought success. Even though India handed Pakistan a thumping defeat, Sana cleaned up Mithali with an inswinger. 'In my head, I was very happy. Mithali was the person I had to dismiss. She was my rival. In the early days, that rivalry was very intense for me. Over the years, though, we became good friends.'

Her fast-bowling career, and the aspiration to emulate Waqar, was cut short early courtesy of a stress fracture. As the Indians would come to realise, it was probably for the better. She had gone unnoticed in her great moment when she dismissed Mithali, but in the next Asia Cup, having shifted to bowling off spin, the opposition observed a promising player in the Pakistan team.

It wouldn't have been as smooth a transition for her without the experience of playing street cricket. 'On the street where we played, we had only one lamp. Since we played with a plastic ball after it got dark, there was no point bowling fast. So, I had to learn to spin the ball if I wanted to bowl after sunset.'

Even though she turned to spin, she says, 'At heart, I am still a fast bowler. Nothing pleases me more than an uprooted stump even now.'

Sana wasn't the most gifted athlete in the team. However, a comparatively greater exposure to the game allowed her to harness her skills better, and also to develop an astute tactical understanding. She was bold and confident, unlike several players who had made it through the ranks for the love of the game and were unsure if speaking out would shatter their dreams, which were under threat at all times.

'I had noticed early on that in Pakistan girls aren't very confident – in their households, in schools. From whatever background they come up, they are not encouraged to ask questions. The idea is that if you're an obedient girl, you're a good girl. So, they try to be like that.'

She was well exposed to different cultures, having lived in cantonments of different cities. As a leader, she was a comforting presence for the players, whom she could empathise with and aid off the field. It wasn't always like that though. Recalling her first train journey with the team – from Karachi to Islamabad – for a domestic tournament in 2007, she says, 'The moment we reached the railway station, we found that third-class bogies had been booked for us. The windows were broken, the doors were just about hanging on. Being from an army background, I had only travelled with my family, in my father's own car. I was very protected. When we went there, I saw the bogie and looked at my father. He just said, "If you have to be a leader, you have to go with the team. I can pay for a ticket for you to travel by air. But if you want to be a leader, you should travel with your team."'

A sharp communicator, she won trust easily. The Sufi-inclined Sana gets spiritual when explaining her approach to people management, quoting Prophet Muhammad: 'None of you has faith until you love for your brother (or sister) what you love for yourself.'

It helped that she had led Karachi to back-to-back titles in 2007 and 2008, and in Urooj's absence she seamlessly became one of the leaders in the group during the national side's training camps. She developed a better understanding of her teammates and even gained the backing to assert authority in match situations, something that Urooj couldn't do so well.

The 2009 World Cup became a showcase of that power transfer.

The team, despite the victories against Bangladesh, wasn't allowed to prepare for Australia without distraction. Heading into the tournament, taunts of going on a paid vacation had already hurt several of the players. After a long flight to the southern hemisphere, crossing the Pacific Ocean, Nain Abidi recalls being greeted with the return tickets on arrival at the airport from the tournament organisers. 'It was annoying,' points out Nain. 'We had just arrived. How dare they think that we were going to return early! We hadn't even played.'

Despite fairly good performances in the warm-up matches against the West Indies and South Africa, their showing in the opening encounter against India must have justified the organisers' planning. Pakistan were cleaned up for 57 in Bowral, a total India chased down without losing a wicket.

The move to Canberra for the next match against Sri Lanka wasn't any more pleasant. Put up in a hotel located in the city's red-light district, the sights outside the windows left several players unsettled. 'By then, we were quite angry, and maybe that even fired us up,' notes Nain.

Sri Lanka, who had traditionally dominated their Asian counterparts, slipped in the big event. Even as Pakistan's struggles with the bat continued, with most batters getting dismissed after steady starts, the players worked their way to a fairly healthy 161 for 7. It proved to be enough for them, as Qanita Jalil cleaned up Sri Lanka's top order with three wickets, and the middle order brought on their own downfall with three of the batters getting run out, including Shashikala Siriwardene, who had scored a fighting half-century. Sana Mir picked up a brace, and Sri Lanka were bowled out for 104, handing Pakistan their maiden win in a World Cup. The victory also enabled the team's passage to the Super Six, despite losing to England in the last match of the group stage. Against the organisers' expectations, the flight back to Pakistan had to be rescheduled.

Pakistan further enhanced their reputation with a victory against the West Indies in the Super Six. Electing to field, left-arm pace bowler Almas Akram ripped through the West Indian top order, dismissing three batters lbw and reducing them to 24 for 4 in the 12th over. Stafanie Taylor's half-century helped the West Indies post 132 for 9, but it was a total well within Pakistan's range.

Armaan Khan's unbeaten 48-ball 43 proved handy enough in the tricky chase to escort the team to a four-wicket victory.

With two wins in four games – when none had been expected – Pakistan had already overachieved. But with success, the players' own expectations rose.

In the next two games, they were comprehensively beaten. Australia secured a 107-run win and New Zealand smashed them by 223 runs – in a match where skipper Haidee Tiffen (100) and Suzie Bates (168) registered their highest individual scores. Although victory seemed impossible, Nain Abidi waged a lone battle for herself, at a time when even personal landmarks were rare.

'When I reached 46, I was tempted to play a big shot. The thought that I would be scoring my first 50 was running through my mind, and I panicked. Out of nervousness, I kept sweeping every ball, a shot that I rarely played. I just couldn't find my timing. I kept missing the ball and getting hit on the pads. Urooj, who was at the other end, just asked me to turn the strike over. I was so excited in that moment that I got out soon after reaching the landmark.'

All that she got in return for her first ODI half-century were a few pats on the back from the opposition players and a standing ovation from her brother, who was a part of the crowd.

But when the New Zealand batters kept smashing Pakistan bowlers, the players were looking for direction, and there was a feeling that captain Urooj Mumtaz's instructions weren't being heard. Suggestions were being taken from vice-captain Sana Mir instead.

Pakistan returned home following a defeat in the fifth-place play-offs against the West Indies, but despite new successes, Shamsa reveals that Urooj was informed at the airport that she wouldn't be leading the side any more.

Was it really surprising though?

Not for Sana Mir, who claims that an offer was made to her to lead the side even before the World Cup, which she declined, citing the importance of the tournament.

The change in guard was imminent, though, a by-product of the change in the political leadership. On 9 September 2008, Asif Ali Zardari was elected as president of Pakistan, less than ten months after his wife, Benazir Bhutto, had been publicly assassinated during a political rally.

The political environment in Pakistan had taken a turn for the worse by then. The Taliban had grown stronger than ever in Musharraf's regime, and even Pakistani civilian lives were under threat due to a massive surge in suicide bombings.

Musharraf, without many powerful allies, was under threat of impeachment and resigned from office. Control had shifted once again into the hands of the Pakistan Peoples Party, which had a trickle-down effect on the PCB leadership, with Yousaf Raza Gilani becoming patron-in-chief of the board.

Ijaz Butt, the former national cricketer, was elected chair of the board, replacing Nasim Ashraf, a doctor in the UK who had returned to Pakistan to join as a minister under Musharraf. Ijaz, even after retirement as a cricketer, was involved with the game in Pakistan. Hailing from the family which owned Servis Industries – a prominent business, popular for making shoes – he had previously served as the secretary of the board and had sponsored Pakistan cricket in various capacities through his business.

Soon after his appointment in October 2008, he also brought in Shirin Javed, his sister-in-law, to head the women's wing. Ijaz's tenure as chair was contentious enough, as he steered Pakistan men's cricket from one debacle to another – and not with much grace. Shirin didn't have it much better. Writing for *The Dawn*, Afreen Qizilbash stated, 'Ijaz Butt and his sister-in-law (Shirin

Javed) seem to be running neck and neck in order to see who creates more controversies in less time.'

So hostile were the times that soon after she took office, the West Indies backed out of their eight-match international tour to Pakistan. Shirin's tenure was, moreover, marred by allegations of nepotism and incompetency. Even though she attempted to defend her position, her arguments rarely had enough merit.

Her time in charge was further rocked by allegations of sexual harassment by long-time aide Azra Parveen, who was serving as an advisor with the women's wing. Azra asked a journalist to write stories about Shirin and team manager Ayesha Ashar's alleged 'sexual tendencies'.

Azra was dismissed from her position, and, in turn, she demanded compensation of PKR 10 crore from the board, whose members were reeling from the after-effects of a terrorist attack on the visiting Sri Lankan team bus. By then, the West Indian team, which was set to play five ODIs and three T20Is backed out of their tour in October 2008, citing security concerns.

Shirin was intent on having a leadership reshuffle, with the captain not being someone who enjoyed the trust of the long-time rival faction. Sana was tasked with steering the team through the mess of this transition. To assist Sana, Nain Abidi was appointed as deputy for the tour to Ireland.

It was a unique outing for the team, where they began with a 20-overs-a-side international contest. The shortest format of the game had gained success in global men's cricket, and the international governing body believed that it would be a useful vehicle to drive the women's game to a more prosperous future. But very few understood the tactics of the format.

The mad rush of scores and a change in the approach towards batting in the men's game had prompted the women to believe that T20 cricket would be all about slam-bang hitting. To Pakistan's horror, it turned out to be not that simple.

Playing for the first time in Ireland, after heavy rainfall which had reduced the match to a 15-overs-a-side affair, Pakistan's players could barely keep their hands out of their pockets, let alone hold on to a cold leather ball. To remain inside the hut for as long as possible, among other cricketing perks, they chose to bat on winning the toss on 25 May 2009.

With opener Nain Abidi dismissed off the second ball, the next batter Marina Iqbal had little time to comfort herself in the pavilion at The Vineyard in Dublin. For her, it was about following the plan of action that had been decided in a small meeting of batters the previous evening.

'We had reached a consensus that not a single delivery could be blocked. We had to play aggressively,' Marina recalls.

That approach didn't work, especially for Marina, who tottered her way to a 28-ball 14. 'It took us some time to realise that even though the format is different, we needed to put some sense into our approach. We couldn't swing our bats blindly without caring for our body alignment and footwork.'

Pakistan had managed to score 80 for 3 in 15 overs, which was a fair total to begin with but not enough to win. Isobel Joyce, the Ireland opener, was much wiser, targeting the Pakistan bowlers towards the shorter part of the ground. Her brisk, unbeaten, 32-ball 56 helped Ireland chase down the total in just 10.3 overs.

It was a harsh lesson in the new format, but the Pakistan players worked on their mistakes and came back stronger in the T20 series which followed soon after, involving Ireland and Nottinghamshire from England. Pakistan won all their four games comfortably across two days, with Sana Mir being the standout performer with the ball. Nain Abidi too seemed to have come to grips with the format early, ending the series with a run-a-ball 55 against Ireland and 45 against Nottinghamshire.

It was a fairly successful tour of Ireland, with the two T20 events interspersed by a one-off ODI which Pakistan won despite the odds stacked against them. In the quintessential Irish conditions, where a constant drizzle meant that there wasn't enough time for the pitch at the Clontarf Cricket Club Ground to fully dry up, the chances of winning relied heavily on the toss. Sana Mir, having poked her finger at the wicket, was sure that they had to field to have any hopes of winning the match. 'Of course, I didn't win the toss.'

Put in to bat, Pakistan worked their way solidly to 141 despite having three batters run out. Sajjida Shah's 52 played a critical role before a testing opening spell by Qanita Jalil and Asmavia Iqbal helped Pakistan make a contest out of it. The Irish middle order did consolidate but Sana Mir's four strikes reduced them from 112 for 5 to 114 all out.

In England, at the inaugural women's T20 World Cup only a month later, Pakistan adjusted well to the conditions as well as the format, which was novel for most other participating teams. Yet, when they were pitted against India, England and Sri Lanka – in Taunton – the side was outclassed. Barring Bismah Maroof's half-century in their tournament opener against Sri Lanka, there wasn't much to write home about.

The invention of the shorter format was a blessing for Pakistan. The longer the duration of the games, the greater the likelihood that a better team would make a comeback and win. For the Pakistan side, their main concern was in the batting department as they hadn't fully mastered the art of playing out 50 overs. They were capable of doing well in short passages of play, which meant that T20 was best suited to their pursuit of victory in international cricket. With the next edition of the T20 World Cup set to take place in 11 months, there was a possibility that they could improve on their showing. However, in that period, they didn't play a single international match.

In the aftermath of a terrorist attack on the Sri Lankan team bus, no team toured the country and no board agreed to host the Pakistan women's team. Shirin Javed's health had started to deteriorate, and the T20 format, which had been introduced in the domestic calendar as a four-team tournament in the previous season, was reduced to a one-off game played between the top 22 players divided into two teams – PCB Greens led by Sana Mir and PCB Blues captained by Nain Abidi. It was a closely contested, low-scoring affair in which Sana Mir's unbeaten 54 helped her side clinch a four-run victory.

Several significant developments took place on the domestic front, which included the national Under-17 championship being replaced by an Under-19 tournament, while schools cricket was left out of the system. In senior 50-over cricket, three new departments were introduced – ZTBL, Pakistan Education Board and Pakistan Universities. ZTBL, in particular, was significant since it also provided employment to its players. And as a result, ZTBL could get the services of some of the best players in the country. Sana Mir was roped in as captain, and in the final of the national championship, she top-scored (75), also returning the best bowling figures (3 for 14) to guide her side to a massive 182-run win over the weakened Karachi team. The State Bank of Pakistan joined in the domestic competition the following season and paved the way for a classic departmental rivalry over the next few years.

But the lack of high-quality cricket from one T20 World Cup to another meant that Pakistan's results didn't really change. The side lost all three games in Basseterre. Before they were swatted away by India and New Zealand, Pakistan ran Sri Lanka close, only to fall short by one run, with five of their batters getting run out.

By 2010, nearly five years into the merger between the ICC and IWCC, it was evident that most cricket boards were reluctant to spend their moolah on women's cricket. The richer bodies could still afford to host a few games, but for the rest, there were too many financial constraints. The international cricket body had to step in to save face. As a measure to hand match practice to the teams ranked below the top four, and in a way also enhance their show in the marquee events, it organised a six-nation tournament, which included South Africa, the West Indies, Pakistan, Sri Lanka, the Netherlands and Ireland.

Sana Mir's team were outperformed by Sri Lanka and South Africa. Their only victory in the tournament came against Ireland, by a mere five runs, and they finished fourth. In the ODI leg, they didn't fare much better. Having faced off against all the five teams, Pakistan registered trouble-free wins over Ireland and the Netherlands but were as easily beaten by Sri Lanka, South Africa and the West Indies.

It wasn't the best of tours for Pakistan, but it was the start of a transition. Veteran pace bowlers Qanita Jalil and Almas Akram weren't picked for the tour. A new pace bowler with a slinging action – 18-year-old Kainat Imtiaz from Karachi – made her debut alongside Nida Dar – a promising all-rounder.

The relationship between Sana and Urooj had already turned cold, if not bitter, by then. During the training camp ahead of the tournament, the PCB received an email from Urooj stating that she wouldn't be able to join the team. She had left for the UK to pursue her master's in dentistry and never returned to play cricket.

But many years after her retirement, she did return – in an all-powerful position – and in a way facilitated Sana Mir's exit from the game.

A GLIMPSE OF A NEW IDENTITY

PAKISTAN CRICKET WAS in denial in 2010.

Just when it seemed like the taint of match fixing had left the cricketing world, left-arm pace bowler Mohammad Amir delivered the most infamous no-ball in the history of the game, at the Oval on 18 August.

It would have seemed like an unusual but routine overstepping of the crease had reporters from the *News of the World* not been spending time with Mazhar Majeed, a bookie who had predicted that exact scenario.

The 19-year-old Amir, who many had hoped would be the next Wasim Akram, wasn't the only one to be caught in this scandal. His senior pace partner Mohammad Asif, who had already troubled several top batsmen around the world with his artistry, was also embroiled in the spot-fixing outrage. The newspaper also alleged that skipper Salman Butt and four other players were involved.

Even though the UK's anti-corruption chief feared that there wasn't sufficient evidence to nail the bookie, and the accused players initially refused to accept the charges against them, the world outside had seen enough in the evidence provided by the newspaper. So cornered and frustrated was the PCB chair Ijaz Butt by all that had transpired that, in turn, without any evidence, he made allegations of fixing by the English players when they lost one of the matches in the ODI series which followed. Threatened with legal action, he had to apologise and retract his statements.

As hard as Pakistani players and administrators tried to cover up the actions of the accused players, it was hard for them to run away from the evidence at hand, triggering one of the lowest points in the country's sporting history.

The ignominy in England took place only a year after the Sri Lankan men's team had been attacked in Lahore. Twelve gunmen, hiding behind Liberty Square in the city centre, fired at the Sri Lankan team bus and the match officials who were travelling in a minivan to the Gaddafi Stadium. The players and officials survived despite the attackers being armed with AK-47 assault rifles, hand grenades, rocket-propelled grenades and more.

Six policemen and two civilians (including the minivan driver) died in the attack, while two cricketers – Thilan Samaraweera and Tharanga Paranavitana – were hospitalised, along with umpire Ahsan Raza, who was seriously wounded. The security provided was heavily criticised in England by former cricketer Chris Broad, who was the match referee in the series, and it seemed then that international cricket would take a long time to return to the country.

Pakistan's reputation had taken a beating at home and abroad, and it needed a boost of the highest order. The women's team, of which very few had even heard then, provided that in the most unexpected of ways.

And Nida Dar, a 23-year-old all-rounder from Gujranwala, was the star of the show.

✧✧✧

Only a few years earlier, Nida's performances for Lahore University were credited to 'Aaina Naaz'; a pseudonym offered to her by local newspapers to help her avoid the attention of her brother, who was against her playing cricket.

She terms it 'brotherly possessiveness', but for him to have his sister play a sport – conventionally believed to be a 'manly' act – was a matter of embarrassment among his friends in Gujranwala, the 'city of wrestlers'.

Nida had grown up playing cricket with her brother and her cousins in the 1990s in the small industrial town, which had been a hotbed of ethnic cleansing during the partition four decades earlier. It later became the prime settlement for Muslim immigrants from the Indian cities of Ludhiana, Amritsar and Patiala. As a kid, it was easy for her to escape the gaze of passers-by. 'I was the only girl playing cricket, and since I had short hair and dressed like a boy, I could escape being noticed,' she recalls. 'Many believed that I was a boy, and I was happy to let that misconception be.'

However, family tradition dictated that girls stop playing sports after hitting puberty. Nida had already witnessed one of her cousins, who played the best straight drive she has ever seen, give up on her love for the game after getting married early.

Nida didn't want her life to shape up like that, but even though she got permission from her parents to continue playing, it was upon the condition that her brother shouldn't find out about it.

In order to meet this challenge, she would play for her university on weekdays, when her brother stayed in Lahore for work, and pretend that she had given up sport when he returned home at the weekend.

The arrangement was working well until she led her team to an inter-university title win. The request not to mention her name in the newspapers was duly met, but the picture desk wasn't given this instruction and a photo of her was added alongside the article by mistake. When her brother spotted her face in the newspaper the next morning, she had to feign ignorance and deny that it was her.

But the secret wasn't to last too long. Through her performances, she became one of the most prominent figures on the local circuit and was picked for the national team camp after a selection trial. 'I wasn't too excited about it,' she recalls. 'I knew even though I had the national cap in sight, I couldn't go any higher. My coach could see my disappointment and he came home to convince my family.'

Her parents agreed to let her play and, much against his wishes, she also secured her brother's consent. But this was only because they thought they knew better. Nida's father, Rashid, was a first-class cricketer, and was certain that there was no future for women playing sports in Pakistan – no fame, no financial security. They were confident that her aspirations would soon be dashed. As far as her family were concerned, her career was a ticking time bomb and could end at any moment. Even though she played in the 2009 World Cup, had it not been for Pakistan's 2010 Asian Games campaign, they would have prevented her from playing any further.

In April 2007, the Olympic Council of Asia (OCA) had announced that the proposal to include cricket for the first time in the Asian Games had been approved. The decision had come on the back of a key assumption though. The OCA president Sheikh Ahmad Al-Fahad Al-Sabah had stated: 'India and Pakistan were the drivers [for cricket's inclusion at the Games] . . . and they will come with their best teams because it will be a big competition. Asia's four (men's) Test-playing nations have committed to sending their best available teams.'

However, in June 2010, only five months ahead of the event in Guangzhou, China, the BCCI announced its decision not to send its players (both men and women) for the 16th edition of the Asian Games.

While the BCCI had financial reasons for withdrawing from the Games, the Indian Olympic Association felt ashamed of its actions.

India's withdrawal from the tournament might have had only minor financial repercussions for the tournament, but not everyone was complaining. Sri Lanka also didn't send a team for the women's competition, since it was scheduled to play a home series against England in mid-November. Its men's team had representation, though, through a second-string side, while the main players were taking part in other cricket assignments.

The withdrawal of Asia's two strongest women's teams meant that Pakistan had a clear passage to the gold medal, with an improving Bangladesh the only possible threat in the 20-overs-a-side competition.

To win the gold medal, though, the players had to go through four knockout contests. By then, the several distractions at the Asian Games village had already turned their heads. The massive village was unlike anything they had seen before, with lavish facilities and extravagant celebrations. It was also a rare opportunity for them to mingle with players from other sporting disciplines of the country.

At a small outlet of McDonald's, they found their go-to spot to unwind. 'Back then, there was no concept of fitness and diet,' Kainat Imtiaz recalls. 'We were living on a diet of burgers and fries.'

Nida remembers that all too well: 'Who doesn't like McDonald's? Back then, in Pakistan, there weren't too many outlets, so we rarely got an opportunity to eat there. In the Asian Games village, we had a meal pass for unlimited food from McDonald's. So, we stuffed ourselves with fries and then packed some more and brought it to our rooms to share with the rest of the teammates.'

Fortunately, none of that distraction was to affect their cricket. They swatted aside the challenge of Malaysia with off-spinner Sana Gulzar picking up four wickets and Nida snaring a brace to clean them up for 49. Nida and Javeria Khan then led the chase with the bat to complete the win in 8.3 overs.

China didn't add much to their challenge the next day either. Having restricted the hosts to 60 for 5, Pakistan won by nine wickets. Nida top-scored again, with a 29-ball 27.

Japan, who had lost to Bangladesh in round two, made it to the semi-finals after winning its repêchage match against Thailand. Even though Japan had been on the competitive circuit since 1995, two years before Pakistan, its cricket hadn't developed as significantly. In the semi-final, it came a distant second. Nida's all-round showing (1 for 13 and a 29-ball 27*) powered Pakistan to another untroubled victory.

It was with that win that the news that Pakistan were guaranteed a medal reached home. Those were still early days in the tournament, but the country had yet to win a medal. Even though many in Pakistan had been unaware of the existence of a women's cricket team, they were now glued to the final.

Friends and relatives, even those who had been deeply cynical about their sporting ambitions, turned up at the homes of the players; and those who couldn't make it called up the family members to congratulate them on their daughters' achievements. The support the players had long craved was finally with them – but with it came a new pressure to perform.

In the final, they would face their most competitive match. Bangladesh, a country that had shaped its independence from

Pakistan in 1971, had players with similar motivation. Having endured years of neglect by their erstwhile government, they also wanted to be seen as equals to their men's team.

On 19 November, at the Guanggong International Cricket Stadium, Sana's luck with the toss continued and she elected to field. Bangladesh, unlike Pakistan's previous opponents, didn't make the contest all that easy. After losing Fargana Hoque early, Rumana Ahmed broke free, blasting a couple of boundaries, but once she was trapped lbw on 16 by Nida, the rest of the line-up collapsed. Salma Khatun put up some resistance, but Bangladesh were bowled out for 92, having played their full quota of overs. Nida, yet again, was the wrecker-in-chief, picking up four wickets.

Having chased in all their previous games, 93 wasn't a score Pakistan had yet accumulated. Against the best bowling attack in the competition, it was a stiff total, and the challenge was heightened as much of the run-scoring had been done by openers Nida and Javeria, leaving the other batters mostly untested in the conditions. To make the contest exciting, all that the Bangladesh bowlers needed to do was get past the openers.

But they couldn't.

Javeria, who was still new to the demands of opening the batting, kept steady from one end while Nida cut loose. 'We knew 93 was a par score,' Nida reveals. 'There was no pressure on me, because I had been scoring in the previous games. So, even on the day of the final, I didn't stop myself. I whacked everything that came my way.'

Nida's batting was uncomplicated. She idolised Shahid Afridi and tried to bat like him – with a no-caution approach. It paid off that day as she breezed away to an unbeaten 43-ball 51 and helped Pakistan overhaul the total in only 15.4 overs, securing a win by ten wickets.

The momentary jubilation and celebration notwithstanding, the gold medal win had a long-lasting effect on the personal lives of the players and on the state of women's cricket in the country.

Asif Ali Zardari, the president of Pakistan, was quick to note that the win was 'a gift to the nation riding on a series of crises'. While the more prominent cricket team in the country was dealing with a spate of controversies, the efforts of the women's team brought joy at a time of mass human tragedy – with over 21 million people affected by devastating floods that monsoon season.

The people of Pakistan celebrated the win and gave the players a royal welcome on their return to the country. Some had landed in Karachi and some in Lahore. Kainat Imtiaz, who had landed in Karachi, doesn't even recall the players who walked out of the airport with her. All she remembers is the crowd that flooded the airport arrival zone and the dazzle of thousands of camera flashes.

In Lahore, the scenes were even more dramatic. Several media vans followed Nida's car for two hours to Gujranwala. 'The street where we lived was so packed with people that when I reached home I couldn't open the door of my car and get out.

'The scenes were stranger inside my house, where there were people I didn't even recognise. They were claiming to be my distant relatives. I had never seen their faces before. They were congratulating and hugging me. Some were playing the *dhol* [a percussion instrument]. I couldn't understand where these people were coming from. Everyone wanted to talk and take pictures with me.'

The grand celebrations continued with the teams and the players individually being feted by several individuals and institutions – from universities to various sports federations. There were hoardings and banners congratulating them. Local politicians and wealthy businessmen announced cash prizes for the winning team. The president, as well as former prime minister Nawaz Sharif, hosted a feast in their honour.

'There were so many people coming over to meet me over the next few days that I had no time to even eat my food,' recalls Nida. 'The interesting bit about success is that the relatives you didn't know existed suddenly appear out of nowhere to flaunt their connection to you.'

Nida's house, like that of many others, had become the hotspot of media attention. Not to miss out on the celebration of that victory was her brother, who had long been ashamed of his sister playing cricket. 'That day, he was extremely proud and went around singing songs and playing the guitar on local news channels. That acceptance was a big change.'

Nida Dar continued to play for Pakistan and went on to become one of the country's finest-ever players.

Beyond the glamour, which lasted for a while, the Asian Games victory gave women's cricket a major boost around the country, and the PCB handed central contracts to the players for the first time. At a time when even some of the top countries in the world hadn't given their players this financial security, Pakistan offered contracts to 19 cricketers. (Sania Khan was listed to be given the contract but it was held back due to her injury.)

The board also started awarding match fees to the players, who had until then been given only daily allowances as low as PKR 300 for non-ICC tournaments. The inclusion in the domestic cricket set-up of ZTBL and State Bank further improved the financial condition of the cricketers, which proved to be a key motivator for more parents to let their daughters pursue the sport.

Despite the financial support and a one-off reward, women's cricket still wasn't a hugely followed sport. It needed greater star

The 1997 World Cup team.
Back row: Kiran Baluch, Kiran Aitezaz, Asma Farzand, Saeed, Nazia Sadiq,
Farah Deeba, Shazia Hassan.
Middle row: Jodie Davis, Shaiza Khan, Nazia Nazir.
Front row: Maliha Hussain, Sharmeen Khan, Sadia Bano, Meher Minwalla. *PWCCA*

One of the many letters
written by Shaiza Khan
to Jodie Davis before
the Australian could
fly down to Pakistan
to coach the team.
Jodie Davis

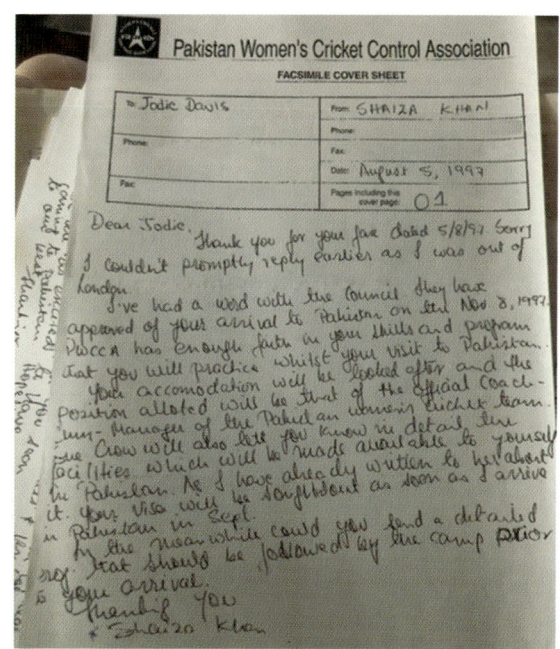

Jodie Davis giving catching practice to a few girls aged 11 to 14 in a private school near Lahore. Such events were often organised by Shaiza to spread the word about women's cricket. *Jodie Davis*

The cricket ground developed at Saeed Khan's carpet factory by Aziz Saheb, the curator of the National Stadium in Karachi. *PWCCA*

The Kookaburra cricket balls used by PWCCA. They had to be specially manufactured as the required size wasn't available in Pakistan at the time. *Jodie Davis*

Practice facility at Shaiza and Sharmeen's house in Karachi. *Jodie Davis*

The Lahore Garrison grounds were available to the PWCCA players for practice after 2:30 p.m. every day. The gates were manned to keep the players safe. However, in the absence of nets, most of the training was limited to basic skills like catching, batting and fielding. *Jodie Davis*

Shaiza Khan during a team meeting ahead of the first-ever match played by the MCC women's team. *PWCCA*

Shaiza Khan walking out to open the innings for MCC in their first-ever match after membership was opened for women after 212 years. *PWCCA*

Shaiza Khan, Sharmeen Khan and Kiran Baluch – the three players instrumental in running the affairs of PWCCA – with John Major at Lords. *PWCCA*

Ahead of Asia Cup 2006 – Pakistan's first international series under Urooj Mumtaz's captaincy.
Back row: Sana Javed, Sabahat Rasheed, Shumaila Mushtaq, Nain Abidi, Maryam Butt,
Khursheed Jabeen, Bismah Maroof, Sajida Shah.
Middle row: Umar Rasheed, Asmavia Iqbal, Tasqeen Qadeer, Qanita Jalil,
Batool Fatima, Sana Mir, Mohammed Tariq Siddiqui.
Front row: Shahnaz Sohail, Shamsa Hashmi, Imtiaz Ahmed, Naseem Ashraf, Urooj Mumtaz,
Javed Zaman, Nadia Compton. *PCB*

Bushra Aitzaz, like many other protesters in Lahore in February 1983, was roughed up,
teargassed and arrested during a protest organised by the Women's Action Forum
against the rule of Zia ul Haq. Almost three decades later, Bushra went on to become
the general manager of PCB's women's wing. *Azhar Jafri/BBC*

Domestic cricket prospered with departments entering the system. In 2012, six teams participated in the inaugural edition of the Shaheed Mohtarma Benazir Bhutto Women's Cricket Championship. In 2019, the departments left the system and the domestic structure was shrunk to only three teams. *PCB*

Qanita Jalil getting awarded Player of the Match in a triangular domestic tournament. Prize money, which was as little as PKR 2,000 (around £8.50) in 2012, went up 10 times in the next 10 years. *PCB*

ZTBL was a powerhouse in domestic cricket, being able to acquire the services of some of the best players in the country. They won the inaugural edition of the Shaheed Mohtarma Benazir Bhutto Women's Cricket Championship among many other tournaments during their brief involvement in domestic cricket. *PCB*

Pakistan's cricket took an upswing during the tenure of Sana Mir and Mohtashim Rashid.
Mahwash Rahman/Women in Green and Beyond

The integral members of Pakistan cricket's journey (*from left to right*): Sidra Ameen,
Iram Javed, Aiman Anwar, Sidra Nawaz, Nain Abidi, Nahida Khan and Anam Amin. *PCB*

A few record-holders for Pakistan in one picture. *From left to right*: Nain Abidi, Javeria Khan and Batool Fatima, along with left-arm pacer Masooma Junaid.
Mahwash Rahman/Women in Green and Beyond

Sana Mir and Asmavia Iqbal were the pillars of Pakistan's bowling attack, retiring as the team's most successful spinner and pacer respectively. *PCB*

Mohtashim Rashid giving a word of advice after a wicketkeepeing session with Rabiya Shah. *PCB*

The batters' conference: past, present and future. *From left to right:* Nain Abidi, Bismah Maroof, Muneeba Ali, Javeria Khan, Nida Dar, Omaima Sohail. *Mahwash Rahman/Women in Green and Beyond*

The players thank the crowd for their support after their win over Bangladesh in 2015. It was the first time they got a chance to play an international match in front of a home crowd since 2005. *PCB*

Bismah Maroof introducing the team to Najam Sethi in 2017, soon after she became the ODI captain and Sethi was re-elected as PCB's chair. In the background, the pranksters of the team – Javeria Khan and Nida Dar – can be seen sharing a joke. *PCB*

Training drills, fitness regimes and results changed drastically during the reign of Mark Coles (*sitting, fourth from left*), Andy Richards (*sitting, extreme left*) and Gemaal Hussain (*standing, extreme left*). PCB

A tradition within the team has been to start off training sessions or match days with a prayer *PCB*

David Hemp took over the reins of women's cricket at an uncertain time. With the COVID-19 pandemic raging, cricket training and matches were massively affected. *PCB*

After her performances in 2021, Fatima Sana became the first Pakistani
to be awarded the ICC Emerging Cricketer of the Year. *Ahsan Nagi/PCB*

Players from the Pakistan national team visited Peace School and College in the conservative
city of Abbottabad as part of PCB's Skills2Shine programme designed to interact with young
girls and introduce them to the game. *PCB*

The Class of '21. *Back row:* Ayesha Naseem, Sadia Iqbal, Ayesha Zafar, Aliya Riaz.
Middle row: Aiman Anwar, Syeda Aroob Shah, Fatima Sana, Nahida Khan, Omaima Sohail,
Diana Baig. *Front row:* Anam Amin, Sidra Nawaz, Nida Dar, Javeria Khan, Kainat Imtiaz,
Muneeba Ali, Nashra Sandhu. *Mohammad Arbaz/PCB*

Bismah Maroof with her daughter, Fatima. In 2022, Bismah became the first Pakistani
cricketer to return to play international cricket after childbirth. *Ahsan Nagi/PCB*

power. Zeb Bangash, a popular singer, became one of the earliest stars to offer her support to the team.

It was a chance encounter between Sana Mir and Zeb in August 2011, when the Pakistan team were heading for their tour of the West Indies, that sparked the connection. Sana and Zeb met accidentally on a flight when the latter asked the Pakistan captain for her autograph.

It was the start of a friendship which would play a quiet role in helping to improve the visibility of the team and its players. Over the coming years, Zeb spent time with the team, watched their matches, cheered for them and, most importantly, helped them network better and secure various endorsement deals.

'She was the first celebrity who put her weight behind us and saw this team for what they were actually doing,' says Sana. 'She saw something in us that we couldn't see. At that point, we felt that we were just playing cricket, but for her, we were changing the fabric of Pakistani society. She had a bigger vision and saw things in a different perspective.

'She made us understand that it wasn't just about the wins and losses. What we were doing was big. Your parents and friends tell you that, but in your heart you still feel that they are saying it only because they love you. When a stranger who has a standing in society says it, it makes a bigger impact.

'She is very modest about all that she has done for us. She doesn't bring it up much on social media. But she was also there at a time when we were quite low as a team, when we weren't winning. That support was huge for us.

'When she started seeing us as heroes, we also started seeing ourselves as heroes.'

8

IN THE AGE OF SANA MIR

THE 2010 ASIAN Games gold medal, the first across any sporting discipline for Pakistan in eight years, brought the women's cricket team firmly into national consciousness and paved the way for Sana Mir to become a star over the coming years – not just because of her on-field performances but also the impact she would have on the careers of her teammates and Pakistan cricket over the next decade. However, the success at the Games would have only been a momentary high for Sana, as well as the team, had she not found the support of Bushra Aitzaz in the four years to follow.

In November 2010, Bushra took over as general manager of the PCB women's wing from her long-time friend Shirin Javed. Not only had Shirin's two-year tenure come to an end, but her health had also deteriorated significantly. While there was a change in leadership, the new vision was only an extension of what had been started under Shirin's tenure.

Bushra was the wife of eminent lawyer Aitzaz Ahsan, who was also a member of the ruling Pakistan Peoples Party. Even though he hadn't contested the previous election due to the Lawyers' Movement for restoration of deposed judges, he was soon to become the leader of the House of Federation, the Senate of Pakistan.

Under Bushra, Sana got a free run as a trusted leader, which allowed for stability and steady progress. She was given greater control of team selection and the backing to work towards a long-term vision. That support allowed her ample time to experiment, shape ideas, build a culture and back a set of players who she, along with the coach, trusted would come good over a period of time. This was despite the chaos in the PCB – with the chair changing six times through the course of Bushra's four-year stint as the general manager of the women's wing.

Unlike the previous captains, who were affected by external trouble, lack of resources, numerous controlling hands and uncertain pathways, Sana's road under Bushra was clear. It didn't come easily though. In June 2011, she was pulled up by the PCB for speaking her mind to the media over the need for a foreign coach.

Her demand wasn't met fully, but she found an ally in Mohtashim Rasheed, who was appointed as the head coach ahead of the 2011 ICC Women's World Cup qualifiers, set to be held in Bangladesh. Hailing from a family of cricketers, Mohtashim wasn't the most talented coach available in the country, nor did he assert his authority like most of his predecessors or successors did, but he understood many of the problems which had beset women's cricket over the years. A lot had changed in the cricketing set-up since his brother Mehmood had coached the team under Shaiza, but many problems still existed.

Before taking over full-time, Mohtashim had served as the bowling coach in the preceding series in the West Indies, where he caught the first glimpse of the team he was to take charge of.

Pakistan were outplayed in the first two ODIs, before winning the third match of the series. In the T20s, the visitors gave a much better account of themselves after losing the first two games, of which the West Indies had won the first match by a solitary run (Duckworth–Lewis–Stern [DLS] method). The most dominant of the displays came in the third contest though, where, led by Javeria Khan and Bismah Maroof's 83-run stand for the fifth wicket, they reached the 116-run target in 17.3 overs.

The most interesting encounter was the last match of the tour where, after being limited to 72, left-arm spinner Sadia Yousuf and Sana kept their West Indian counterparts in check and dragged the game to a Super Over. Sadia conceded only nine runs, all to Stacy-Ann King. In response, however, the West Indian slow left-armer Shanel Daley gave away just seven runs to Asmavia Iqbal, with both Javeria and Bismah failing to score.

In that match, Mohtashim, an amiable personality, and measured with his words, saw initial glimpses of the team's talent and their inability to handle pressure situations. That also shaped his philosophy of how the team needed to be coached.

'Skill-wise, our team was good, but when they started competing against better sides and beat them, they tended to get overexcited and lose focus on their preparation,' Mohtashim said of his initial impressions. 'We lost that match against the West Indies because they didn't know how to cope with that excitement. At that point, I could have tried to get their feet back on the ground, but it was important for them to go through that experience and face the consequences. Only then would they understand what their mistake had been.'

Mohtashim's ways as a coach were unlike anything the players had experienced before. Most coaches would either follow the strict methods that had been the norm for decades in training boys or be indifferent altogether. Many failed to fully understand the physical capacities of the women and oversaw training in the same way they would a male club session. More significantly, they struggled to understand the difference in motivation, as well as the insecurities, of the women, as compared to the men. Mohtashim *did* understand; he wouldn't scold the players for making errors, nor would he dictate tactics to them. Instead, he pushed them to make their mistakes and learn from them. The players felt empowered by his approach.

'We didn't have a strong grass-roots structure – no club cricket for girls or any other form of competitive games,' Mohtashim explains when analysing his coaching style. 'The start of their formal cricket training began at the national level. As a result, the players coming to the international side were neither particularly skilful nor had the understanding of match situations. But their passion was driving them to learn and work hard.'

He would hand each player the responsibility to analyse someone in the opposition and come back to him with their insights. After that he would add his own input to help refine their plans for the match.

Explaining the rationale of his process, Mohtashim says, 'I wanted to train the players to understand their own game better. Spoon-feeding wasn't going to help them learn and improve in the longer run.'

But with a World Cup qualification hanging in the balance, was there really enough time to let the players proceed by trial and error?

During the Sana Mir–Mohtashim Rashid tenure, there was a sense of stability and continuity in the team. Mohtashim acknowledged that there was a limited talent pool to draw from, and it was better to work on them and help them improve instead of constantly changing combinations to achieve short-term success.

The pack of pace bowlers was led by Asmavia Iqbal and Qanita Jalil. While their bowling styles differed, with the former being an inswing bowler and the latter an outswinger, they were very alike in their demeanour: extremely intense on the field and jovial off it. What separated them were their recovery methods. While Asmavia preferred to sleep as much as possible, Qanita was obsessed with fitness training.

They had both made their debuts in the same game as Sana, against Sri Lanka in the 2005 Asia Cup. However, while Asmavia took time to make an impact with the ball, Qanita had picked up a 5-fer in only her second international tournament. In Bangladesh, though, during the 2011 dual World Cup qualifiers, their major contributions came with the bat.

In the ten-team competition, Pakistan were grouped alongside Japan, Ireland, the West Indies and the hosts. The top teams from each group would qualify directly for the semi-finals, and with it to the 2012 World T20 as well as the 50-over 2013 World Cup. The second- and third-placed teams from each group were to play the play-offs to reach the semis. While the West Indies were the standout favourites from the group, Bangladesh and Ireland offered little room for Pakistan to slip up.

Fortunately for Pakistan, they faced these two tricky opponents first up, and registered clinical victories. Bismah Maroof's 75 and Nida Dar's 4-fer helped secure a 73-run win over Bangladesh before Sadia Yousuf's four-wicket haul paved the way for a comfortable eight-wicket win over Ireland.

In the Ireland game, much against received wisdom, the opening pair of two bowling all-rounders – Sana Mir and Qanita Jalil – found success. It was an idea which the captain was forced to come up with following the reluctance of several front-line batters to face the new ball. Even as the team was gaining momentum, by the Sri Lanka series it was clear that the side hadn't settled on a strong opening partnership – despite Javeria Khan's good run in the new position.

Qanita didn't possess the best batting technique but was a powerful hitter. Her role was to go after the new-ball bowlers, while Sana stayed steady at the other end with her more limited skills.

'In the previous few series, no plan was working out for us,' Sana explains. 'At that point, our batters feared facing the new ball. It wasn't about a lack of skills; it was a psychological issue; they just weren't backing themselves enough. I promoted myself up the order for two reasons. Firstly, I knew that the competition was big, and we couldn't make too many mistakes. Secondly, we needed a mentally strong person to set the tone for the team. We couldn't go and show the opposition that we were afraid.

'I decided to open for the team not only to show the opposition but also our players that if I could do it with my limited technique, others could do it as well. We couldn't afford to lose the qualifiers just because players were afraid to tackle the new ball. I'd opened once in domestic cricket, and I had that confidence in myself. I trusted my ability to pull it off. There were times I failed as well, but it was enough to give my teammates that motivation.'

She scored 49 against the West Indies in a match where all the other batters, except Nain Abidi, struggled. Anisa Mohammed, the West Indian off-spinner, took a return catch to dismiss Sana one short of 50 and went on to finish with figures of 5 for 26. An eight-wicket humbling dashed Pakistan's hopes of qualifying directly to the semis, but the team thwarted Japan's challenge, courtesy of Nida Dar's 139-ball 124 (in a match which did not have ODI status), to keep themselves in contention for the play-offs – where they were to meet the Netherlands, who had finished third in their group.

The Netherlands, much like Japan, didn't pose much of a challenge. Sana Mir, opening the innings, was dismissed for 49 again – this time trapped lbw by Esther Lancer. However, 50s by Nida Dar, Bismah Maroof and Javeria Khan helped Pakistan to a healthy 277 for 4, before the bowlers skittled the Netherlands for 87.

In the last league match against Japan, Sana dropped back to her usual lower-middle-order position and Marina Iqbal was sent out to open. Marina, a batter who could bowl medium pace, was brought back to the 11 alongside Kainat Imtiaz, a medium-pacer who could bat. Neither made an impression in that contest, but they were both inspired by what they witnessed from Asmavia Iqbal only a couple of matches later.

In qualifying for the semis, and with it for the two World Cups, Pakistan had achieved the larger goal of the competition. In doing so, the side had also beaten the teams they had been expected to beat. Moreover, they had done so clinically, with all the batters and bowlers playing their part. Winning anything further was a bit of a stretch, especially against Mignon du Preez's South Africa – who had been almost untouchable in the group stage.

Pakistan didn't have a lot to lose at that point, so they decided to compete hard.

Asmavia was already feeling unwell following a case of food poisoning after the previous night's dinner. She agreed to play despite not feeling fit. Not surprisingly, her stay on the field didn't last long. After having the South African opener Shandre Fritz caught off her bowling, she left the ground and started to throw up. (Coach Mohtashim wasn't feeling much better and had to rest up inside.) She returned towards the latter half of South Africa's innings and picked up two late wickets to restrict South Africa to 180 for 9.

It was a stiff total by Pakistan's standards, and South Africa's 23-year-old Shabnim Ismail, who was gunning to be the fastest bowler in the world, unleashed her pace on the Pakistanis. Ismail was too hot for their top order to handle, and they suffered an early collapse, down to 43 for 4 by the 16th over. Javeria Khan tried to revive the chase with a couple of handy partnerships, but when she fell in the 42nd over, Pakistan needed 41 runs in 50 balls – with only the last four wickets remaining.

Asmavia, who still hadn't fully recovered, joined Marina, who had settled in well by that point, at the crease. Two overs into her stay in the middle, she started to throw up again, in the middle of the pitch. The condition of the coach, who was in the doctor's room, had also worsened and he was unable to give any direction to the players. His only message to the team was, 'Take a call as you deem fit.' With the qualification for the World Cup secured, Asmavia didn't have to continue, but she did. After all, Pakistan were in with a chance of beating South Africa for the first time ever.

'The management asked her to come out,' Marina recalls. 'I looked at her, and we knew our only chance of winning the match stood if we both batted till the end. I didn't say anything, but she looked at me and got the message. She wouldn't leave.'

The duo had decided that they wouldn't exert themselves too much by trying for quick runs, and instead targeted boundaries. In the 46th over, Asmavia swept Dinesha Devnarain for a four, and followed it up with two more against Shabnim Ismail in the next over to close in on their target.

With only seven runs needed in the remaining three overs, Asmavia didn't want to drag things out any longer than necessary. Her condition had begun to worsen. In trying to stretch the ailing Asmavia, Devnarain helped out with a wide delivery outside off. After five dots, the last ball of the over fell in Asmavia's swinging arc and she middled it over the fence at long off for a six to end her misery and help Pakistan to a historic win.

'Asmavia is a fighter, and in that match she inspired me,' the then 19-year-old Kainat admits. 'The story of that innings has been told so many times over that it inspires you to do something similar for your country.'

For as inconsequential as that win was in the context of the tournament, Sana believes it held a larger importance. 'After that match, the team started believing that we could be as big as South Africa. Crossing that line was crucial.'

'Until then we were under the impression that only Bangladesh and Ireland were our competitors,' adds Mohtashim. 'That we could beat South Africa made us feel that we'd achieved something significant.'

That win also gave Pakistan the confidence to push for a victory in the final with the much-fancied West Indies, against whom they had enjoyed a few recent successes. However, the final against Merissa Aguilleira's team proved to be a one-sided contest. Contrasting half-centuries by Juliana Nero and Deandra Dottin powered the West Indies to 250 for 5. And Pakistan, despite a quick-fire 50 by Qanita Jalil, fell off track in the chase – yet again to Anisa Mohammed's off spin. Anisa returned her career-best figures of 7 for 14 to bowl out Pakistan for 120.

'We wanted to win the qualifiers,' Sana claims. 'We had qualified for the World Cup, but we wanted to improve on that. Even if we could beat our own previous performance, it would have been a significant improvement. Losing to the West Indies after getting a start from Qanita was disappointing. We weren't happy about it, but we did enjoy beating South Africa. That feeling lasted for a really long time.'

Mohtashim was certain that Asmavia had the qualities to become a useful all-rounder and, over the years, spent several hours training her in the nets – for basic technique as well as power hitting. At the heart of it though, much like Qanita, she was a pace bowler.

Although many women were inspired by the numerous fast-bowling greats the Pakistan men's team had produced, it wasn't a skill they could all excel at. Some didn't have the pace, some weren't physically strong enough. The poorly maintained pitches they often played on didn't help their skills develop either. Quite early into their careers, Sana Mir and Nida Dar's fast-bowling aspirations were cut short due to injuries. Asmavia, much like Qanita, was part of the rare breed who excelled despite the innumerable hindrances.

She grew up in Multan, the ancient city of Sufi shrines located on the banks of the River Chenab in Southern Punjab, aspiring to become a fast bowler like Shoaib Akhtar. If not for the support of her father, who was a regional hockey player, playing the sport wouldn't have been possible in the conservative society. Even while playing with the boys at a local academy, she had to miss several training sessions if her brothers weren't free to drop her off and pick her up from the training ground.

Cricket would have remained nothing more than a hobby had she not figured out, during a 2003 summer vacation stay with her grandmother in Faisalabad, that the PCB (led by the PWCA) was organising trials for women cricketers. As a 16-year-old, she was called up for the camp and was all set to make her international debut, but with Shaiza Khan's group getting the rights for representation at the 2003 IWCC qualifiers, Asmavia's hopes were dashed.

Nonetheless, when the PCB fielded its debut team in 2005, Asmavia delivered the first ball. Over the years, she became one of Pakistan's leading wicket-takers, with the high point coming during the England tour of 2012 – when she became the first woman cricketer to bag a T20I hat-trick. In the second match of the series, played at the Haslegrave Ground in Loughborough, she claimed the wickets of Sarah Taylor, Arran Brindle and Danni Wyatt.

The wickets were spaced out. Off the fifth ball of the ninth over of England's innings, she broke a strong partnership between Charlotte Edwards and Sarah Taylor by trapping the latter lbw. Arran Brindle's stay was nipped in the bud as she was cleaned up off her first delivery. Asmavia, having bowled three overs at that point, didn't return to the attack till the last over of the match – by which time Danni Wyatt had counter-attacked Pakistan and tilted the balance in her team's favour. Her innings was brought to an end by the first ball of the 20th over – with a return catch – with which she completed her hat-trick.

One of the major hurdles for pace bowlers in Pakistan, and especially frustrating for Asmavia and Qanita, was the poor standard of fielding. They didn't have the fittest or the most agile fielders who liked to throw themselves around in the field. The ground conditions in the country weren't safe enough for players to match the fielding quality of some of the better teams. As a result, there were plenty of dropped catches or catches that could have been. Nain Abidi, though, was an exception to the rule.

Sana Mir believed Nain's world usually swung between two extremes – confidence and overconfidence.

Brought up in the cosmopolitan city of Karachi, Nain was a hyperactive child who wanted to emulate Jonty Rhodes – the South African fielder who had showcased new standards of athleticism in the 1992 World Cup by running out Pakistan batsman Inzamam-ul-Haq. That highlight remained one of her earliest cricketing memories.

Growing up as the only girl among five siblings, her activities revolved around what her brothers were doing – including playing cricket on the streets. 'There were a few neighbours who were very happy to see me play with all the boys,' Nain recalls.

'It was sort of a novelty back then. Some would peep out of their windows, some through the gates. Some of them would sit outside their house with a cup of tea, watching us play.'

But as much as Nain wanted to become a cricketer, she didn't see a pathway for herself to take up the game professionally. She focused on her academic life, fulfilling her mother's ambition for her to become an engineer. 'Engineering was one of the most respectable professions, much like becoming a doctor. But to become a doctor I would have had to study a lot, so I chose engineering instead.'

While Nain was preparing for her 2004 entrance exam for NED University of Engineering and Technology in Karachi, her mother came across a newspaper interview with Kiran Baluch – soon after she had scored the record double century against the West Indies. In that same paper, there was also an advertisement for trials by the PWCCA for women cricketers. She suggested Nain give them a try.

'I was a little surprised at first, even a little annoyed at that time. I was wondering what had suddenly come over my mother. What was I supposed to prepare for – the engineering exam or this cricket trial?

'But we didn't really have a choice. We had to listen to everything that our parents said, such was the respect we had for them. Even today, we don't lift our heads while talking to our parents. Even with engineering, I chose to do it because my *waalda* [mother] wanted me to, even though I was poor at maths.'

Eventually, Nain took the entrance exam as well as attending the cricket trials and got selected for both. Now, the decision about where her life should head was taken at the dinner table that evening. 'My parents said, "Do something different and make up for all the broken lights in the house and the plants destroyed in the garden. Show your skills on the big stage and make an impact."'

Nain, as always, agreed with their decision.

Among hundreds who had turned up for the trials, inspired by the feats of Kiran Baluch and Shaiza Khan, six were selected by the PWCCA – Nain and Sana among them.

However, with the power tussle going on between the Shaiza Khan group and the PCB, Nain didn't get a chance to play for Pakistan for two more years. While she was a good fielder, her batting needed improvement. She didn't get selected for the national camps but she made friends with a few of those who did. 'I would talk to them in the mornings before they left for training, and again in the evenings after their session, asking them about their routine.'

She would then try to mirror them. Waking up at 4.30 a.m. and running on her terrace, while it was still dark, she switched on a light bulb and practised knocking with a rubber ball so that it wouldn't wake up others at home. To understand the training routines she was being told about, she would go to the National Stadium and observe the players practising there.

While her family supported her aspirations to become a cricketer, there were hindrances that came along when she took up the sport professionally. 'I belong to a conservative, Shia family. We follow religious practices quite strictly. Islamic scholars would come to our home. So, the environment was such that it was awkward to talk about cricket for girls. Some of my relatives believed that, as a woman, cricket wasn't for me. It was a gentleman's game.

'Several of our relatives ended ties with us because my father and mother were supportive of my decision. They believed my parents had turned me into a *baaghi* [rebel] by allowing me to play. But thankfully my father told me, "Do whatever you wish, but respect the boundaries of the family. Fulfil your dream and make a difference in society."'

In Nain's early teens she wasn't allowed to attend local matches, organised under lights, which her brothers were playing in. In order to find a way around this, she would pack sandwiches in a box and take it for them and their teammates to eat during the innings break. In return, she would ask for a favour – to swing the bat in the middle for a few minutes.

'I would make a puppy face,' she reveals. 'Some of them would eventually relent and bowl at me.' Those ten minutes were enough to make her day. She would return home extremely happy, having fulfilled all that she desired. Little did those boys playing local cricket matches know that they had caught glimpses of Pakistan's first woman ODI centurion.

For nearly nine months after the ICC World Cup qualifiers in Bangladesh, Pakistan didn't play an international match. The barren phase ended on 22 August 2012, when they took on Ireland in the opening encounter of a tri-nation series, also involving Bangladesh, in Dublin.

Nida Dar and Qanita Jalil provided a quick start, putting on a half-century stand before the former fell to Isobel Joyce in the 11th over. On a flat wicket, against a fairly undemanding bowling attack, Nain Abidi also cashed in. Qanita departed soon after, eight runs short of a 50 – getting cleaned up by Joyce. Barring Joyce's left-arm medium pace and Eimear Richardson's off breaks, there wasn't much trouble for the Pakistan batters. In the company of Bismah Maroof, Nain steadied Pakistan's innings with a 74-run partnership. They were helped along the way with several extras – 22 of them wides.

However, as Nain approached the 90-run mark, she began to get nervous. Pakistan players weren't used to big individual landmarks, and Nain herself was aware through her past experience that overcoming that mental barrier wasn't easy. She was the first Pakistan player to score a T20I 50 but she also fell several times in the 80s and 90s in club cricket that year.

'It didn't matter to my father how much I scored,' she recalls. 'He would just say, "Don't worry. You work hard and leave the rest to Allah. Trust him to take care of everything." His reaction would remain the same at all times, but my mother and brother constantly pushed me to do well. They were never satisfied with my 50s and 60s.'

So, when she reached the 90s, she panicked again. 'I replayed all the criticism that I had received, especially from my relatives.' And in a moment of pressure, she neatly tucked a ball to the cover region and sprinted across the pitch for a quick single to bring up the historic century.

'It was the first time that my mother used the word "excellent" to compliment my innings. It meant so much to me. For me, the significance of it is beyond just a three-figure score, because such knocks inspire others,' she said, possibly from her memory of being inspired by Kiran Baluch's feat.

While she was closing in on the landmark, Javeria Khan went into overdrive in the final overs and powered the team to 254 for 3. Rain affected play thereafter, and Ireland were left chasing 224 in 39 overs. They seemed up to the task for most of the game, courtesy of Clare Shillington's 66, but eventually fell 42 runs short. Although the Pakistan bowlers had trouble containing the opposition, they were top-class on the field. Javeria Khan and Sadia Yousuf effected a run-out each, while Batool Fatima was at her athletic best with two stumpings and as many run-outs.

That was an emphatic start to a multi-format series they went on to dominate, winning all four games – two ODIs and two T20Is.

Even though Pakistan lost in the subsequent tour to England, where Asmavia took a hat-trick, it was clear that they were a team on the rise. The results of their growth since Sana Mir had taken over as captain started to bear fruit in 2012, not only through individual landmarks but also through their performances – in victories as well as defeats. Mohtashim's coaching methods were proving effective.

The most significant victory that year came against India in the 2012 World T20. It was not only the first win for the women's team over their neighbours, but also a laurel which their men's team had yet to achieve at that point.

Pitted in Group A – alongside Australia, England and India – even the odd lucky match wouldn't have helped them sail through to the semi-finals. The slow and turning pitches in Galle would have aided their spinners, but it was too tall a task to win two of those three games. Expectations were low, and in the first two games, they were outplayed by England (bowled out for 90 in a 134-run chase) and Australia (restricted to 38 for 3 in nine overs of a rain-hit match where they were chasing 64). They had collectively failed. Barring Sana Mir's bowling effort against England, there was no individual performance of note.

India had found themselves in a similar position with their results – losing to Australia by eight wickets and to England by nine. By the time Pakistan were up against them, neither of them had a chance to qualify any further. But when India and Pakistan, two countries with a tense political history and emotional cricket fan bases, contest against each other, it rarely needs an additional context.

Only a day earlier, Virat Kohli's unbeaten 78 had powered the Indian men's team to a comfortable eight-wicket win over Pakistan in Colombo, and the focus had shifted to their women counterparts at Galle on 1 October.

Electing to bat, Sana Mir and Nain Abidi made steady starts after losing Qanita Jalil early. However, once Sana was caught behind off debutant off-spinner Rasanara Parwin in the tenth over, Pakistan's line-up fell apart. Veteran pace bowler Jhulan Goswami and off-spinner Anuja Patil bagged a brace each, while a couple of run-outs added to Pakistan's woes. The innings struggled to gather momentum and the players were eventually restricted to 98 for 9.

On a sluggish pitch, it was a defendable score, especially as India didn't have the longest batting order, relying heavily on bowlers who could bat a bit. Mithali Raj and Punam Raut displayed fine skills on a challenging wicket to help India to a steady start after losing wicketkeeper Sulakshana Naik early on. However, on the last ball of the tenth over, Nida Dar had Punam tricked with her off break and stumped. In her following over, she returned to dismiss Mithali and Harmanpreet Kaur, breaking the back of India's batting and reducing them to 51 for 4.

With some help from Reema Malhotra and Amita Sharma, Jhulan pushed India towards the target, but the penultimate over of the match proved decisive. Bismah Maroof, who had barely started to bowl a year before, delivered a match-turning over – dismissing Jhulan and Amita and conceding only three runs. That left Sana Mir with 14 runs to defend in the final over, where a few swipes by Niranjana Nagarajan brought the equation down to four runs off the last ball. Niranjana tried to slog again but it didn't go for a boundary. She, along with Anuja, sprinted two runs and attempted a third to level the scores, but she was run out by a relay throw from Asmavia to Batool to Sana.

In the most sensational of finishes, Pakistan had achieved their first World Cup win over India.

Even though Pakistan hadn't qualified for the semi-finals and lost badly to South Africa in the next match – which served as a qualifier clash for the next edition of the World Cup – it didn't matter. A victory against India was a rare high for a sport that needed attention in order to reach the hinterlands, creating awareness and acceptance that girls were stepping out and playing. 'That victory gave women's cricket in Pakistan the visibility it needed,' Sana notes. 'The girls who were part of that match got an extraordinary level of attention afterwards. That victory made parents proud. It made them understand that what we were doing [playing cricket] was meaningful. A win like that boosts you for a couple of years. We were quite lucky in that sense to get those wins. The 2008 qualifiers, the 2009 run in the World Cup, the 2010 gold medal, the 2012 win against India – every one or two years, we were able to produce those performances.'

The high of 2012 continued in the Asia Cup, in Guangzhou, later that month. Pakistan crushed Thailand (bowling them out for 32, courtesy of Marina Iqbal's 5-fer, after posting 129 for 7) and Hong Kong (scoring 157 for 7 before bundling the opposition out for 15). The victories, even though expected, were an indication of how dominant Pakistan had become on the Asian circuit. The team lost its last Group A match to India by eight wickets but qualified for the semis.

Up against Bangladesh, who had beaten Sri Lanka and topped Group B, Pakistan had a comfortable outing, largely due to the all-round efforts of Bismah Maroof (27* and 2 for 9) and Nida Dar (25* and 2 for 13), winning by six wickets to schedule their third match of October 2012 against India – this time in a final.

India were without their most experienced batter (Mithali Raj) and bowler (Jhulan Goswami), both of whom were ruled out due to injuries. To add to their woes, India lost openers early after electing to bat. Punam Raut and Harmanpreet Kaur steadied the innings briefly with a 32-run partnership for the third wicket before Bismah broke the stand in the ninth over and Sana triggered a collapse to have India all out for 81.

Even though it was a challenging surface, victory was in sight for Pakistan. However, as on so many occasions in the past, the possibility of a big win got them excited, and they lost momentum. A collective effort by the Indian bowlers wrapped up their innings in 19.1 overs – 18 runs short of India's score.

Nonetheless, pushing India so close was a proclamation

that they were out there to compete for the title of the best country in Asia, which would have been inconceivable three years earlier. Bismah Maroof, who had topped the run charts with 113 runs and five wickets, was named the player of the tournament.

By then, under Sana and Mohtashim, Pakistan had undergone a significant change: there was less chopping and changing and each player had a clear role. Practices and training had a structure, and the vision for the team was becoming clearer.

For the first time in its cricketing history, Pakistan had reasons to be hopeful as the players prepared for the 50-over World Cup, scheduled to be played in India in February 2013.

The visit to India was Pakistan's first since the 2006 Asia Cup campaign.

It was a rare opportunity to cross the border, but there were more reasons to be excited with the World Cup games scheduled to be played in Mumbai, the home of Bollywood. Since the partition in 1947, the two countries had experienced almost constant political tension, but formally and informally enjoyed a strong cultural exchange – Bollywood movies being the prime cultural crossover from India.

As much as the tour was about cricket, for many players it was also about exploring their roots, about which they had heard, read and romanticised. Families and friends of the players expected them to bring home everything they had heard was popular in India, irrespective of how irrelevant it was to their own culture. Demands for three things topped most lists: sari, sindoor and Fevicol.

While the desire for saris and sindoor came from Indian shows and movies, the demand for Fevicol had emerged from a popular song of the same name in a Salman Khan film, which had been released in December 2012.

While the players readied themselves for an exciting trip, the political situation in India wasn't as welcoming as they might have hoped.

The 2008 terrorist attacks in Mumbai had soured relationships between India and Pakistan, which until then had been mending after 2004 with annual men's tours. Political tensions rose, and cricketing ties were cut. Small efforts were made to improve matters through cricket. President Zardari was invited along with Shahid Afridi's team to travel to India for the semi-finals of the 2011 men's cricket World Cup. The following year, the team was hosted for another limited overs, bilateral series held in India. There were attempts made to broker peace, but relations were far from healed.

In January 2013, tensions mounted again when two Indian soldiers were killed in a ceasefire violation at the India–Pakistan border. With the national elections set to take place in mid-2014, anti-Pakistan sentiment was on the rise, and several opposition parties in India had already started to object to the presence of Pakistani artists in Bollywood. An anti-Pakistan stand was not only a way to gain popular support but also one that would help gain instant media attention.

Shiv Sena – a Hindu, right-wing political outfit – was adamant about not letting the Pakistanis perform or play in Maharashtra, a state where its members commanded strong control despite not being in power. In January 2013, around 100 people had gathered at a stadium in Mumbai – the capital of the state – protesting against the presence of four Pakistani players in a hockey league.

With the World Cup matches set to be played across four venues in the city, there were concerns as to whether or not

Pakistan would be allowed to play in the tournament. The BCCI requested several state associations take on Pakistan's games, but, with the election season coming up, none wanted to assume the risk.

Naveen Patnaik, the chief minister of Odisha, was an exception.

A writer and former socialite whose circle included the likes of Mick Jagger and Jacqueline Kennedy, Patnaik had drastically switched his lifestyle after entering politics following the death of his father. Since becoming chief minister of Odisha in 2000, his control in the region had rarely been challenged. His liberal outlook and politics ensured that Sana Mir's team could find a safe haven in the state. The Odisha Cricket Association agreed to host them, and on 25 January, six days before the start of the tournament, the ICC announced that Pakistan's matches would be shifted to Barabati Stadium in Cuttack.

Despite the Odisha government's support, there were still major security concerns, with fringe, right-wing outfits like Bajrang Dal, Kalinga Sena and Vishwa Hindu Parishad threatening to disrupt the matches. These groups had protested at Bhubaneshwar (Odisha's capital) airport, outside the police commissioner's headquarters and the hotel where the ICC delegates had arrived to discuss the security arrangements with state officials ahead of the tournament.

Ahead of Pakistan's arrival at Cuttack, security was beefed up, the crowded Buxi Bazaar marketplace was shut down and numerous political workers were detained for threatening to disrupt the team's stay.

Mohtashim Rashid had no clue what to expect in Cuttack, but from his previous experience of travelling to India as the fielding coach of the Pakistan's men's team in 2007, he knew the welcome would be warm. To his surprise, it was anything but.

'There was no one to receive us at Delhi airport,' he recalls. 'We were made to fill in a load of forms and were being questioned constantly. It felt weird with all the protocols. We had to convince the security that we had come to play the World Cup.'

To make matters worse, Bismah was unwell and began throwing up. 'I pleaded with them, saying that one of my players was vomiting. "Can you send a doctor instead of questioning us?" It was extremely shocking. It wasn't like that the previous time.'

The team was quickly transferred to another flight from Delhi to Bhubaneshwar. 'As soon as we got out, there were a few buses lined up outside the airport. Some of us wanted to go to the washroom. They didn't allow us to go and instead made us sit inside the bus, where it was completely dark. It was so weird. We had no clue where we were heading. We couldn't even see each other, it was a complete blackout. It didn't feel like we had come to play a World Cup.'

The uncertainty remained throughout the 40-minute drive. 'But as soon as we reached Cuttack and the door of the bus opened, it was a surprise. There was a grand welcome for us with a lot of noise, and they showered us with love.'

In a short space of time, the Odisha Cricket Association had constructed a structure within the stadium complex for the players' accommodation. As they couldn't step out of the complex, a few indoor games, a swimming pool and a massage chair were kept for their recreation in the lobby. The shopkeepers were also called in so the players could buy whatever they wanted. They brought jewellery and saris, both of which were popular buys among the players – and were then stunned by the bizarre demand for Fevicol.

The organisers did all that they could within their means to make the team comfortable, but the effects of restricted movement were obvious. Whether it was the living conditions or the fact that Pakistan hadn't played a one-day international since their Ireland tour in August 2012, their on-field performance was disappointing.

'It's a shame because the last time I came to India, my image of India changed a lot,' Sana told ESPNcricinfo during the World Cup. 'Despite the historic rivalry between the two countries, the people here were really amazing. And we took a lot of love back to Pakistan. And I just wanted this new generation of Pakistan girls to feel that love and warmth. Unfortunately, due to the circumstances, we couldn't have that.'

Their morale was hit early after being beaten by a state side – Odisha XI – in the warm-ups. Even though they started their campaign well, bowling out Australia for 175 in the first match, they were thoroughly outplayed in the three games. The intensity was evident in the first match, especially with Asmavia going after the Australians. Lisa Sthalekar, the Australian all-rounder, remembers, 'She had steam coming out of her ears, ready for a contest. Every time I played and missed the ball, she came after me. They were up for it, not caring who we were.'

The early aggression dwindled quite quickly as the tournament progressed. They were bowled out for 84 against Australia, New Zealand chased down their 105-run target with seven wickets in hand and more than 20 overs to spare, and South Africa bundled them out for 81 after scoring 207 for 5.

Through the course of these games, several local political factions threatened to disrupt the matches, especially when Pakistan were scheduled to play India for the seventh-place play-off. While the games were eventually played out without interruption, Pakistan's misery on the tour didn't end there.

Nain Abidi and Nida Dar scored 50s against India, but their team total of 192 for 7 was overhauled quite effortlessly courtesy of Mithali Raj's unbeaten century. Except for the last match, they never looked the part.

'For a player, it wasn't an ideal environment,' Mohtashim notes. 'All they could do was go out and play. Once the match was done, they had to remain locked up. As a player, you need to relax, especially in such an intense competition. To make matters worse, those who were assigned to look after our food wouldn't always understand our instructions well. There were times we had to make our own meals. The organisers tried to make us feel relaxed in every way they could, but we didn't have the freedom that the other teams did. Even the Australian players came and offered their sympathies to us.'

Such was the discomfort for the team in the series that instead of being disappointed with the results of the matches, Sana Mir admitted that the players felt relieved to be returning home. 'Yes [I'm relieved]. I can say that now because it was one of the toughest tours I have ever played in. Everything – like my own performance, my team's performance and the whole situation – it was one of the toughest tournaments.

'It's a mixed feeling. It has been tough. But we have seen a lot of people supporting us, especially all the people at the Orissa Cricket Association Academy and the OCA staff in the dressing room. They all helped us a lot. Overall, it was a tense tournament for the Pakistan team, but still we managed to do it and for some reason it's good that we are going home now.'

The poor performance in the series notwithstanding, Pakistan's showing in international cricket was on the rise and a steely core was being forged. Even with their disappointing showing at the World Cup, several took note of the skill levels, which unfortunately weren't backed by high fitness standards and physical strength.

Javeria Khan and Bismah Maroof were forging a steady batting line-up in the company of Nain Abidi. Sana Mir and Nida Dar remained the premier all-rounders in the side, with Qanita Jalil and Asmavia Iqbal looking after the pace department. Batool Fatima remained reliable behind the stumps, while Sadia Yousuf was the premier left-arm spinner. Masooma Junaid, Nahida Khan and Marina Iqbal too made frequent appearances for the side that was pushing Pakistan cricket forward.

Not only were the players developing individually in terms of skills and match awareness, but they were also pushing the boundaries as a team. One of the most significant yet uncelebrated moments came in the 2013 tour to England and Ireland. While Pakistan as expected lost both their ODIs to England, they beat Ireland in the two 50-over contests. In the one-off T20I, Javeria Khan registered her maiden 50, Sadia Yousuf – much as in the one-day leg – delivered her best spell, and Batool Fatima effected four dismissals behind the wicket.

However, the most memorable of those matches was the second T20I against England. After losing the first match by 70 runs, Pakistan returned only a few hours later to the same venue – the Haslegrave Ground in Loughborough – to register a historic win and level the series on 5 July.

It was a series in which England were experimenting. In the first match, they had handed four debut caps – to Amy Jones, Nat Sciver, Lauren Winfield-Hill and Tash Farrant. In the second game, the experiments were extended further.

Pakistan won the toss and chose to bat. It didn't matter much initially as they were soon cut to 40 for 4. Sana Mir and Nain Abidi rescued the innings with a 55-run partnership, but they were eventually restricted to 116 for 8. It wasn't a massive score, but the improved batting performance had given the bowlers enough of a cushion to pose a challenge.

England, as part of their experimentation, decided to shuffle the batting order. Wicketkeeper Sarah Taylor was rested and skipper Charlotte Edwards, who had scored a 33-ball 46 earlier in the day, did not walk out to bat until the fall of the seventh wicket. Pakistan used England's mercies to their advantage. The spin trio of Sana Mir, Sadia Yousuf and Nida Dar didn't allow the fairly inexperienced England top order to break free in the chase. The turning point came in the ninth over, when not only did Yousuf bowl a maiden but England also lost two wickets –

Susie Rowe run out by Bismah and Danielle Hazell stumped by Batool.

Arran Brindle (née Thompson) kept England in the chase with a 27-ball 39, which included two boundaries in the penultimate over and a six in the last, bowled by Bismah. Needing three off the last ball, she failed to connect with her swing, and the edge flew towards the third-man area. Arran ran the first run quickly and was sprinting for a second to level the score. However, collecting a ball thrown from the deep by Nahida Khan, despite an awkward bounce, Batool dived to run out Arran.

Even though the win came against an England side that hadn't treated the match as a stiff contest, the enormity of the victory makes Sana Mir believe, 'From a cricketing perspective, I think this victory was our biggest achievement.'

The confidence gained from that win showed in the ICC Women's World T20 qualifiers, where Pakistan remained undefeated, dominating against Thailand, the Netherlands and Zimbabwe in the group stage, before comfortably winning against Ireland in the semi-finals. The final against Sri Lanka was washed out.

The successes weren't to end there.

For the first time since the 2005 Asia Cup, the PCB decided to host a series for the women's team. With no international matches being held in the country since the 2009 attacks on the Sri Lankan team, a multi-format tri-series was organised in

Qatar, in January 2014. It was quite unlike any international assignment, outside of the ICC tournaments. Accommodation, food and all the fanfare around the series were lavish, almost festive.

'We haven't been fortunate enough to play at home,' Sana had told reporters ahead of the series. 'Mostly, we've had to rely on matches overseas. We've played a lot in England, Ireland where the conditions have helped the bowlers. That experience is beginning to show now, and hopefully even on these pitches, they'll be able to make an impact.'

While Ireland lost all their league games of the ODI leg, South Africa beat Pakistan in the only match that was possible in that stage before scraping through for a win in the final, where after bundling out Pakistan for 94, they struggled against the spinners before eventually overhauling the total in the 44th over, with four wickets in hand.

In the T20 leg, the hosts asserted their dominance. They began by beating South Africa in the first match before crushing Ireland's challenge. The Mignon du Preez-led side did pull back one in their last league game against Pakistan, but both teams had managed to set up another final date.

'More than 10,000 people had come to watch us for the final,' Javeria Khan recalls. 'We were not used to that kind of a crowd. We were used to playing in front of cuckoos and crows. Finally, we got a chance to play in front of a human crowd.'

The spinners tested the South African batters yet again. Barring Marizanne Kapp, who stroked a 48-ball 40, none of the others managed a double-digit score. In fact, only two boundaries were hit in the innings.

Pakistan, much more accustomed to the slower conditions, were guided masterfully by Javeria Khan in the chase. Her 46-ball 38 helped Pakistan register a seven-wicket win.

The progress of the team was obvious, and yet again they were ready to head to a world event with promise. But things started to go wrong during their tour to Bangladesh, just ahead of the 2014 World T20.

Even though Pakistan won both the T20Is against the hosts, the losses in the two ODIs preceding that were alarming. The inconsistent batting was yet again the leading cause of Sana

Mir's worries. It was to eventually show up in the flagship tournament.

In the first match of the World T20, Lizelle Lee and Dane van Niekerk's unbeaten 163-run opening stand crushed Pakistan. New Zealand and Australia also posted big wins. By the time Pakistan beat Ireland in the last group game, their chances in the tournament were over. Moreover, Pakistan also lost the match for the qualification play-offs for the next edition of the tournament against India. All the players had left to salvage from the contest was the seventh-place play-off against Sri Lanka. After posting 122 for 5, courtesy of Bismah Maroof's 62, they restricted Sri Lanka to 108.

The performances at the 2014 World T20, much like the 50-over World Cup in 2013, were an indication that Pakistan were underperforming in big tournaments, and it wasn't a true reflection of how skilled the players were when the pressure was off.

The introduction of the ICC's ODI women's championship, announced in July 2014, proved to be a game changer.

As per the requirements of the tournament, all the top eight sides had to play against each other in the 2014–16 cycle. The top four teams from those would qualify directly to the 50-over World Cup in 2017, while the remaining four were supposed to go through the qualifiers, which would include six other ICC regional qualifiers. This rule by the ICC meant that Pakistan would get a chance to play regular international cricket, and against all the top sides. This would help the players gain more experience, develop skills and build high-pressure match temperament.

Australia was their first challenge. In what was expected to be a one-sided series, Pakistan displayed why, outside the World Cups, they were a rising force on the international stage. Even though the team lost 4–0, they gave a good account of themselves, competing well in at least three of the four matches, which included a win for Australia with only three balls to spare in the rain-marred second one-dayer. Additionally, there were several noteworthy performances, with Bismah Maroof and Javeria Khan registering half-centuries.

While they were outplayed as expected in the T20Is that followed, Javeria acknowledges, 'It was one of those series where we were very happy with our performance despite not winning any of the matches.'

Within a few months, when the ICC launched its rankings for women, eight Pakistan players made it to the top 20 across categories. In sticking with a core group of players, there was a trade-off and allegations that some of the weaker performers were being given a longer rope than they deserved. But it had started to pay dividends, with an improved team performance and a few individuals like Asmavia Iqbal and Nain Abidi grabbing headlines, bringing greater visibility to women playing cricket and achieving recognition on a global stage.

Beyond the victories and losses, this period showed what a bunch of Pakistani women could achieve in sport, despite its numerous challenges, if all energies were focused towards a common goal without external disruptions.

9

IT'S GOLD, AGAIN

FEW SPORTS, POSSIBLY none, are as dependent on rain and other weather interruptions as cricket. Just a brief spell of rain on 26 September 2014 at the Yeonhui Cricket Ground in Incheon during the Asian Games was enough to send the Pakistan players into a panic.

The half-an-hour innings interval had stretched way past its stipulated time, but there were signs of the pitch drying just about enough for play to resume. At 4.00 p.m., their hopes for a second Asian Games gold medal were on the way down with the setting sun.

Unlike 2010, Pakistan had headed to the 2014 edition of the tournament with expectations of returning as champions. 'That made the task more challenging,' reveals Nida.

For the tournament that was set to begin on 19 September, the selectors had announced the squad more than two months in advance. Apart from the Asian Games, the team for the preceding Australia tour was also declared.

Some controversial calls were made ahead of the big tournament, which included rewarding the high-performing players in the domestic circuit in preference to the more experienced cricketers. While opener Nahida Khan was dropped, pace bowler Kainat Imtiaz was recalled and a promising all-rounder, Aliya Riaz, was handed her maiden call-up after a prolific run in the domestic competition. Twenty-year-old wicketkeeper Sidra Nawaz was also included to fill the big boots of the recently retired Batool Fatima.

Yet, it was a far improved squad – both skill-wise and in terms of game understanding.

With the BCCI again refusing to send its representation for the tournament, Pakistan were left with only two strong competitors – Sri Lanka and Bangladesh. China, Hong Kong, Japan, Malaysia, Thailand, South Korea and Nepal were, in the mildest terms, making up the numbers.

On the basis of the rankings, Japan, Pakistan, Sri Lanka and Bangladesh earned direct entry to the quarter-finals while China, Thailand, Hong Kong and Nepal made it to that round through their performances in the group stages.

Sri Lanka and Bangladesh, as per the draw, would have had to play each other in the semi-finals. As a result, Pakistan's road to the final was expected to be untroubled. Not surprisingly, the side broke little sweat in beating Thailand in the quarters and China in the semis.

In a rain-hit quarter-final clash, Pakistan scored 97 for 5 in 14 overs, led by Nain Abidi's run-a-ball 40, after being put in to bat. In response, Thailand were restricted to 46 for 7.

In the semi-final, Pakistan elected to field and bowled out China for 37 runs in 19 overs. Nida bagged four scalps while Bismah Maroof picked up a brace. After losing Marina early in the chase, Javeria and Bismah reached the target in eight overs and cruised to a nine-wicket win.

When the morning match at the Yeonhui Cricket Ground wrapped up early, Pakistan's attention diverted to the next game at the same venue – Sri Lanka vs Bangladesh. Lata Mondal's unbeaten 43-ball 34 helped Bangladesh to a competitive 95 for 4 after they elected to bat. Although Sri Lanka were a fairly competitive and experienced team, against Panna Ghosh's seam-ups they came second best on the day.

Panna ripped through the top order, and although skipper Shashikala Siriwardene and Chamari Polgampola tried to revive the chase, Sri Lanka succumbed. In 18.2 overs, the innings folded for 70, and the 25-run win helped Bangladesh set up yet another final against Pakistan.

'We knew our passage to the final was going to be smooth,' Nida, the star performer of Pakistan's previous Asian Games campaign, reveals. 'But we had to win the gold medal. It didn't matter to us who played us in the final. After our previous experience, we knew the rewards and recognition that we would get. But this time, we were under the pressure of expectation.'

Even as Pakistan were the favourites to win the contest, they were wary of their opponents, who had already caused an upset. 'Bangladesh's bowling was always their strength, and they also had a few batters who could hit. And for some reason, they had always troubled us.'

By then, Pakistan had matured into a better side – collectively and individually. As a group, the communication between the players had improved, and the understanding of each other's strengths and weaknesses was far sharper. On the cricketing front, the ability to read conditions and adjust game plans had also matured.

Bangladesh's cricket was on a similar trajectory to Pakistan's and, more importantly, the team had turned up with similar aspirations. The side came into the big game having beaten favourites Sri Lanka, and Pakistan too were dealt an early blow with the dismissal of in-form opener Javeria Khan. Going slow on a sluggish pitch was a safer option, but the pressure of the occasion forced the players to pick up the pace. Bismah Maroof remained calm and helped her side to 55 for 3 in the 13th over, in the company of Marina Iqbal and Nain Abidi. The foundation was set for the big hitters to power on from there, but it never happened. Rumana Ahmed's miserly spell of 2 for 13 in four overs restricted Pakistan to 97 for 6 and gave Bangladesh a real sniff at the gold medal – an achievement none of the other Bangladesh athletes or teams had managed at the Games that year.

To help their cause, a rain break followed. When play resumed, they were left needing only 43 runs in seven overs. It simplified their plans and forced Sana Mir to recalibrate hers. Much like Bangladesh, Pakistan hadn't won a gold medal in the 2014 Asian Games (across all sporting disciplines) until that point.

'We had checked the forecast that morning and no rain was predicted,' Nida recalls. 'When it started raining, we felt as if the match had slipped from our hands.

'We knew they had a few good hitters in their side. With ten wickets in hand, they just had to swing their bats and they would've crossed the target.'

Bangladesh's opener, Ayesha Rahman, did just as Nida expected – she swung her bat. Asmavia Iqbal, beginning Pakistan's defence, was swinging as well. Her first delivery swung far too much and was called wide. A few balls later, Ayesha's swing found the middle of the bat and flew over the mid-wicket fielder for a boundary. With ten runs from the first over, the chase had come down to 33 in 36.

'We lost our motivation after that over,' remarks Nida.

Sumaiya Siddiqui's medium-pacers tidily kept the run flow in check. Two overs down, the equation had come down to 31 in 30, with all ten wickets still in hand.

Although the ball was fairly new, on a sticky pitch which was holding up slightly, Sana Mir brought herself on to bowl the third over. Rumana Ahmed swept the first ball to long leg and sprinted for a run. She contemplated a second before backing out of the call. However, by then keeper Sidra Nawaz picked Javeria Khan's throw from the deep a few feet away from the stumps and effected a direct hit, which caught Ayesha fairly short of the crease on her return. It seemed just a consolatory wicket but offered a much-needed rush of excitement for the fielding team.

Rumana Ahmed reverse swept Sana Mir for a boundary later in the over, but off the next ball another confusion in calling resulted in her being run out. Despite taking two wickets in the over, the game still rested in Bangladesh's favour at 20 for 2. They knew, however, that they were finding themselves in a trickier position than they would have liked and attempted to break free from it. In Siddiqui's next over, Fargana Hoque and Salma Khatun pushed harder and picked up nine runs, bringing the requirement down to 14 off 18 balls, with eight wickets left.

'We were expected to win and we could see our chances slipping away,' says Nida. 'I was standing near the boundary and praying to Allah. Maybe the rest of my teammates were also praying.'

In the tense situation, as she often did, Nida resorted to humour. 'I know even the Bangladeshis believe in Allah and must've been praying to him, but I was hoping that Allah would help us this one time. While standing there I even agreed to observe fasts and prayers if we won.'

While her wait continued, the momentum of the contest began to shift. Sadia Yousuf, with her classic left-arm spin, skittled both Khatun and Hoque in the same over and conceded only four runs. Sana Mir, in her second over, had it even better. She foxed Lata Mondal with a doosra as she tried to step forward to the first ball of the over, and Sidra Nawaz neatly stumped her.

Four balls later, Fahima Khatun tried to give charge and was beaten, also by a doosra. This time, the ball hit the stumps. At the end of the penultimate over, Bangladesh needed seven runs, with four wickets in hand.

The occasion called for wise minds to confer. All the senior players swarmed in towards the middle of the ground, offering advice to Sana. The dilemma was whether to choose the front-line pace option of Qanita Jalil, or, on the basis of a sluggish track, opt for a spinner. The latter option seemed viable, for which there were options again: Nida Dar's off breaks or Bismah Maroof's leggies.

'The weather was pleasant yet we were sweating profusely,' recalls Nida. 'Standing at the boundary, I was looking elsewhere to see whether my teammates were as tense as me.

'Sana summoned me, "Dar aao" ("Come, Dar") and asked, "Are you confident?"

'I said, "Today, I'll either end up as a hero or zero."'

Sana held her by the collar and said, 'Tum mere sher ho! Kar do!' ('Go, tiger!')

'Nothing else was mentioned. No plan given. We were still trying to figure out what tactic would work best for us. Back then, I didn't even have any variations or a wide skill set to understand change of pace and the other techniques of outsmarting batters. I had my limitations as a bowler.'

The Bangladesh batters had their own limitations. Swinging the bat or playing behind the stumps were their go-to modes of scoring, and Pakistan had set the field for it. With her cap on, and green-coloured zinc on her cheeks, Nida began the battle. Off the first ball of the last over, Nuzhat Tasnia's attempted swipe hit the top edge and ballooned up. As two fielders converged under it, Nida gave a loud call before settling under the ball.

After a dot, Shahnaz Parvin reverse swept to backward point for a single. Panna Ghosh, who was witnessing the game slip out of their control from the other end, was finally on strike. She drilled the next ball towards mid-wicket and pressed for a second run. Asmavia Iqbal's throw to the bowler's end found Parvin short by a yard, but importantly Panna had retained strike.

With five off two needed, Panna changed tactics and attempted to hit the ball down the ground. While executing the plan, she failed to get the elevation, and Nida's reflexes were sharp enough to catch it above her head. She broke into a Shahid Afridi celebration pose. With that wicket, the contest was almost sealed.

The new batter, Shaila Sharmin, had only one way to steal Pakistan's moment of glory – to clear the ground. And her best bet to do that was a hard swing. Nida wanted to eliminate that option, and she darted a delivery wide of the off stump and away from her swinging arc. The batter could only manage to swat it to the leg side for a single, and Pakistan had scripted the most miraculous of comebacks.

'Winning the 2014 final the way we did was a big deal,' says Nida. 'We couldn't believe how we managed to turn the game around and win it from such a difficult position. It was almost as if we had taken the medal from the Bangladeshis and put it around our necks.

'We were crying. The Bangladeshis were crying as well.'

IZZAT, ON TRIAL

THE 2014 ASIAN Games win had a far-reaching impact on the lives of many, including those who were not a part of the team, like Nahida Khan who, according to Marina Iqbal, is the real superstar of Pakistan cricket. The achievements of Sana Mir's team had made cricket aspirational for more women and a lure for many parents who wanted their daughters to be seen on that same pedestal.

Nahida was the first international cricketer to emerge from the war-ravaged region of Balochistan. Her home was in Chaman – a small town near the Pakistan–Afghanistan border which has been a centre of constant violence, witnessing five insurgencies in six decades, with public infrastructure and educational institutes being routinely attacked. Violence between separatist groups and the state has been a constant in the province since Pakistan's independence in 1947.

But the violence outside the house wasn't the only deterrent for the softly spoken Nahida, who grew up in the Pashtun tribe-dominated region. Playing sports wasn't an honourable act for women even among the peace-loving people of the community.

'I grew up playing cricket with my brothers and cousins. It was fine when I was a kid. Once I grew up, I was shamed for it,' reveals Nahida.

Through most of her growing-up years, cricket was played in secrecy.

In 2011, two years after making her international debut, when she headed for practice to the training stadium in Quetta, clad in a salwar-kameez to avoid detection, she was confronted by a rickshaw driver who had noticed her kitbag.

'Looks like you're going to play cricket. There is another girl who lives here, Nahida Khan, who plays the sport. Do you know her?' he asked.

Such was the fear of being identified that she swiftly responded, 'Yes, I do. She comes there to play with us.'

Looking back, she says, 'I didn't want any trouble. I just wanted to play cricket. Even when journalists came home to interview me, I wouldn't show my face. I was scared that if someone found out I was playing, my cricket could stop all of a sudden.'

The fear stemmed from being admonished by relatives when her photo was published in a local newspaper as the standout performer in a college cricket tournament. Praise was far too much to ask. 'Girls are expected to uphold the honour of the house, and playing sports wasn't respectful for girls in our region.'

That fear never left her, and even after playing five years of international cricket by 2014, she preferred to keep her identity a secret from people in her locality. If not for the support of her father, it would have been impossible for her to pursue her ambitions.

While Nahida's fears lasted a few years, the events at Incheon in 2014, in the far east of the continent, had a catalytic effect on the lives of the people in Chaman, much as they did in the rest of

Pakistan. It was the only gold medal for the country in the 17th edition of the Asian Games, and thus it had as much effect on the lives of those who were a part of the win as it did on Nahida.

Although it took Nahida three more years thereafter to feel secure being seen in public, she had become an 'acceptable' star in Balochistan. After that, she had the company of more girls from Chaman and the towns nearby while training. 'The same people who stopped me from playing cricket for all those years were now showing interest in sending their kids out to play,' Nahida points out. 'With time, mindsets can change, and when they did, it helped me to open myself to the rest of the world.'

Over the years, the battlegrounds for women to pursue cricket have changed from the early days when the elite strata of society were at the forefront of the fight against the rigid, societal norms which marked Zia-ul-Haq's regime. For them, the fight to play was external – taking on fundamentalist, religious groups with ulterior motives, or others of their ilk. In their pursuit, they were backed by the oligarchs, the financially and politically influential – businessmen, bureaucrats and lawyers.

Once the PCB took control of running the sport's affairs, the reach of women's cricket stretched beyond the grasp of the rich and the famous to the hinterlands. The problems arising after that were slightly different.

For a cricket-loving country like Pakistan, gaining success in the sport is the ultimate form of *izzat* (honour). And yet, several women who have attempted to play the sport testify to the *beizzati* (dishonour) their families fear it will bring.

In small towns and villages, mostly in the countryside outside Lahore and Karachi, families exist in close-knit communities where upholding traditional values in the face of modern influences remains the touchpoint of *izzat*. It can be driven by any emotion – ego, fear or control. In most of these regions, for women to even seek out higher education isn't acceptable. Pursuing a professional career and playing a sport are lofty fantasies.

In the successful rise of almost every cricketer to have represented Pakistan, as in the case of Nahida, there also lies a tale of a father and mother who were willing to put their honour in question by going against the cultural expectations and allowing their daughter to pursue her ambitions.

But there are stories that go beyond that. Just about everyone, irrespective of their family background, faced resistance of different kinds. Nazia Nazir, hailing from an affluent feudal family in the small town of Haveli Lakha in Okara, played cricket secretly, unknown to her family, much as Saba Nazir did nearly 200 kilometres away in Muridke while balancing the financial challenges of the house. In Gujranwala, Nida Dar kept her cricket a secret from her brother, who felt embarrassed talking about her hard work with his friends.

There were also those who were apprehensive about their daughters playing cricket, including parents in the more progressive environments of army cantonments, like Marina Iqbal's mother.

The recognition gained through cricket, however, proved to be their card for upward mobility. For Saba Nazir, it was the income which helped her take care of the family's financial needs and help her father to retire from work. For Nida Dar, it was the glory of the 2010 Asian Games win that eventually made her brother proudly strum the guitar and sing songs of celebration on local news channels.

For many others, it was the *izzat* which was showered by those close to the family – relatives, friends and neighbours, and strangers in media and politics.

By 2014, society had emancipated significantly from the clutches of its regressive beliefs, and the gold medal at the Asian Games had pushed women's participation in cricket further in the cosmopolitan urban centres – Lahore and Karachi – as well as some of the orthodox regions in the far corners of the country, like Chaman.

Celebrations of the gold medal win were loud if ephemeral, but the social impact of it was positive and slow. Even more than half a decade later, several aspiring and professional cricketers became the subject of ridicule for playing the sport.

In early 2021, Nida Dar was mocked on national television for having strong hands by a former men's cricketer, Abdul Razzaq. He stated, 'In order to match up to men, our women cricketers have become like us. Look at her [Nida Dar's] hands. If you shake hands with her, it feels as if you're shaking hands with a man.'

Even as Nida tried to calmly explain herself, another woman on the show interrupted and questioned the need to have short hair 'like men'. Everyone around laughed at her again. Several months later, when the video clip became viral on social media, Razzaq called up Nida and apologised, explaining that he had simply been trying to be funny on a comedy show.

That an international cricketer of repute, who had brought glory to the country and was the chief architect of both the Asian Games gold medals, was a subject of public humiliation by another cricketer – who had played and understood the requirements of the profession – was only a glimpse of how women playing sports are viewed. Even though there was an uproar on social media over the comments, the laughter which accompanied those jibes on the show had only served to reinforce them.

Even Shahid Afridi, one of the most popular cricketers in the country, had packaged his resistance towards his daughters playing outdoor sports in the guise of 'cultural and religious reasons'.

In several regions of Pakistan, as Nahida made clear, a girl playing sports brings shame to the family, for whom all acts of raising a daughter lead ultimately to her marriage. A woman playing sports makes her an undesirable bridal prospect.

That link of cricket and marriage, as a prominent cricketer explains, becomes a hindrance for women to continue playing the sport, even if they achieve fame and accolades. It's worse for those who don't achieve either and want to play the sport merely for the love of it.

Most often, there is a 'select one' option between playing cricket and marriage.

As a result, most cricketers have stayed away from the game after marriage. Those who have continued have either played for only a few months after tying the knot or taken up administrative roles.

It's a topic of such sensitivity that players don't want their identity to be disclosed while explaining the issue. But as a senior cricketer says, it's a matter of great concern.

'Most players start feeling this pressure from the age of 23, depending on their family's support. As a woman, after a certain age all that people around you keep asking is: "Are you married or not?" That's all that matters to them. Relatives ask your parents about it and your parents put that pressure on you.

'After initial resistance, they give you time, hoping your opinion on marriage will change. When it doesn't change even after six months or a year, they start pressurising you into it. And when that pressure mounts too much, it starts affecting us. Once you get married, you have to live up to the expectations of two houses and not just one. That's when we have to give up on all our personal aspirations.

'The problem is the pressure doesn't end with marriage. A few months after you marry, the pressure mounts on you to have a kid. How do you get out of it now? If you're in your mid or late twenties, you will lose out on your prime years. If you're in your thirties and you decide to become a mother, you lose a year of your cricket and there is no coming back from there.

'When we look at Australia, there are players who have kids and they are still playing. That's not possible in Pakistan. There are girls who are 28 or 29, and they're already under pressure. If you're 28 or 29, they make you feel insecure that you won't get a "good" husband if you don't marry right away.

'There are pressures from all ends, and the support system is limited. I know I have to get married but I'm worried. After marriage, if I don't perform well in a couple of games, I don't know what will happen. Every player goes through good and bad patches. But after marriage, the perception is such that the player is not serious about her cricket. We don't get that margin for error after marriage.'

Another player quips, 'Parents of some of the players are supportive and confident that their daughter will take the right decision and won't marry unless she's happy with her partner. They let them take that decision for their happiness. But that's not a luxury everyone has.'

Slowly the glass ceiling for married cricketers is breaking. Nain Abidi, who got married in January 2017 and left cricket a year later, made a return to the competitive game after childbirth – in the USA, her adopted land. But it's Bismah Maroof who has blazed the trail for her teammates, having an uninterrupted career since marriage and even childbirth.

'Before marriage, I'd seen that all the girls who got married had to quit cricket,' Bismah said in mid-2021. 'I was worried that I too would have to leave cricket after marriage. So, I was initially reluctant about marriage.

'Thankfully, my husband and in-laws were supportive of my decision. I'm married within my family [to her cousin]. So, they had seen my struggle all these years. They comforted me and assured me that I wouldn't have to leave cricket. Marriage is a commitment and it brings a lot of responsibility. But cricket is independent of that. The demands are different. I have to be away for long periods, training and playing. Being the captain of the team, there are other things to take care of as well. To give me that much space wasn't easy. But without the support of my family, I wouldn't have been able to concentrate on my cricket.

'The perception I had earlier that women can't continue playing after marriage changed for me as well. It's important for us to understand each other's desires. You can't overlook family responsibilities, either. You won't be at peace otherwise.'

In her concluding line, though, lies both her bliss and the agony experienced by many others. 'I've been lucky. I've had that support. I'm under no pressure to leave cricket.'

The support system which Bismah has been fortunate to have has not been everyone's luxury. While the PCB had come a long way by 2021, offering a strong maternity policy to reintegrate players into the game after motherhood, in 2014 the administrators were at their wits' end handling the sport, especially the concerns at the grass roots.

Most of Pakistan's constraints in advancing women's cricket stemmed from societal pressures and the fear of families regarding the safety of their daughters. The PCB, as the governing body of the sport, didn't help significantly relax those apprehensions. The most questionable aspect of its handling took place a year before the Asian Games, while dealing with claims of sexual harassment against Multan Cricket Club's chair Maulvi Muhammad Sultan Alam Ansari.

On 7 June 2013, five Multan cricketers – Seema Javed, Hina Ghafoor, Kiran Irshad, Saba Ghafoor and Haleema Rafiq – made allegations against Alam Ansari, a man of religious influence who served as a judge and was later an elected member of the Provincial Assembly of Punjab.

Accusations of unfair treatment were also levelled at Express News's TV show *Takrar* regarding the PCB's regional woman representative Shami Soltan and other members of Multan CC management – Agha Ehtisham and Javed Ahmed.

The PCB set up a two-member committee, which included national head coach Mohtashim Rashid and team manager Ayesha Ashar, to resolve the situation. Eminent advocate Shahbaz Ali Rizvi was appointed to offer legal assistance.

But on 11 July, the day of the inquiry, the allegations shifted with the defendants becoming the complainants. The women who had accused Alam Ansari and the others in Multan CC management were character-assassinated for consuming alcohol and indulging in 'objectionable acts'. It was further stated that the cricketers were trying to take revenge for being punished for their 'acts'. On the other hand, the women who had turned up for the inquiry didn't make any allegations of sexual harassment to the committee.

The eventual report filed after hearing from all the members involved was in some ways trivialising, starting with Point 1 which concluded: 'The general attitude and demeanour of the Players during the TV programme and the interviews raises questions about their own mental calibre.'

If the seriousness of the inquiry, or the lack of it, has to be understood in greater depth, the answer lies in Point 4. By then, the original accusation had already been painted as a farce, and the discussion had moved to the snooker table and plant nurseries of Multan CC.

It read: 'In the TV programme it was alleged and Multan CC management admitted that they have a snooker area, restaurant and other commercial activities going on within Multan CC premises. While it is logical for a club to have on its premises a canteen, gym or to allow some commercial activity due to which the club earns income, it does not appear to be consistent with the objects of the club to have a snooker playing area which is used by the general public, or that the restaurant/canteen is used by the general public. We are also unable to understand the establishment of a plants nursery in the club.'

The more critical aspects of the inquiry weren't absent though. In the last point of the report, the committee noted – with proof – that the players were threatened to not appear at the inquiry. In the point just before that, it also mentioned that Multan CC had no record to present regarding the allegations of banning the players for their conduct.

Yet, in the absence of proof of sexual harassment, the report suggested that the players 'should be severely reprimanded for their acts and misplaced and motivated interaction with the media'. The PCB eventually slapped them with a fine and a nine-month ban from all cricket for 'breach of discipline and for bringing women's cricket into disrepute'.

It was only three years since the Prevention of Sexual Harassment for Women at Workplace Act had been passed in Pakistan. It was still a time when allegations were met with scepticism, and across the corporate sector it was believed that more efforts were being made to silence allegations than to investigate them. The PCB, a male-dominated organisation, also carried its set of biases rather blatantly in judging a case of harassment through the lens of personal lifestyle choices.

It was believed that the committee was set up in good faith, but without the effort of finding the right personnel who could understand the complexity of the case. In a way, it was an opportunity lost by the PCB to show itself as an organisation that could protect its women cricketers from harassment.

The misery didn't end there, though, for the cricketers. Alam Ansari filed a defamation suit of PKR 200 million against the five women who had accused him and the two journalists who reported the story.

On 13 July 2014, Haleema's brother came across a report in the newspaper which stated that all five cricketers accused of defamation had to appear for a court hearing, as per the order of the judge. On hearing the news, Haleema went to the bathroom and ingested a bottle of drain cleaner. She was taken to hospital soon after, but passed away that night.

Her death wasn't reported as a suicide, which is a punishable offence in Pakistan. Even her own family members chose to blame the hospital for failing to pump the acid out of her stomach.

The handling of the sexual harassment case by the PCB didn't help make women or their parents feel any more secure – indeed, apprehensions about the safety of female players only grew. For as long as cricket has been played in Pakistan, men who are not family members of the players, special invitees or part of the coaching and organising set-up have not been allowed entry to women's games. However, such restrictions have not been possible in the matches played abroad or telecast live.

For many family members, the knowledge that the women of their house are being watched by strange men is discomfiting. Yet, over the years, many parents have entrusted their daughters to the likes of Shaiza Khan and Sana Mir against the promise that their daughters would be safe.

But the road to *izzat* is long and hard. It has required a lot of assurance and reassurance.

AND THEY ALL FALL DOWN

UNDER THE TRIO of Sana Mir, Mohtashim Rashid and Bushra Aitzaz, it seemed as if Pakistan were heading towards a golden age of cricket. But, aware as they were that relationships weren't going to be as smooth moving forward, even they couldn't predict the turmoil that would follow.

In the same way that the country had a hung parliament following the 2013 general election, before the PML(N) managed to form a majority, the PCB was also without a head following Zaka Ashraf's suspension as chair by the Islamabad High Court.

Technically, it was the first time that a democratically elected government had completed its five-year tenure in office, signalling stability, but the PCB was in complete chaos following the attacks on the Sri Lankan team and the match-fixing scandal. A change in government only added to that unrest.

Ashraf, who had studied with President Asif Ali Zardari in Cadet College Petaro in the southern province of Sindh, had no links to cricket apart from having served as chair of ZTBL, a prominent sponsor in both men's and women's domestic cricket. He was removed from his post on the board for lack of transparency in the election process. Sharif, leader of the right-wing conservative party PML(N), became prime minister of the country after forming a coalition government, and with it became the PCB's patron-in-chief.

Bizarrely, Najam Sethi – a left-leaning journalist and Hilal-i-Imtiaz, the second-highest civilian honour in Pakistan, who shared a bitter history with Sharif – was elected chair of the board. Events had come a long way since May 1999 when Sethi was picked up by Punjab police for giving an interview to the BBC, which was planning to report on corruption in the Sharif government. He was detained incommunicado in Lahore for nearly a month before international pressure mounted on Sharif demanding his release. His freedom was eventually granted following an order by the Supreme Court, which stated that there was no evidence for the charges laid against him.

By early 2013, however, the relationship had taken a different turn. As a political analyst, Sethi was effusive in his praise for Sharif's work behind PML(N)'s growing popularity. When there was a hung parliament, with no party winning the majority, Sethi's name was suggested by the Pakistan Peoples Party as the caretaker chief minister of Punjab, and this was agreed upon by PML(N).

Once Sharif became prime minister in June, Sethi left his position in the Punjab government and took over running the affairs of the PCB. But this stint wasn't to last too long. In January 2014, Zaka Ashraf was again reinstated as chair by the Islamabad High Court, with a two-judge bench accepting the intra-court appeal against the previous decision.

Zaka's return as chair was also a short one. In less than a month, using his powers as the patron-in-chief of the board, Sharif dissolved the PCB's governing body, sacked Zaka and formed an eight-member management committee, with Sethi again appointed chair.

The musical chairs at the top continued as Sethi made way for Shahryar Khan in August 2014. For as long as the tumult lasted, the administration of the women's wing remained unaffected. Sana, supported by Bushra Aitzaz, was able to retain control of running the team and had the luxury of setting plans for long-term goals. Once Sharif became prime minister, it was obvious that Bushra's second tenure wouldn't get an extension, and that she would have to make way at some point – if not immediately.

With gifts and praises, the PCB bade goodbye to her services in a fairly harmonious farewell on 21 November. Shamsa Hashmi, who had served as secretary of the women's wing in Shahryar's previous tenure, was brought back to the fold – this time as general manager.

As with all leadership changes, it was bound to have a trickle-down effect on the team – in much the same way that Shirin Javed's appointment in October 2008 had led to the change in captaincy. The difference when Shamsa came on board was that Sana had established her mark by then – as an accepted leader within the side and the most popular face outside of it. Under her captaincy, the team had improved, and several players had become world-class.

One among them was Javeria Khan.

In professional sports, teams that tend to lose more often than win, blame games and finger-pointing can be common. Even though Pakistan largely escaped such behaviour with a singular leader in Sana Mir, such teams require individuals to keep their spirits and motivations high. Add a prankster and a musician to the mix, and it transforms the vibe completely. With a guitar for company, Javeria – popularly called 'Jerry' in the group – was both.

Along with Batool Fatima and Nain Abidi, Javeria led the unofficial team choir, humming popular Indian and Pakistani songs if not the usual celebratory tunes of 'Dil Dil Pakistan'. She hailed from the Pathan clan of a region in the interior of the country which doesn't have an official name. Locals call it 'Kaala Dhaka'. Her parents had moved to Karachi, where she was born. Her sense of humour – dry, at times sarcastic, and full of mostly clever retorts – was indicative of her roots, as was Nida Dar's – the other 'funny woman' in the pack, who would leave everyone in stitches with her loud Punjabi one-liners.

As much as she liked cricket, it was a profession Javeria had got into by chance, in an attempt to avoid her economics classes. Attending the PCB trials organised in her college in 2008 was a way of escaping a lecture she had no interest in sitting through.

But her elevation was way too quick. She was picked for the national domestic championship that year, where she gave impressive performances with the ball and made some handy contributions with the bat. It opened the door to the national camp and then to the national team for the 2008 Asia Cup. However, much like the cricketer she most wanted to emulate – Muttiah Muralitharan – in 2010, she was called for chucking while bowling off spin. Despite multiple attempts, she couldn't clear her action, and with her primary skill rendered illegal, many were apprehensive about picking her in the team. 'It felt like my world had come to an end,' Javeria recalls.

But Sana Mir, who had captained Javeria in domestic matches, was aware that there was a lot more value to unlock beyond her bowling skills. Within two years, it was also obvious that Javeria was among the sharpest cricketing minds available at a time when most female cricketers had come through to the national team without ample exposure and guidance. She was also self-driven, fit and agile on the field. Unlike Sana, Nida Dar and Almas Akram, who had switched from bowling pace to spin, an effort was made to hone Javeria's limited batting abilities.

'I had seen her play the cut and pull very well in domestic cricket,' Sana notes. 'I saw that she could play those shots well.

She didn't play the drive often, but I thought with a bit of hard work we could have a very good cricketer on our hands. Also, she was quick between the wickets and fielded well.'

The attempt to accommodate Javeria as an opener in the 2010 ICC Women's Cricket Challenge in South Africa didn't leave the former off-spinner too pleased. 'It was Sana Mir's idea that I should open the batting,' Javeria says, pointing the finger of blame at her captain. 'It came just as an idea in a conversation, and I was not at all confident about it. I feared that if I failed as an opener, my career could come to an end.'

'She was reluctant to give up on her bowling and become a batter,' recalls Sana. 'She didn't talk to me for the entire tour.'

In her first match as an opener, though, Javeria scored a useful 37-ball 25 – finishing as the highest run-getter – and helped Pakistan beat Ireland. And in the Asian Games that followed, she had a prolific spell along with Nida Dar.

'Even after scoring 25, she was angry with us,' Sana recalls. 'But we left her with no option. Anyway, back then, our batters were scoring only 20–30 runs on average. And I could see that we could develop a cricketer to play according to the situation.

'Earlier, all our batters were one-dimensional. Reading the situation wasn't their forte. Those who were brought up playing on big lawns would just swing their bat hard. Those coming from smaller houses would only block. I knew we could develop her. But she wanted to clear her bowling action. We worked on that for some time, but it didn't happen. It was taking too much time, so we told her to concentrate on her batting.'

With the presence of several off-spinners in the team, it wasn't much of a sacrifice for them, but despite her success with the bat, Javeria continued to feel the urge to bowl. 'When I'm not scoring runs, I feel bad that I gave up on my bowling. But on days when I score runs, I feel, "Oh, it is good that I started concentrating on my batting."'

In 2015, she tried to clear her action again, this time, successfully. However, by then she had lost touch with the art and had carved a space for herself as arguably the best batter in the team.

She had scored two 50s in Australia, which in itself was a mark of her class, but her glory moment came in the 2015 series against Sri Lanka – when she registered her maiden international century.

Since the 2009 attack on the Sri Lankan team, the United Arab Emirates (UAE) had become the home base for Pakistan's men's team. The women's side, barring the triangular in Qatar, hadn't hosted an international game. The matches in the UAE, despite being hosted by the PCB, felt as far away from home as any other tour for the players.

Nonetheless, it was here, in 2015, that they truly stamped their authority over Sri Lanka. Having won the two Asian Games gold medals without facing them, Pakistan hadn't properly established themselves as the second-best Asian side.

In the first of the three-match ODIs, Marina Iqbal's 69 helped Pakistan cruise to a fairly effortless five-wicket win in a 179-run chase. The second match, though, was closely fought. After being limited to 138 for 9, Bismah Maroof and Sadia Yousuf picked up three wickets apiece to help Pakistan to a narrow 12-run win. The series victory was sealed, but the challenge levelled up when the side attempted a clean sweep.

Riding on the advantage of a fresh, flat pitch, Sri Lanka's in-form opener Chamari Athapaththu scored a brisk 99 before playing an uppish drive off Asmavia Iqbal to the cover fielder. She may have missed out on her third ODI century by a run, but her efforts had helped the side to 242 for 5, a score Pakistan had never before chased.

Even though Sri Lanka's spinners were unlikely to prove as effective on a belter of a track, it was a stiff task. Javeria, who had failed to convert any of her six previous 50s into a three-figure total, had come into the match encouraged by her teammates to go for a big score. Self-motivated as she was, her competitiveness – which often bordered on the extreme – was also a motivator in helping her improve as a cricketer. There were few in the team who were as intensely driven.

She made a slow start to the innings, after her attempted drive off the second ball caught the outside edge and flew past the slip fielders. Despite the mountain of runs required, she went about the chase in a measured manner, frequently collecting singles and twos. In fact, for a period of ten overs – from the 12th to the 22nd – she didn't hit a single boundary, and yet kept up with the scoring rate.

Her composure took a beating once she reached the 90s. Nervousness crept in and led to a few false strokes. In the 34th over, while batting on 91, she attempted to loft over the infield but failed to connect fully. The fielder at mid-off, though, despite settling well under the ball, failed to hold on to it. Javeria took that as a gift and ensured that Sri Lanka didn't get another opportunity.

With Sana Mir taking the onus of attacking, Javeria took the less demanding route of sauntering towards her century with singles, the last of which was a soft dab towards the leg side. She went on to score 133 – the highest individual score by a Pakistani in ODIs – and helped her side register their highest run chase and also complete a 3–0 series win.

Sri Lanka provided tougher competition in the T20Is. After losing the first match by eight wickets, Pakistan returned to square the series in the second match, courtesy of Sana Mir's all-round exploits. The captain scored an unbeaten 48 before returning four wickets to bundle out the opposition for 69 runs. Nonetheless, the visitors secured a series victory by winning the decider.

Despite not ending on a high, Pakistan's march ahead continued with a T20I series win against South Africa two months later.

The Mignon du Preez-led side's tour to the UAE had started poorly, with a loss in the first one-dayer. In what was Bismah's first piece of misfortune with centuries, she was run out on 99, but helped her team to a healthy 216. Some tight spin bowling by Anam Amin and Sana Mir restricted the visitors to 159.

South Africa lost the opener but returned to their dominant selves for the remaining matches of the series, with a narrow three-wicket win in the second one-dayer and an easy five-wicket victory in the third.

In the T20Is, it took them more time to overcome their opponents. By the third match, when they eventually overhauled Pakistan's total off the last ball, they had lost the series.

The performances in the twin series in the UAE had put Pakistan on a par with Sri Lanka and South Africa, a clear improvement in their global standing as a cricket team. To add to their gains was the effort of the board in bringing back international cricket to the country for the first time since the 2009 terrorist attacks.

Inviting a women's team to tour Pakistan seemed like the easiest way to achieve this as there would be less of a security threat. Unlike the red carpet that would be rolled out for the Zimbabwean men's team, who were lured into touring the country in November with offers of more than US$10,000 for each player and high-level security in Lahore, with security guarding a perimeter of more than a kilometre around the Gaddafi Stadium, a lighter security presence was in place for the Bangladesh women's team.

Instead of the more high-profile National Stadium, all the matches in the Bangladesh series were played at the Southend Club Stadium in Karachi, which also had facilities to accommodate the players,

The Bangladesh Cricket Board had offered the players the right to refuse to tour, but since the team hadn't played a representative match since the epic 2014 Asian Games final, it was an opportunity the players were looking forward to. For most of their Pakistani counterparts, it was an even bigger occasion – the first chance to play an international match in front of their home crowd. Having mostly played at venues with negligible crowds or ones that supported their opponents, to be cheered on by the fans in the stadium would be an unusual feeling, unlike anything they had experienced before.

There were restrictions on who could attend the matches though. While women were allowed, the only adult men who could enter the stadium were family members of those who were playing or those who were a part of the organising team. Javeria, who hailed from Karachi, had her own reservations, meaning that she wouldn't let her family watch the match at the stadium.

'I am extremely uncomfortable playing in front of my family. There is a lingering fear that I will disappoint them if I fail. Their presence makes me nervous. I don't want them to even see me play on TV, or while practising in the nets. I tell them to not watch me play, but they would of course know the schedule of my matches and would watch the games on TV.'

The atmosphere, despite the limited attendance and it being a low-key affair, was lively, mainly thanks to the attendance of students from several schools who had been invited to watch the matches. The cricket-loving country was so deprived of its favourite sport that women's cricket got more attention than it otherwise would have. It was an important series in terms of visibility for the women's game, irrespective of how Pakistan performed. With international cricket being a rarity in Pakistan in those days, the women's team had received barely any coverage. But now, any and every cricket match became a reason for the local media to turn up and find space in their publications to showcase the achievements of the players to a larger audience.

The on-field action, though, was low on excitement with the hosts keeping control of the proceedings almost throughout the two T20Is and two ODIs, clean-sweeping the visitors across formats.

By then, Bismah Maroof had become a regular contributor with the ball. When Javeria's action was called for chucking in 2010, coach Mansoor Rana needed to fill up the lost slot in the bowling department. He summoned Bismah as well as Nain Abidi, who hadn't bowled until that point, to roll their arms over in the nets. The coach didn't feel the latter would be an able substitute, so went with Bismah – who bowled slow and loopy leg breaks. The lack of pace was her biggest strength.

Her primary asset, however, was batting. Ever since she made her debut as a 15-year-old, Bismah had been the standout left-handed batter in the team – not the most elegant, but among the most reliable scorers. In the home series against Bangladesh, she continued her consistent run – with a quick-fire half-century in the low-scoring, first T20I, and scores of 92 and 41 in the two one-dayers. Even though all the innings came in winning causes, the 92 was especially painful.

It was her second dismissal in the 90s in a span of four innings, the count of which would rise to three a few months later. Despite being one of the best batters in the side, a three-figure total evaded her.

'I didn't feel as bad missing out on a century against South Africa,' Bismah observes. 'Before that series, I hadn't scored a lot of runs. So, I was under a bit of pressure. I was slightly scared going into that match. I was too focused on my own game and wasn't looking at the scoreboard. It was only when Asmavia walked out to bat that she made me realise that I was closing in on a century.

'I didn't want to think about it because I knew I would get distracted and put myself under too much pressure. So, I tried to ignore that. In ignoring that, we reached the last over of the innings. Off the last ball, I needed two more runs. That was my only chance to score a century. I attempted to run two and got run out in the process. Even though I missed a century, it felt like I had achieved something significant, so I was happy about my performance.'

But in the first ODI against Bangladesh, that wasn't the case. She had ample time, but with eight wickets down, she wasn't sure if her two remaining batting partners would survive till the end. So, instead of closing in on the mark cautiously, she went for big hits. In trying to swipe the ball through the vacant deep mid-wicket region, she got caught eight runs short of the mark. Ironically, her batting partner then – Rabiya Shah – remained unbeaten till the end.

'Of all my 90s, that dismissal bothers me the most. It bothers me even more when I think about it now, because I haven't been able to score an international hundred.'

Javeria and Bismah now formed the core of Pakistan's batting, alongside Nain Abidi. A host of all-rounders were also improving on their secondary skills, which was enabling Pakistan's growth as a team. The individual and collective enhancement notwithstanding, Sana was slowly losing the board's favour as leader.

Whether it was due to the ICC's introduction of the ODI Women's Championship – which ensured that the top eight teams got plenty of matches – or due to the vision of the PCB chair Shahryar Khan, which had failed to take flight in his first tenure as chair, Pakistan had hosted three bilateral series in a year for the women's team (the series against Bangladesh wasn't a part of the IWC). This was something the PCB had never done since taking control of the women's game.

But with Shamsa Hashmi's appointment as general manager of the women's wing, it was obvious that there would be a knock-on effect on the leadership of the team, especially since both the captain and the coach enjoyed the trust of Bushra Aitzaz, who had sparred for decades with Shamsa's allies.

A leadership change was imminent, but to dethrone Sana Mir from the captaincy was going to be a complicated and unpopular move. Sana's aura within the team went far beyond that of a cricket captain. As Mohtashim would put it, 'She was a mother, a sister, a mentor and a friend to the players.'

Sana's leadership was critical for Pakistan cricket, especially at the point when she was appointed. Most of the players coming through to the national team had fought their way to the top – with social and financial insecurities, despite all the support from their families. Sana's journey hadn't been as hard. She was well supported by her family, both financially and emotionally, and as a result, she was a highly self-confident individual. Thanks to her own tact but also her fame, she didn't flinch when she made demands to the authorities.

Additionally, being a guardian figure came naturally to her. Even in her early twenties, parents of players would trust that Sana would look after their daughters while they travelled the length and breadth of the country to play unrewarding domestic matches. She also doubled up as a personal tutor for the players.

It was a foresight that many hadn't paid attention to – that cricket careers hinged heavily on form and fitness, with no financial security. To pursue their passion, several cricketers with unstable financial backgrounds had given up on their education and didn't have a backup option ready. To secure their futures, through the entire stretch of her cricket career – from Bismah in 2005 to Fatima Sana in 2019, and many others in-between – Sana sat and helped her teammates prepare for their university exams.

Bismah, who had served as Sana's long-time deputy, shed light on her contribution. 'She is an extremely selfless person. Very few people had the vision to take Pakistan cricket as far as Sana took it. We didn't have any resources or facilities, but she would often go and fight with the top management on behalf of the players. It was in-built in her. And it helped women's cricket enormously.

'Whether in professional or personal lives, if any player went to her with a problem, she would go out of her way to help them and ensure they were relaxed. Back then, there was no concept of a therapist. She ensured that everyone in the team was mentally in a good frame of mind.'

For all her diplomatic skills, Sana was extremely headstrong and vocal with her opinions. Bushra was often able to calm down situations that got a little fiery, but at other times, Sana would have serious clashes with administrators. Her leadership was dynamic. For someone who had forged strong bonds throughout the team during her early days, she began to maintain a distance after taking up the captaincy. The change, according to her, was triggered when accusations of favouritism were flung at her for backing Javeria Khan as a batter in 2010.

Over the years of her captaincy, Sana became a fairly feared individual within the set-up. She was authoritative, a respected trait for a leader in Pakistan. 'One of the factors that made people fear me was the unpredictability,' she admits. 'If a player makes a mistake, I might hold them accountable three or four years later if they make the same mistake again because I expect them to know better. After a while I started getting a bit pushy with the players because I felt that it was time for us to evolve as a team.'

Yet, her ability to set things in order, especially in moments of crisis, made her a go-to person for many junior cricketers. She had established herself as an undisputed leader. Her esteem among her teammates extended far beyond the boundaries of the field. Naturally, she enjoyed their support – something Shamsa was well aware of.

She saw this support in a different light though: 'lobbying' in nature. In a way she was right; when Sana picked fights or raised issues, she always had several backers, which didn't allow the administrators to have their way easily.

'Except Mohtashim, every coach complained that Sana used to force player power,' Shamsa opines in rather harsh terms. 'Sana was running the show during Bushra's tenure. Five or six top players were in her pocket. When I took over, the entire PCB was of the view that Sana should be sacked. Everyone knew of Sana's monopolisation, but she had strong communication skills and a massive fan following.'

For Sana to be removed as captain, the pressure had to be mounted in a different way. Batool Fatima, a long-time friend, had retired in 2014, and selectors were insistent on bringing in newer players, which put additional pressure on the older ones – especially Qanita Jalil, Asmavia Iqbal and Nain Abidi. With two World Cups set to take place in 2016 and 2017, Sana wanted to persist with those whose skills and game plans had been honed over several years. She assumed younger cricketers, despite all their talent, would need time to settle in, given that they were coming into the national set-up without much quality training and game time behind them. Even as several talented youngsters were producing good performances on the domestic circuit, Pakistan cricket wasn't at a stage where players could step up and deliver straight away on the international stage.

'We were encouraging of younger talent and wanted to back them, but not in a World Cup,' Sana points out. 'Our stance was that we didn't have a structure where players could come in from the domestic circuit ready to perform in international cricket. We couldn't expose them on a global stage like the World Cup. We needed to build them up for at least two or three years before we played them at the World Cup. That was the main issue with us and the management.

'We weren't convinced when the selectors and the board suggested a new name and we were reluctant to make wholesale changes to the squad. Some people think that we got stuck there. There were a lot of good young players around, but there's a right time for everything. You just can't put players in difficult situations that they have not experienced before and expect them to instantly flourish.'

For as fit as Qanita was, her fielding standards weren't great, and her performances were dropping. Even though Sana valued her, with the promising 19-year-old Diana Baig waiting in the wings, the oldest member of the squad was the first to face the axe following the Sri Lanka series in 2015.

Qanita was soon followed out of the door by another of Sana's long-time teammates, Nain Abidi, who was dropped for the 2016 World T20 and replaced by the uncapped 19-year-old Muneeba Ali.

The third person from Sana's support system to get the boot was coach Mohtashim Rashid. Despite having aided the team's progress for half a decade, he was removed from the post after Pakistan were beaten 3–0 in both limited overs three-match series in England in July 2016. It was the second successive failure on tour for Pakistan, with the previous one a 3–1 loss in the Gros Islet ODIs and a 3–0 defeat in the St George T20Is on the tour to the West Indies soon after the home series against Bangladesh.

'We were just six months away from the one-day World Cup when he was axed,' says Sana bitterly. 'He had brought a lot of stability to the team. He was backing the players. He knew what we had in the squad – whether they would score runs or take wickets. I think we had to be patient till the World Cup at least before making so many changes. You just can't expect younger players, who had not been in a good system, to deliver immediately.'

Mohtashim, who Shamsa believed was nothing more than a 'rubber-stamp' coach dancing to Sana's orders, was shifted within the PCB set-up to look after age-group cricket, following the England tour later in the year. Shamsa didn't rate Sana too highly as a cricketer either – an average bowler at best, who stat-padded her way up, according to her.

Yet, there wasn't a way to get Sana out of her position. 'There would have been a double disaster if we had sacked the captain and coach in one go,' Shamsa confesses.

Qanita's exit paved the way for Diana's entry into the line-up, more than two years after having first been picked for the squad. Marina Iqbal was phased out too, opening the door for 23-year-old all-rounder Aliya Riaz.

In between the two spaced bilaterals, though, Pakistan had a fairly reasonable outing in the 2016 T20 World Cup, where they yet again beat India. After losing the first match of the tournament, by a narrow five-run margin against eventual champions the West Indies, Sana Mir's team upset the hosts in a rain-marred encounter.

Electing to field at the Feroz Shah Kotla Stadium, Pakistan restricted their arch-rivals to 96 on a slow track. Sidra Ameen's assured, run-a-ball 26 provided a steady start in the low run chase. Even though a few wickets fell in a short time and India strangled the run flow, Pakistan looked at ease heading towards the target. However, in the 16th over, nervousness crept in, and reckless running resulted in the dismissal of Asmavia Iqbal and Sana Mir in successive deliveries. While Asmavia was run out courtesy of a fine throw from the deep by Smriti Mandhana, Sana fell to a skilled effort from wicketkeeper Sushma Verma.

Pakistan could have caved under pressure, but rain ensured that there was no further play. Pakistan had just about crossed the victory line, two runs ahead of the DLS target. The win, beyond being significant for their own fortunes, also came on the day the Pakistan's men's side was beaten yet again in a World Cup against India. Ironically, the team was led by Shahid Afridi – the man who had recently brushed aside the idea of Pakistani women playing cricket with the words 'our women make good cooks'.

Sana Mir's side followed up that effort with a dominant nine-wicket win over Bangladesh, courtesy of Sidra Ameen's unbeaten half-century. With two successive wins, the players gave themselves a strong chance of qualifying for the next round. However, England crushed them by 68 runs in the final match of the group stages, which ended a fairly impressive campaign.

Despite the jubilation of the win over India, Sana resigned from her position as the T20I captain. 'When I became the captain, I didn't have a lot of leadership around me and I didn't want that to be the case with the next leader. I stepped down in 2016 to be there with Bismah, so that she could take over a settled team.'

The changes to a once settled team led, however, to a period of transitional pandemonium, which included numerous changes to the coaching panel during the six months leading up to the 2017 World Cup qualifiers. The first to take charge after Mohtashim's exit was Basit Ali, a former batter who had represented the Pakistan men's team 69 times in international cricket in the 1990s.

On 13 November 2016, Pakistan would have hoped that its miseries in New Zealand – this was their first bilateral series in the country since the historic tour Shaiza had led nearly two decades earlier – had come to an end. Following three thumping defeats in the ODIs, at the Bert Sutcliffe Oval, the tour caravan was set to move to Nelson.

However, at two minutes past midnight, an earthquake measuring 7.8 on the Richter scale, with its epicentre in Kaikoura, shook the country. It was soon followed by a tsunami which caused devastation along the eastern coastline.

Panic ensued everywhere, even in the Pakistan camp, which was put up at the Crown Plaza Hotel in Christchurch. While the rest of her teammates were running downstairs when the first tremors were felt, Javeria Khan, who had just come out of the bath on the seventeenth floor of the building, had other priorities. She ensured her towel was neatly hung to dry, located her phone, and went around knocking on the doors of her teammates, only to realise later that everyone had already made a quick dash to the ground floor.

'Everyone was scared, especially Anam Amin and Iram Javed. They started reciting the *kalma*, and look at my stupidity,' Javeria remembers. 'It never struck me that the building could collapse at any moment.'

Fortunately, they were all safe. In New Zealand, though, two lives were lost, and more than NZ$1.8 billion worth of damage was caused by the calamity. The players were shaken, and cricket became an afterthought amidst all the destruction.

On the field, the results for Pakistan didn't improve, and they lost the last two one-dayers easily. Javeria Khan was the standout batter, scoring two half-centuries to cap two impressive years of batting, while Bismah Maroof's fancy 90s continued as she stroked an unbeaten 91.

Despite the loss, it wasn't a series with many regrets for Pakistan. Even though points earned in the five ODIs counted towards World Cup qualification, Pakistan never had a realistic chance of winning any of the matches. However, leading up to the tournament, there had been signs of an improved cricketing side – against a team that was considerably stronger on paper and had the motivation to push harder for wins. New Zealand needed four victories to secure direct qualification to the World Cup and, led by Amy Satterthwaite's three successive centuries, the team registered a clean sweep.

In the lone T20I, the spin duo of Sana Mir and Sadia Yousuf restricted the hosts to 118 but Pakistan couldn't chase down the total. A late surge by No 10 Aliya Riaz only helped Pakistan reach 14 runs short of the score.

Those improvements in the players' performances were reflected in the results they achieved later in the month, when they sailed past all their opponents – except India – in the T20 Asia Cup, held in Bangkok. While victories against Thailand and Nepal were expected, they also thumped Sri Lanka and Bangladesh. Led by Javeria Khan's unbeaten 56, they eased past Sri Lanka with an eight-wicket win in the second match, and then bundled out Bangladesh for 44 to secure a nine-wicket victory. They ran India close in the league game but were comprehensively beaten in the final to finish as runners-up.

Despite fairly good returns, Basit Ali's tenure was short-lived. In the last week of December, during a domestic one-day tournament, played at Karachi's National Stadium, he allegedly slapped former cricketer Mahmood Hamid. In response to his action, Shahryar Khan said, 'The PCB will not tolerate physical violence. We will launch an investigation to figure out whether the incident actually happened and then take action.'

On 2 January, Basit Ali was relieved of his duties and Iqbal Imam, who was serving as the fielding coach under Basit, was made the interim coach for nine days during a training camp in Karachi.

On 11 January, the PCB appointed former Pakistan pace bowler Kabir Khan as Basit's replacement. A hard-nosed coach, his training methods were rigorous and a big change from those of Mohtashim, which the players had become accustomed to. He also brought in Shahid Anwar, a former Pakistan international cricketer, as his assistant, to replace Imam Iqbal. Kabir had not seen enough women's cricket to understand where the team was at that moment, and where the general international standards lay. His first task was to help them through the qualifiers for the World Cup, which were scheduled less than a month after his takeover.

In Colombo, Pakistan achieved the larger purpose of qualification for the World Cup, which was to be played in England later in the year, but the players' performances didn't scale up. While they beat Bangladesh, Papua New Guinea, Scotland and Ireland, they were outplayed by South Africa and India, and Sri Lanka also registered an easy win. In those defeats, there were a few positives. Nain Abidi stroked a slow 62 against South Africa, while Javeria Khan and Nahida Khan hit 50s against Sri Lanka.

India's twin wins in the Asia Cup notwithstanding, the BCCI's decision to not play bilaterals with Pakistan – courtesy of the government's anti-Pakistan stand – meant that India presented a walkover, giving Pakistan three additional wins in the IWC. In the qualifiers, where they finally had a chance to compete with India in a 50-over contest, they exposed their weak link – the batting – which was improving but was found out on the day as they folded for 67, courtesy of Indian left-arm spinner Ekta Bisht's 5-fer.

The tournament offered Kabir Khan a glimpse of what standards were expected in the women's game. On their return to Pakistan, he arranged a two-week training camp, where he pushed the players hard to hone their skills. It may not have been an army boot camp of the kind that Yasir Ali had organised in 2014, but it was sapping enough for the players who weren't used to practising over such long hours.

Bismah views his methods differently. 'I really liked his cricketing philosophy. He would make me bat from morning to afternoon and then bowl from afternoon to evening. It would tire me out, but eventually I was able to bowl ten overs in a match because he pushed us. During practice, though, often I would get so tired that the ball would land in the adjacent net while I was bowling.'

Neither his methods nor his stint lasted too long as, just over a month after that camp, Kabir was also sacked. His dual jobs – as an employee of a bank and as national team coach – was reportedly cited as the reason for the termination of his job. The next in line for the hot seat was Sabih Azhar, a former first-class medium-pacer.

By then, the trust levels between the players and the management had completely disintegrated. Sabih, in his role, couldn't improve matters. He had two and a half months to work with the team before they headed to England for the World Cup, and during that period, the team environment deteriorated and became worse than ever.

Not only were the captain and coach not on the same page with regard to team selection and combinations, but the players didn't enjoy Sabih's style of coaching. Sana eventually had her way, being able to retain the players she wanted, but it came at the cost of heavy friction.

The coach had turned rude and sarcastic towards the senior players, who then united against him. Amidst this, the juniors found themselves in an unappealing situation as they approached the World Cup. Irrespective of who was right, the power struggle eventually impacted a team that had been on the rise and at its strongest ever in the run-up to a World Cup. A 30-day camp in Abbottabad and 15 days of training in Leicester ahead of the tournament did little to help repair those bonds.

The 2017 World Cup was structured in such a way that all eight teams would get a chance to play each other once. This would give Pakistan a fair indication of where it stood among the top sides. The campaign began at Grace Road in Leicester on 25 June against South Africa – a side Pakistan had competed with fiercely over the previous few years.

Put in to bat, Nahida Khan continued her rich vein of form from the qualifiers, leading the way with a 101-ball 79. Although none of the other batters made a significant contribution, handy knocks from the rest allowed them to post a competitive 206 for

8. They were aware that they were 20-odd runs short, but it was a total they felt capable of defending.

The South African openers Lizelle Lee and Laura Wolvaardt didn't take any prisoners though. They blazed away early and put on a 113-run stand for the opening wicket before the former was trapped lbw by Sana Mir in the 26th over. That wicket derailed the innings, and in the next 20 overs South Africa lost six more for only 64 runs, turning the contest in Pakistan's favour.

It was Pakistan's game to lose. And they did. Shabnim Ismail swung her bat around in the 49th over against Kainat Imtiaz and picked up three boundaries to get her team over the line with three wickets and an over to spare.

Despite the defeat, the Pakistan players realised there were only minor areas to improve upon. Giving a tough fight to the Dane van Niekerk-led side boded well for them. However, the situation inside the dressing room wasn't helping. Even as Sana lauded the effort of her team at the post-match presentation, the coach wasn't too impressed.

In the next match, against eventual champions England, the team stood no chance. The hosts, led by centuries from Heather Knight and Natalie Sciver, crushed Pakistan's bowlers and registered a massive 377 for 7 after being put in to bat. It was a rain-delayed start, and more showers were expected, which should have eased Pakistan's worries. But the players were unable to chase the target, particularly when Katherine Brunt sent the in-form duo of Nahida Khan and Javeria Khan back to the pavilion early. Ayesha Zafar fought hard with a valiant half-century but couldn't keep up with the pace of the chase before the innings was halted due to rain in the 30th over. At 107 for 3, Pakistan were 107 short of the revised total, as per the DLS method.

The loss had significantly dented their net run rate. But it didn't really matter. All their opponents eased past them. India, the eventual runners-up, were restricted to 169 for 9 in Derby, but Pakistan were undone again by Ekta Bisht's 5-fer. Barring Nahida Khan and Sana Mir, no one could register double-digit scores as the side folded for 74.

As expected, Australia also crushed them – by 159 runs. New Zealand followed the Aussies and delivered an even bigger thrashing. The side cruised past the 145-run target in a mere 15 overs, with Sophie Devine dashing all celebrations of Sana Mir's landmark 100th ODI.

Pakistan ran the West Indies and Sri Lanka close but couldn't gain a single point. Against the West Indies, the team was taken apart for 285 runs, courtesy of hard-hitting Deandra Dottin's maiden ODI century. Nahida Khan's 40 and Javeria Khan's unbeaten 58 kept them in the chase before rain ended play after 24 overs, at a time when Pakistan were just 19 runs short of the total.

Until the loss against New Zealand, Sana had publicly backed her players – the batters who played too many cross-batted shots, the fielders who dropped catches, and the bowlers who were leaking too many runs in the crucial final overs. She was crediting the opposition and spoke of believing the team would come good. After the loss against the West Indies, she didn't have many excuses left and admitted to poor planning and the lack of responsibility taken by the batters.

The horrors of the tournament came to an end on 15 July when they lost by a narrow 15-run margin to Sri Lanka. In what proved to be the last one-dayer for Nain Abidi (a 68-ball 57) and Asmavia Iqbal (a 45-ball 38*), the duo were the leading run-getters for the team as the side was bowled out for 206.

It was a tournament Pakistan had headed to with a host of key players injured. Sidra Ameen, who was in good form, got injured before the tournament, while left-arm spinner Anam Amin was hurt in the qualifiers and leading batter Bismah Maroof in the second match of the World Cup. Javeria Khan also had to miss the game against Australia due to an injury.

These injuries were only an addition to the disarray already caused by the constant changing of the head coach. Each came in with his own set of ideas, had no experience of working with a women's team and wasn't aware of what the standard of women's cricket was like within Pakistan, let alone in other countries. By the time the World Cup started, players were left so confused that many found better value in reaching out to players from opposition teams to gain clarity than from those within their own set-up.

This disappointing campaign was expected to have repercussions on the leadership, but it turned into an ugly fiasco.

Sabih sent a 14-page report to the board explaining the reason for Pakistan's performance, with a scathing assessment of Sana Mir. The report was conveniently leaked to the media. He described her as 'self-centred, egotistical and being wrapped up in oneself'.

He further added, 'Her denial to accept self-centredness overshadows her good qualities of confidence and the esteem she is held in.

'Too many of our so-called role models don't give a hoot about anything except themselves. To them, the "team" is nowhere near as important as the "me". "What's in it for me? I want more playing time. I should be starting instead of them! My average, my stats, my salary, etc." Similarly, Sana Mir's "me-whining" affected the mindset of aspiring young players to understand how important teamwork really is to success and any team game is not about "me", it's about "we"!

'The captain was so negative in her approach that, on a number of occasions, she inculcated fear among other team members during team meetings. She used to praise opponent players a lot instead of backing her own players to do well. Eventually, the captain's negative approach did damage to the confidence of our batters and bowlers, and they couldn't play their natural game during matches.'

He further criticised Ayesha Ashar, who had served as the team's manager for nine years, for her biased attitude. He claimed that she would only pay attention to a few senior players – Sana, Javeria, Nain and Asmavia – and remained cold with the juniors.

Adding to what Shamsa believed, he wrote, 'The captain selfishly used to pick herself to bowl at such a time during the match when she knew that the batters wouldn't go after the bowling, meaning that her bowling figures wouldn't be damaged. She was jealous if other bowlers took a wicket or two and had an extended spell of bowling.'

Among his recommendations was that the head coach should have full control over selecting the team and who was selected as assistant coaches.

Three days later, Sana responded to the report with an open letter explaining her position and issues with the coach, which had started from the time she insisted on the selection of a young and in-form Diana Baig. For validation of her behaviour with younger players, she simply wrote, 'Journalists are free to ask our junior players about our attitude towards them. No one can have a 100 per cent record, but it's disheartening to see a coach maligning the senior players who have given confidence and guidance to the youngsters for so long.'

She concluded the report stating: 'I do not intend to continue in the future with the current set-up of the Women's Wing in any capacity.'

It was an emphatic statement. Not only was she putting her career on the line in this battle with the administration, but she was also testing how powerful and popular she was. 'Leading up to a World Cup, you can't change so many coaches, and get in those who had no idea about women's cricket,' Sana explains.

'When you do that, you can't expect good results on the field. It doesn't work like that. You either get serious about women's cricket like you are about men's cricket, or you can't do it. We'd worked very hard leading up to the World Cup, but the eventual results were heart-breaking.'

The outgoing PCB chair Shahryar Khan didn't want to meddle further with women's cricket, and left it for the incoming Najam Sethi, who was elected unanimously, to deal with the issue. Early in his tenure, Sethi's focus was elsewhere, however, with the ICC set to send its representative men's team to Pakistan. Once the high-profile, highly guarded and big-moneyed three-match T20I series – titled the Independence Cup – was over, he could take stock of the situation in women's cricket. Much as Shahryar had done earlier, he didn't waste time trying to find the culprit; instead, he just cleared the decks.

Shamsa Hashmi was removed from her position as general manager of the women's wing; Ayesha Ashar's nine-year stint as team manager was brought to an end; Sabih Azhar's contract wasn't renewed; and Sana Mir was no longer captain (it remains contentious whether she resigned or was sacked).

In her parting shot, Shamsa remarked, 'I do respect Sana as a player and, since she is captain, I wanted to give her a graceful exit. But as far as her manipulation and hegemony is concerned, I told her we should abide only by merit.'

I'LL GIVE IT A DAMN GOOD GO
AND NEVER GIVE UP

THE TUMULT WHICH followed Pakistan's performance in the 2017 World Cup led to such disarray in the team that it actually allowed them to start afresh. To lead this new dawn of Pakistan cricket, Bismah Maroof was elevated to the post of ODI captain as well, just a few months after Sana had made way for her in T20s.

Even though she was only 26, Bismah had been around the set-up for more than a decade. As the youngest player in the first Pakistan team to enjoy sustained success, having been drafted into the national team in 2006 as a 15-year-old, she had seen the transformation of Pakistan cricket while undergoing a transformation herself – both for the better. In fact, her personal journey and evolution as a player vividly mirrors the evolution of the Pakistan team.

Growing up as the youngest of an 18-member Kashmiri family, Bismah wasn't alien to being treated as the 'little kid' of the group. Naturally quiet and shy, she had been something of a recluse during her early days in the national set-up.

However, unlike most of her other teammates, she had a family which pushed her towards playing the sport they all loved. Playing cricket at home was always a family affair. Her brother had hoped for a boy when Bismah was born, but only so that he could have someone to play cricket with. His disappointment was only brief, though, for almost as soon as she could walk, Bismah wanted to emulate everything he did, and playing cricket became their primary recreation.

While her father and paternal uncle had played club cricket, it was supposed to be only a bit of fun for her, to be played at home. However, in 2005, one of her relatives came across an announcement of a cricket trial held by the PCB for women and urged her family to put Bismah to the test. Nobody had a clue what women's cricket was like, but they would do soon enough.

Playing against a leather ball for the first time, it was a tough initiation for the left-handed batter. But as a 13-year-old, her skills impressed selector Imtiaz Ahmed, who suggested she play more hard-ball cricket to hone her skills. Her father, acting on Imtiaz's advice, enrolled her in a cricket academy in Model Town.

A clean and hard hitter, Bismah was a standout find and she was swiftly promoted to Lahore's Under-21 side, from which seven players made it to the senior national team's camp that year. Having impressed there, she got her maiden call-up to the national team for the 2006 series against Hong Kong.

'Initially, I resisted the opportunity to play,' Bismah admits. 'I was the youngest at home and pampered by everyone in the family. It was difficult for me to stay away from them . . . I would cry, thinking, "Where have I been sent?" It used to feel lonely.'

Being the youngest in the squad meant that she was unburdened by expectation and was able to play the game with complete freedom. And with that approach, it didn't take long for her to become one of the best batters in the team. A self-motivated individual, she threw herself into fitness training in 2009 to further improve her game.

The lure for most girls to take a stand against social rigidity by playing cricket had largely stemmed from the aspiration to either swing the bat or roll their arms over – following in the footsteps of their favourite male players. Fielding was an afterthought, an activity they would much rather avoid. As a result, the drive to work on that aspect of their game was also limited.

At a time when diet plans didn't exist and the need to be ultra-fit hadn't hit Pakistan cricket, Bismah had understood the difference such things could make to her game. She was only 18 when she observed how easily some of the top teams were outrunning Pakistan – in both speed and stamina. In the 2009 T20 World Cup, she noticed that their opponents were able to press for an extra run or cut down runs while fielding, which she – like most of her teammates – wasn't equipped to do.

As a result, she became one of the pioneers of gym training in the squad. Working on fitness – which remained an otherwise boring activity for most of her teammates – became a part of her daily routine. Even when she was not with the team, she would train with the boys in her academy after morning prayers, followed by gym sessions in the afternoons. Improved fitness levels and a considerable loss of weight showed results in her stamina and speed. Once she began to enjoy the perks of putting in the hard yards, there was no looking back.

Even though Bismah was softly spoken, her maturity and hard work weren't difficult to spot. In 2014, Sana Mir believed that the 23-year-old Bismah could be honed to take up the leadership role after her and suggested she become her deputy.

'Honestly, I didn't think that I would play for as long as I did,' Sana admits. 'We were initially grooming Nain to take over, but after a point we wanted someone younger. The question was – who will be the one person who will be in every captain's team for the next five years? The answer was Bismah. She was guaranteed a spot; there was no match for her. She was the only leftie in the side, her fitness was outstanding, and, as a cricketer, every captain would want her. Her other asset was that she wasn't greedy. She didn't see others as competition. She was ambitious, but in a positive way.

'There were other players who were intelligent and maybe had better cricketing sense, but for me, it was about finding the person who would give others the confidence and see them grow. I saw all of that in Bismah.'

But Bismah, in her own mind, wasn't ready. Not only was she very young, but she was also unlike Sana in every way: too shy and calm, not fitting the traditional Pakistani idea of a leader. Several people questioned whether she was 'captaincy material', but over the years, in her own unique way, she developed her leadership skills.

For Sana, the reason to consider Bismah as an ideal successor came as much from her own experiences during her stint as captain. 'For me, leadership is about the quality of human being that you are. It's not about being charismatic or having an extrovert personality. For women's cricket in Pakistan, we've had many obstacles, many people pulling us down – knowingly or unknowingly. There was a lack of finances, infrastructure, willingness and belief. We needed a leader who was nurturing and secure enough to give everyone in the team the same level of confidence.

'Some of the captains that I've seen very closely had greed for themselves, wanting the spotlight on themselves. In the process, if the leader is like that, the team becomes like that – selfish.'

By 2017, with several players having retired, Bismah became one of the most senior cricketers in the team. She wasn't the 'baby' any more, as she believed she was. As many of her fellow players would describe her, she had become the 'mother of the team'. A patient listener, Bismah was viewed as an assured and selfless figure. She might not be authoritative, but she had gained the trust of the players even before becoming captain.

As Diana Baig, the pace bowler in the team explained, 'Sana Mir gave a lot of confidence during her captaincy. She made us feel comfortable and confident. Bismah, on the other hand, gave authority to the players and empowered us to make our own decisions.'

Bismah's first task, though, was to bring Sana back into the team.

In September 2017, Sana had sent a detailed report to the PCB stating several changes that she felt needed to be addressed immediately following the World Cup debacle. She insisted that she wouldn't return to cricket unless these proposed changes were made. Among these was the demand to hire a foreign coach, who would come in without any biases to work with the team.

The PCB agreed to this and hired the services of New Zealander Mark Coles. The board sacked Shamsa Hashmi and accepted several recommendations that Sana had made. However, not all changes were agreed upon.

As a protest, Sana refused to attend a training camp held ahead of the new IWC cycle. The board urged Sana to continue in her role as a leader. So did the newly appointed captain and coach. But it was eventually at the insistence of her spiritual guru, Shahbano Aliani, that she agreed to return.

Aliani reasoned that since seven of her ten recommendations were agreed upon, she shouldn't continue to fight. 'It was very difficult, I had burnt all bridges,' Sana confessed. 'I was still extremely angry and bitter at that point and didn't want to go.

'But some part of me also wanted to go back and show the world that we're a better team than we had shown at the World Cup. Also, I wanted to be there for the next captain. That sense of responsibility was constantly on my mind.'

The ultimate responsibility to take the team forward, and also integrate a disgruntled senior player back into the set-up, lay with Bismah, who had been backed, tutored and trained by Sana in multiple aspects of life and cricket. And in doing so, she also had to ensure that she had control of the team.

'Our World Cup campaign was a tough one, and there were a lot of controversies that dogged the team,' recalls Bismah. 'I wondered how I would navigate through it all. It was a challenge, but I'd been groomed for the leadership role for several years as a vice-captain. It would've been weird if I'd run away at the last moment when the team required me to take up the captaincy.'

Mark Coles had come in with his own plans and he knew he had a fresh slate to work with. 'I felt a bit sorry for them, to be honest, after the World Cup, watching them get beaten by seven teams – and convincingly. They had a bit of a challenge, but they were a mess. Sana was thinking about leaving the game. There were numerous coaches who had come and gone. We needed to put a line in the sand and start afresh.

'We didn't know whether Sana was going to play, and she expressed that she didn't want to. I remember having that first meeting with her, just outlining what I wanted to achieve in two years and where I thought she could be individually and, as a leader, how she could help the team.

'Both Bismah and I spoke to Sana. We still wanted her to play a leadership role. And that was on the field as well. She is the ultimate professional. It helped that Bismah and Sana shared a good relationship.'

To add to that challenge, Najam Sethi had a diktat for the coach too. 'He called me to a meeting and said, "Look, Mark, I don't mind losing by three or four wickets, or 20 or 15 runs, but we can't lose by nine wickets and 150 runs." I told him, "Listen, sir, I'm a cricket coach, not a magician. But I'll give it a damn good go and never give up."'

One of the lures for Mark to take up the job, apart from the obvious appeal of coaching a national team, was that his personal life had hit rock bottom. He was a recovering alcoholic and had at one stage contemplated suicide. His career as a cricketer had never taken off and he was training kids in an educational institute in New Zealand when he saw Pakistan being battered by New Zealand in a World Cup match. His ambition sat well with Sana's suggestions. For as uncertain as his wife was about him travelling to Pakistan, Mark had other ideas.

It didn't take long for him to realise that, much like his aeroplane ride from Auckland to Lahore, Pakistan was culturally a long way away from his home country. 'I remember lying on the hotel bed when I first arrived, thinking, "You got yourself into this. This is what you wanted, remember? You can't go home. You're stuck here now, so, you're just going to have to pull up your socks and get on with it, because there's no way out."

'I remember my first meeting with the team. There were 30 Pakistani girls standing in front of me. Some didn't speak English. Many were looking at me, like, "Yeah, I have no idea what this white bloke is saying." My glasses kept fogging up and I couldn't stop sweating.

'I said, "Look, I don't really know what has gone on here in the past. But I've watched you play against New Zealand, and we're playing them again in a month's time. We need to get ready. All I ask is that you do your very best. That way, no matter if we win, lose or draw, we've still won."'

In his maiden series, played in the UAE, Mark discerned that the norms were different. Once, while having a chat with Shahid Anwar, the batting coach, the loudspeakers came on and he turned to see that all the girls were sitting down.

Amused, he enquired, 'Girls! Why are we sitting down? We don't have time to sit down.'

Shahid promptly explained, 'It's prayer time, Mark.'

'Oh, that's fine. Girls, carry on then!'

Prayers were an important part of the day, the routine led by Bismah. 'I knew from then on that whenever the speakers came on, everybody would be sitting, and I would be sitting with them,' said Mark. 'I felt that was really important, just like learning Urdu was. It was important for me to understand their culture.'

In trying to fit in, he once even attempted to fast with the players during Ramadan in 2019 in South Africa. To begin with, the idea of fasting throughout the month of May wasn't the greatest for someone who wasn't used to it. That he didn't know of the concept of sehri (morning meal during Ramadan), only made it worse. He went without food and water for almost 20 hours and was left in awe of the players who were fasting while playing cricket for eight or so hours under the hot sun. When the players found out that he was fasting with them, they enquired, 'But we didn't see you during breakfast.'

Mark, a little confused, asked, 'Was I supposed to eat in the morning?'

The players were in stitches, but they had already become used to seeing him stuck at the cultural crossroads. Once, at a training camp, Javeria offered him a gulab jamun as a post-meal dessert. Out of courtesy, he admitted to having liked it. So, she offered him a couple more. Eventually, he ended up eating seven.

'I couldn't fall asleep until four in the morning and I had no clue what the reason was. The next day when I checked for the ingredients, I was told that it was made up of 90 per cent sugar.'

Mark's efforts to fit in were hugely appreciated by the players. It didn't always go down well, however. Sidra Nawaz once suggested that he should try a mutton delicacy. 'She had mentioned that it was just mildly spicy. Blimey, it wasn't mild! I was sweating.'

Irrespective of all the food disasters Mark experienced, the team environment had changed for the better, starting with his first series. Under the combined leadership of Mark and Bismah, Pakistan headed into one of their most productive years in international cricket.

The options were limited – vanilla, strawberry and chocolate.

Mark was unsure what more he could do to help a team down on morale than take them for an ice cream treat. Even if that didn't cheer them up, he was at least happy to take care of his own sweet cravings.

Pakistan had lost the first two ODIs of the three-match series in Sharjah. The result was expected, even though they pushed New Zealand hard in the first encounter. Led by half-centuries from Javeria Khan and Nahida Khan, followed by Bismah's 41, Pakistan started out well in the 241-run chase. But the middle and lower orders faltered, and they eventually fell eight runs short of New Zealand's total. In the second game, Suzie Bates's team cruised past them in an undemanding seven-wicket win.

'We should've won the first game, but the girls had got so used to losing that they'd forgotten how to win,' was Mark's early assessment. 'The second game we lost pretty badly, and I thought to myself, "Goodness, this is going to be a very short term for me."'

The players were not bred in a culture where they were rewarded for losing, let alone indulging in guilty pleasures. But after losing two games, Coles dropped a message on the team's WhatsApp group asking the team to turn up for ice cream.

The confused players asked, 'Why are we doing this?'

His response was rather obvious: 'You like ice cream, don't you?'

'Yes, but we lost.'

'We are losing, but we might as well do something that we enjoy.'

'Are we having a meeting after this?'

'No, see you tomorrow.'

'What should we do?'

'I don't know. Go shopping or something. I don't care, it's up to you. I'm going back to bed.'

The ice cream treat was a sign of how the team culture was to develop over the coming months. It is unlikely to have brought about an instant transformation, but the team went on to beat New Zealand the next day – for the first time ever.

Sana Mir claimed four wickets as the visitors were bowled out for 155. Led by a steady top-order performance, Pakistan overhauled the total with five wickets in hand. Even though they were smoothly rolled over in the five T20Is, it didn't matter. They were heading into a happy space.

'After the World Cup, we were all down,' Bismah reveals. 'We all knew where we had faltered. We knew that we were better than we had shown. That had hurt us deeply. We came together as a group and had honest conversations. There was no denial or embarrassment.

'Whatever had to be said, had to be out in the open – it didn't matter if it hurt someone or not, we needed to be honest. Some girls liked it, some didn't. But as a team, we had to follow some principles. We needed to push towards that.

'When Mark came in, he started to own women's cricket. As a result, his comfort level with the girls was quite high. That allowed us to have honest conversations. With the Pakistani coaches previously, we had held back from being fully honest – not wanting to hurt somebody, not wanting to be misunderstood. With Mark, there was a professional attitude. He created a comfortable and safe space.'

What Mark had to his advantage, that a coach like Mohtashim didn't, was that he was free from any baggage from the past or accusations of bias. He was able to take decisions without having his motives questioned. At least initially in his tenure, he would be patiently listened to.

Beyond his understanding of the women's game, Sana noted Mark's ability to empathise with the players despite not fully understanding the culture. 'He was very compassionate. He would pick up on things very easily if something made us uncomfortable. He would respect our prayer timings and arrange our training sessions accordingly. He knew what was important to the players and was mindful and respectful of our cultural needs.'

Mark also realised that he would have to go well beyond the cricket field to be accepted into the system, which wasn't accustomed to foreign coaches, especially those who didn't fully understand the subcontinent culture. Ahead of their next international assignment, an informal meeting over sandwiches, cakes and tea was organised with the parents of the players who were based out of Lahore.

'I was very conscious that I was a Western man in their world,' Mark admits. 'I think it was important for their mums, dads and brothers to know who I was. I thought it was really important that parents were secure in the knowledge that their daughters were going away with this chap for 20 days overseas and they could trust him.'

The impact of the cultural shift in the team soon started to show.

In their next series, in March 2018, they whitewashed Sri Lanka in the three-match ODI series and won the T20Is 2–1. The series, played in Dambulla, was highlighted by Javeria's second ODI ton.

But only a day before the game, she seemed ruffled and unable to middle the ball in practice. Despite several attempts to get it right, it didn't fall into place, and she was left hugely frustrated.

Mark was worried. 'Jerry, you're playing tomorrow. It seems like you have the world on your shoulders. You need to relax and watch the seam. Just try watching the seam as closely as you can.'

In the first match of the series, she continued her purple patch, and even though she struggled for most parts of her innings on a tricky surface, her unbeaten 113 helped Pakistan post 250. Bismah Maroof's triple strike with the ball broke the back of Sri Lanka's middle order as they were halted at 181.

In the next ODI, the captain missed out on another century, but Pakistan repeated the scoreline – 250 for 6. Bismah's dash to the elusive three-figure mark was halted on 89 when her attempted hit over the infield off Sripali Weerakkody was caught by Chamari Athapaththu at mid-wicket. In the friendly battle between good mates Javeria and Bismah, the former was chipping ahead and Javeria's constant banter about her numbers eventually began to get to Bismah.

'When Javeria scored a century in the first game, I felt it was high time to do something about it. There should be at least one century in me. So, I went into the next game determined that I needed to score big. Once I crossed 45, I started thinking about the hundred. But when I got out, it was the same feeling all over again.

'I've been chasing that landmark for so long, and it's kept getting away from me. I start getting excited whenever I reach close to a century. My mind shifts focus from the match to my mark, and my teammates keep reminding me of it. Javeria has kept a one-way competition on. She knows all the stats, gives me all the calculations of where we stand. I can't wrap my head around all this. I'm just like, "Javeria, for God's sake, just shut it."'

And it wasn't just Javeria. Even long-time friend and men's international cricketer Abid Ali, with whom she had started out playing cricket in the academy, reminded her of it. While Bismah made her debut in 2006, Abid had to wait until 2019 to join her. But he made up for lost time with a century on debut in both ODIs and Tests – becoming the first player in the history of the game to do so – while Bismah's chase of that elusive century continued.

Nevertheless, Bismah's efforts, backed up by Sana Mir's four wickets, helped Pakistan secure its second win in the series, and with it, to take an unassailable 2–0 lead. A big factor in Pakistan's success had been control of Chamari Athapaththu, one of the best batters in the world. The plan to unsettle her early with Sana's off breaks didn't yield much success but left-arm spinner Nashra Sandhu dismissed her in all the matches.

In the third ODI, Sana returned four wickets again to bowl out the hosts for 107 in a 216-run chase. Under Bismah and Mark, Sana's career was taking another upswing.

Pakistan continued the winning run in the T20Is, played at the SSC Ground in Colombo. Javeria cracked a half-century as Pakistan reached the target off the penultimate ball in the first T20I. The only stutter on the Sri Lankan tour came in the second T20I, when veteran spinner Shashikala Siriwardene's four wickets triggered a collapse. Pakistan were held to 72, a target Sri Lanka reached with ease. In the decider, Pakistan secured an untroubled 38-run win on a tired pitch.

Even though Sana was not the captain of the team, she was a figure everyone looked up to – often playing the bad cop while Bismah and Mark stuck to their more natural good-cop roles – and she still wielded authority, at times even telling off the head coach.

In the last T20I, Mark wanted to concentrate on analysing the match by himself, so he shifted his base from the dressing room to an empty commentary box during Sri Lanka's run chase. Sana, who had noticed his movements, confronted him at breakfast the next morning.

'Don't you do that again,' she warned.

Mark, a little bemused, asked what exactly she was referring to.

She explained, 'Don't you leave the team and go and sit in that box all by yourself again. We need you with the team.'

'She kept me on my toes,' says Mark with a wry smile. 'Every time she would say, "I need to speak to you," I'd get pretty worried.'

Pakistan had regained some momentum, but a poor showing in the T20 Asia Cup later in the year highlighted a few glaring weaknesses that remained in their game. Even though they had won three of the first four matches, which included a victory against Sri Lanka, the surprise loss against Bangladesh proved costly. The players' only shot at qualifying for the final was if they beat India in their last league game. But against Ekta Bisht, their batting struggled yet again and they were humbled. The victories against Malaysia and a rapidly improving Thailand were no consolation. Yet again, in a multi-nation tournament, Pakistan had performed below expectations. More significantly, it didn't augur well for the side leading up to the T20 World Cup later in the year.

Mark, who had spent close to a year with the team by then, had figured out that certain practices needed to be discarded. For a long time, mostly out of curiosity, he had observed the players' eating habits and, as the desire to get them fitter became increasingly important, Gemaal Hussain was hired as the fitness trainer in May 2018 – just before the Asia Cup. Gemaal, a medium-pacer who had played 34 first-class games in England, had had his career cut short by injury. Aged just 34, he was well aware of the demands of the modern game and knew that for the team to improve their fitness, their diet had to change.

The other change was that the batting needed to be braver. Mark felt that Pakistan were being restricted by their more traditional, conservative style while the top teams around the world, like Australia, England, New Zealand, the West Indies, South Africa and India had all progressed with a modern, more attacking approach. To help with this tactical transition, Andy Richards was hired as the batting coach. Richards, who had coached Queensland Fire in Australian domestic cricket and worked with Brisbane Heat in the Women's Big Bash League (WBBL), was accustomed to being in a high-quality women's cricket environment.

He had a tough task at hand, and only a few months to mastermind a turnaround as the focus shifted to the T20 World Cup, set to be held in the West Indies in November that year. At that stage, Bismah was striking around 89, Javeria 88 and Nida Dar 82. The rest were nowhere close to the pace at which batters of top teams were playing. Richards laid out the bare facts to the team when he joined them. In a graphic displayed on the big screen, he showed them that of the ten teams playing at the World Cup, only Ireland were scoring slower than Pakistan. It was crystal clear that the focus had to shift from crease occupation to taking greater risks in the middle.

Training drills evolved. The players were made to bat with baseball bats in order to improve their swings. Additional incentives were given in training to play bold shots – play over the top and innovate. In scenario simulations, when players would get out playing a reverse sweep, it wasn't considered out.

'We wanted them to practise ugly,' Mark claims. 'If you're not coming to practice and making mistakes, then you're not learning. Getting them to play the reverse sweep in practice without consequence would give them the confidence to keep trying it.'

Richards further stressed the need to use the full length and width of the crease: to step out and step back, to make room and to shuffle across. Similar liberties were given to bowlers to try out the more outlandish approaches that had become part of the international game.

One of the reasons for the success during Coles' and Richards' tenure was their ability to identify that a lot of practices which were common in men's cricket couldn't be applied to the women's game. In Pakistan, despite all of Richards' experience, he figured out there were different challenges which had to be overcome. Compared to Australia, where he had previously coached, in Pakistan, the players weren't as physically strong, the quality of their bats wasn't as good, and many were held back by the fear of repercussions of not executing their plans well.

The approach to power hitting wasn't as straightforward. Javeria Khan, for example, weighed close to 50 kg and Sidra Nawaz was in the early 40s. 'We had to stop them from check driving,' Richards explains. 'Women's cricket is generally a front-foot game, and too many of the Pakistan girls would get stuck on the crease – they wouldn't go either forward or back. There aren't too many bowlers in women's cricket who can put you on the back foot. I spent a lot of time wanting them to come forward. I didn't learn a lot of words in Urdu, but agay (forward) is one that I remember saying the whole time.

'In women's cricket, there isn't as much pace on the ball. The girls have to make their own pace. We needed to get them to have a full swing of the bat. That was a little bit foreign to them. When they tried and it came off, it almost shocked them a little bit. I think they've had a history of coaches shouting at them for not getting things right. I wasn't going to do that. We had to build their confidence. Half the time, they were actually sitting there waiting for me to yell at them.'

It was a complete overhaul of any previous approach a coach had taken with the team – and it helped that Sana Mir had bought into their vision. Although Mark and Bismah called each other 'bossy', Sana remained as influential a figure within the team as she'd been during her captaincy days. 'Sana wasn't the captain, but she was the leader on and off the field,' Richards acknowledges. 'She was a big influence in trying to make that change happen.'

For several players, the biggest incentive to experiment was the desire to shed the fear of failure – whether in practice or in matches. And it eventually began to pay off, beginning with their next tour – to Bangladesh. Bismah, who was suffering with asthma, had been ruled out of the series as she was recovering from sinus surgery. The mantle of captaincy was handed to Javeria.

Bangladesh had not only beaten Pakistan in the Asia Cup, but also stunned India twice to win the tournament for the first time. A few miles east, Bangladesh were seeing a change of their cricket destinies as well. However, in the four-match T20I series, of which the first was washed out by rain, they were beaten 3–0 by the revitalised Pakistan.

In the second T20I, played at Cox's Bazar, the hosts were bowled out for 30 in an 89-run chase. Left-arm spinner Anam Amin, sharing the new ball, bowled one of the finest T20 spells, picking up three wickets in as many overs without conceding a run; Bangladesh could never recover.

They put up a better show in the next T20I, putting on 81 for 8. But Pakistan, riding on useful knocks by Nahida Khan (33) and Javeria (31*) sailed past, untroubled. The victory in the fourth T20I was almost as pain-free – chasing down the 78-run target with seven wickets in hand. They could have returned unscathed, but a low-intensity show in the one-off ODI resulted in their only loss of the tour. Off-spinner Khadija Tul Kubra's 6 for 20 wrapped up Pakistan's innings on 94, which was chased down without much fuss.

Between the high of the Bangladesh series win and the anticipation of the T20 World Cup came a series against Australia, to be played in Kuala Lumpur. Even though Bismah had returned to the side, Javeria was allowed to continue as captain till the World Cup.

Meg Lanning's Australia were bruised. Despite undoubtedly being the best team in the world, it was a rare period in the side's cricket history when they weren't the reigning world champions in either format. Even though the challenge against Pakistan wasn't expected to be the stiffest, the players had a point to prove and, more importantly, they didn't want to leave anything to chance in their preparation for the World Cup.

Pakistan were well aware that winning even an odd game was likely to be out of the question. The Australian women cricketers were the aspirational benchmark – the crème da la crème of the cricketing world. They were strong and supremely fit, had the most modern training methods, were highly paid and sponsored – carrying the heaviest of cricket kits with the most expensive of bats. They were setting the standard for on-field cricket and off-field training routines.

The Pakistanis had mostly watched the likes of Ellyse Perry and Meg Lanning on TV. Outside the World Cup, the two teams had only ever faced each other twice. If not for the IWC, such encounters would have been even rarer. So enamoured were some of the younger players by the star-studded Australian team that, even before the series began, they were requesting selfies and autographs from their opponents.

To be handing over such a psychological advantage to the opposition through the course of the series was a non-negotiable for Mark. In turn, Richards spoke to Australian coach Matthew Mott and arranged for a tête-à-tête with the Australian players at the end of the series.

'It was really good that the Australians came and spoke to our players because it broke the fear factor and awe,' Richards observes. 'We had one girl who didn't know who Ellyse Perry was, so that helped. But once you're familiar, the awe gets lessened, and you realise that they put their pants on just like we do.'

In the games, though, Australia were clinical. The batting and bowling depth, coupled with high levels of fitness which aided quick running between the wickets and in the field, meant Pakistan had to chase throughout. But the underdogs exceeded expectations.

In the first ODI, the Pakistan players were bowled out for 95. However, they didn't let their opposition get to that meagre total easily. Sana Mir's three wickets ensured that Australia had lost five by the time they reached the target. In the second match, the Australian captain led the way with an elegant century as they posted 273 before left-arm spinner Sophie Molineux's 4-fer ended Pakistan's chase on 123. Barring Nahida Khan's 66, there wasn't much for Pakistan to take away from the contest.

In the third match of the series, Alyssa Healy and Ashleigh Gardner stroked quick-fire half-centuries to power Australia to 324 for 7. Pakistan put up an improved performance, but it still wasn't much of a fight. In that match, though, Aliya Riaz stroked her maiden half-century – displaying early signs of a new talent making her mark.

The T20I series followed a similar trajectory. Healy and Gardner's half-centuries had muscled Australia to 195 for 3. Pakistan were never in the chase. But against a strong bowling line-up, the team mustered 131. In the second T20I, the batting failed them. They were bowled out for 101 and Australia took just 17 overs to chase down the score. The tour ended on a disappointing note, Australia romping home with nine wickets in hand and almost half their overs to spare.

Pakistan had taken a bit of a pounding, but there were still reasons to celebrate.

After the 2017 World Cup drama, one of the carrots Mark had offered Sana to convince her to come back into cricket was the tag of being officially the No 1 bowler in one-day cricket.

At that point, she was sixth in the rankings, but reaching the top spot wasn't entirely out of the question. No Pakistani woman cricketer had ever achieved such a feat – indeed, the very idea of it seemed beyond Sana's imagination. But Mark knew that he had planted a seed. 'She sort of looked at me and thought, "That's a bit wild but okay, we'll give it a go."'

Sana enjoyed her best years as a cricketer in the post-captaincy days. Right from the first series under Bismah, she flourished as a player. In nine ODIs since the World Cup, she had picked up 26 wickets – against New Zealand, Sri Lanka and Australia. It had propelled her to the top of the ICC's ODI rankings for bowlers.

Given the nature of women's ODI cricket, allowing each of the top eight countries an equal opportunity against each other, her rise to the top was a testament to consistent performances. Her Twitter bio in her post-retirement phase gives a fair glimpse of what that achievement meant to her. Despite a career filled with laurels, 'Former world No 1' is all that she mentions about her cricket.

'Growing up, I had no doubts that I'd play for Pakistan,' she admits. 'I had no doubts that I'd captain Pakistan. In fact, I was overconfident about it. But being No 1 wasn't something I believed I could achieve.

'Firstly, we weren't playing a lot of games. And as a bowler, you need the support of other bowlers and fielders to put the opposition under pressure. So, a lot depends on that when you come from a country where most of the opposition teams are ranked higher than you. I was in the top 20 rankings for a long time, but I wasn't able to break into the top five for the longest time.

'When I was able to reach the top, it broke a lot of barriers in my own mind. Now, I see that happening with the rest of the team. When someone does it, it makes others also believe. A lot of the times when we were looking for sponsors, the general attitude was, "Why should we invest in women's cricket? They aren't good." When you're ranked world No 1, that's not an excuse any more.'

Sana Mir – one of the faces of Pepsi, a long-term sponsor of the team – was also roped in as the brand ambassador of Uber in Pakistan as part of its global campaign, which included women cricketers from other parts of the world as well.

That one personal feat had a catalytic effect on the team. Celebrities from all walks of life came out in public to congratulate her on the achievement. It not only helped her rise in popularity and become a recognisable superstar in the country, but also drew the women's game to the attention of a larger population. For the uninitiated, women's cricket in Pakistan became almost synonymous with Sana Mir.

As heartening as Sana's rise to the top of the ICC ODI rankings was, and as happy as the team was with its performance in the series against Australia, it was to count for little when the players came up against them again in the opener of the 2018 ICC T20 World Cup, held in Providence, Guyana.

Placed in the 'group of death', Pakistan had a stiff task in the tournament, placed alongside Australia, New Zealand, India and Ireland. Only the top two teams were to qualify for the next round – the semi-finals.

Against a wounded Australian side, they were unlikely to be offered an easy start. Electing to bat, the Australian top order powered away – with Alyssa Healy, Beth Mooney and Meg Lanning scoring quick-fire 40s to help the side to 165 for 5. Pakistan, for their part, never looked to be challenging that total, eventually being held on 113 for 8.

Pakistan's next challenge was against arch-rivals India – a team they had beaten twice in the three previous T20 World Cup campaigns. However, by 2018, despite bitter infighting between the head coach and a senior player, India were one of the powerhouses outside the elite duo of Australia and England. The side had come into the contest having beaten New Zealand and were pushing towards a semi-final spot.

In a critical contest for both sides, Pakistan lost their top three after being put in to bat. However, a 93-run stand between Bismah Maroof and Nida Dar – courtesy of their respective 50s, shifted the momentum. They were ably helped by the Indian fielders, who dropped four catches. But then they slipped. While pacing along in the death overs, the batters kept running on the pitch – a violation that had cost them five penalty runs in the series against Sri Lanka as well.

Against India, they were caught doing so three times and were penalised ten runs, helping India start their 134-run chase at 10 without loss, before a ball had been bowled. It was bizarre that the running on the pitch happened despite the presence of several senior players. On the first two occasions, Bismah and Nida were guilty of it. On the third occasion, it was Nahida Khan and Sidra Nawaz.

'It just killed us,' Richards states. 'In that World Cup, we didn't have the luxury to make such mistakes. It made such a difference to the approach we wanted to take. That was disappointing. That game was our chance to qualify for the next round.'

Even though it may have proved destructive in the short term, it was a part of the learning process for the players. Richards had long realised that communicating while running between the wickets was a problem area for the team and had resulted in several run-outs.

'With the language barrier, I discovered that they all had one call for "no". They all know what "no" is. But because of the different provinces that they come from, they all have a different word for "yes". They were saying "yes" but it really wasn't being understood. A lot of coaching had to happen on the run. Thankfully, they were absolute sponges, an absolute pleasure to coach.'

Even though Pakistan eventually lost that match, they managed to stretch India to the 19th over, courtesy of miserly spells from Bismah and Nida. But the ten penalised runs eventually proved costly.

They briefly made up for that loss with a 38-run win over Ireland in the next game, with skipper Javeria Khan stroking her then career-best 74*. All the bowlers chipped in, with Sana, Aiman Anwer, Nashra Sandhu and Aliya Riaz bagging a brace each to limit Ireland to 101 for 9 in its 140-run chase.

By the time they were set to play their next game, against New Zealand, Pakistan's chances of qualifying for the next round had slipped away. The quality of their performance also fizzled out as they were downed by 54 runs. The bowlers did well to hold New Zealand to 144, but the batting, barring Javeria's 23-ball 36, fell apart, and they were cleaned up for 90.

It was an end to yet another World Cup campaign where they had performed below their potential.

By 2019, the PCB were steadily moving towards bringing international cricket back into Pakistan. A representational team, assembled by the ICC, had toured in September 2017, but it required the PCB to shell out big moolah, with each player offered approximately US$100,000 to play. Too many high-profile players hadn't turned up and, more importantly, none of the cricket boards had shown much interest. The Sri Lankan men's team were the only side that agreed to tour, for a single T20I – while the rest of the three ODIs and two T20Is were played in the UAE.

In April 2018, the West Indies Cricket Board sent its men's team to play a three-match T20I series in Karachi. In January 2019, it agreed to send the women's team as well.

With tight security arrangements in place, the three T20Is were scheduled to be packed into a space of four days, in Karachi, followed by three ODIs in Dubai. The West Indian skipper Stafanie Taylor backed out of the T20I leg of the series citing security concerns. For Pakistan, the captaincy was returned to Bismah Maroof following the World Cup.

It was a novel experience for several players, who had never played an international match in Pakistan. It was as novel an experience for several families to watch their daughters play for Pakistan live. And in some ways, it was unlike anything Richards and Coles had imagined, let alone witnessed – helicopters flying over the ground, snipers on the roof of the stadium, and security officers walking around at breakfast and at the toss.

'In one of the games, during the break, when I took some of the batters and went to the middle, the federal police walked with us. I asked, "What are you doing?" They said, "We have to come with you,"' recalls Richards. 'When I sat there and debriefed the players, we were surrounded by the security guards.'

Bizarre as they found the experience, it wasn't hard to figure out what the experience meant for the players, who were overwhelmed by the occasion. The eventual result of the cricket wasn't favourable though.

After losing the first match convincingly by 71 runs, with the batting letting them down again, they managed to drag the second contest at the Southend Cricket Club Stadium in Karachi to the Super Over. Sana, bowling the 18-run Super Over, was taken apart by Deandra Dottin for two sixes and a four. Pakistan, in response, were unable to mount a fightback. Shakera Selman dismissed Aliya Riaz and Nida Dar for first-ball ducks to close the contest.

The hosts improved in the last match of the series, even though it was a dead rubber. Nida's 40-ball 53 helped Pakistan post the biggest score of the series – 150 for 6 – before Anam Amin's triple strike limited the tourists to 138 for 8. The T20I series ended with a 2–1 scoreline in favour of the West Indies.

Despite the series loss, the hosts were grateful. 'When we won the last T20, the crowd went berserk,' Richards recalls. 'I remember telling Colesy, "Thank God we didn't win the series here, we wouldn't have been able to walk out of the ground."' Sana Mir made a special presentation for the touring team, thanking them for their gesture in turning up and playing in the country while the rest of the cricketing world were still apprehensive. Members of the British High Commission were part of the spectacle at the ground, and their approval was to remain a key factor in bringing international cricket back to the country.

The caravan was set to move to Dubai for the one-day leg. Even though the hosts wouldn't have had home support, several players from the Pakistan Super League – which was going on at the time in the UAE – turned up to cheer for the women's team.

Pakistan had improved significantly against the West Indies during the three previous games, but once Stafanie Taylor returned to the side, they were beaten comprehensively in the 50-over contest. Without Bismah, who was injured in training a day earlier, they were shot out for 70 in a 217-run chase. A key reason for the thumping was the form of Deandra Dottin. The West Indian all-rounder had come into the contest on the back of a sensational showing in the 2018 World T20. At her best, there are few batters in world cricket who can be as destructive and few bowlers who can be as fast. Several injuries had impacted her career, but against Pakistan she was at her peak. Her 139-ball 96 laid the foundation of a 200-plus score for the West Indies. But it was a short-pitch barrage with the ball that caught them completely off guard.

Placed at 46 for 1, Pakistan looked steady in the chase at one point, before one of Dottin's bouncers hit Nahida Khan on the helmet and sent the team into a panic from which they never recovered. Based on Richards's suggestion that women's cricket was predominantly a front-foot game, the Pakistan batters had only recently unlearned some of their previous habits and were working on improving their front-foot play. But against Dottin's pace, that was to prove ineffective. She may have only picked up three wickets in the match, but she exposed their technique and, with it, their mental fragility.

With two more ODIs remaining, it was obvious that the West Indians were going to come after them with more bouncers. The team were rattled, and the leaders in the team weren't in the best frame of mind: Bismah was injured; Sana had lost her mentor, Shahbano Aliani, and couldn't fly back to Pakistan to be at her funeral.

The team was grieving, and the coaches needed to try and find a quick fix. 'One of the first things we needed to do even before coming up with a plan was to get the players to admit that they were scared of facing bouncers,' Richards said. 'Once they admitted to that, we could give each of them a plan to counter that approach.'

Some trained to swerve and duck, some practised to play over the slips. And those who were confident, trained to hook. The West Indian bowlers' plan played out the way Pakistan expected. Barring Dottin, the rest didn't have the pace to rattle them. Bismah, who returned for the match, couldn't execute what she had prepared, but Sidra Ameen and Nida Dar's counter-attack proved effective. Sidra Ameen scored 96 before getting run out, and Dar smashed an 86-ball 81. A 102-run partnership for the fourth wicket helped Pakistan to 240, despite four batters getting run out.

The West Indians couldn't better that. Diana Baig led the way with four wickets, while Sana scalped three as the visitors crumbled for 206.

Riding on the momentum of the win, Pakistan secured the series in the decider. Nashra Sandhu broke the back of the middle order with three wickets, while Diana returned as many to end the West Indian innings for 159. Pakistan were tested in the chase, but Sidra Ameen's second successive half-century yet again paved the way for victory. Sana hit the winning runs as Pakistan secured a four-wicket triumph.

'It was a really tough time for Sana,' Coles recalls. 'It helped that her family in Dubai could come over to be with her. When she hit the winning runs, it was almost fitting. It was as if the sun was shining down on her.'

The series win meant that Pakistan were still in contention for direct qualification to the World Cup. Only nine ODIs were left to be played, of which three were against India. Given the political tensions and the Indian cricket board's refusal to be a part of any bilateral cricketing ties with Pakistan, the latter were likely to result in a walkover again. It eased Pakistan's position, but a tough tour against South Africa and a series against England still lay ahead.

And that would be the culmination of everything the team had learned in the tenure of Coles and Richards.

By May 2019, no team was in a position to set priorities between one-day cricket and T20s. A T20 World Cup awaited them in early 2020, and within a few months the qualification for the 2021 50-over World Cup was also set to be sealed.

Pakistan were heading for one of their toughest series of the cycle. South Africa, however, had more ground to gain on the championship table, and a home series against Pakistan was as good an opportunity for them to do that as they could wish for. Even though captain Dane van Niekerk was absent, recovering from a stress fracture, Lizelle Lee quipped that it was the 'healthiest and the most competitive South African Women have ever been'.

While the visitors had comfortably won the two warm-up games preceding the international series, with the return of the hard-hitting duo Lee and Chloe Tryon back to full fitness, Pakistan's chances of doing well on the tour looked bleak. Fortunately, the pitch in the first one-dayer, held in Potchefstroom, played in their favour. On a wet and turning track, Sana's off breaks proved potent. Her 4 for 11 cleaned up the hosts for 63 – their second-lowest total in ODIs. Pakistan broke little sweat chasing down the target with eight wickets in hand and 212 balls to spare – the team's fastest-ever run chase – to go one up in the series.

South Africa made a quick recovery from the shock loss and drew level in the series, winning the second ODI. The visitors had started well after being put in to bat, courtesy of a half-century opening stand by Sidra Ameen and Nahida Khan. However, medium-pacer Masabata Klass's hat-trick – the tenth in women's ODI cricket – triggered a collapse and they folded for 147. In response, South Africa's batting came good against Pakistan's strong spin attack. Opener Laura Wolvaardt led the way with an unbeaten 74 to help overhaul the total in the 37th over, with eight wickets in hand.

Even though the series was tied 1–1 going into the decider, the batting was yet to come good for Pakistan. Richards had returned home due to personal issues before the series, and all he had to offer before leaving were some plans and a few on-the-move chats with the head coach as the matches progressed.

None of his batting plans was designed for Nashra Sandhu, though, the No 11.

In the series decider, in Benoni, South African batters dominated the proceedings. Openers Wolvaardt, Lee and skipper Sune Luus hammered half-centuries to power the home side to 265 for 6. Only three times in history had Pakistan scored more than 265 (twice against Ireland and once against the Netherlands). Against the pace trio of Marizanne Kapp, Shabnim Ismail and Klass, the players would have to bat as they had never done before. And soon enough in the run chase, they were reduced to 37 for 3, with the in-form openers and skipper Bismah Maroof back in the pavilion.

The chase was kept alive by Javeria Khan in the company of two drastically improved cricketers: Nida Dar and Aliya Riaz. By the time Javeria departed in the 37th over, for a 103-ball 74, Pakistan needed 101 runs in 78 balls, with the last five batters remaining to accompany Riaz.

By then Pakistan had already started accelerating, with Javeria stroking Tumi Sekhukhune for three successive boundaries in the 37th over before departing. Omaima Sohail and Sana Mir also fell after scoring quick-fire 16s. Riaz took the game deep though. In the 46th over, she launched an attack on Kapp, hitting the veteran pace bowler for three consecutive boundaries. Nonetheless, Klass's double strike in the following over – snapping up Mir and Riaz – turned the match in South Africa's favour. Even though the tourists were closing in on the target, the last three batters weren't renowned for their skills, let alone the ability to hit big shots.

Wicketkeeper Sidra Nawaz, their last batting hope, was still in the middle when the ninth wicket fell. They needed 11 off four balls. Two balls later, Nashra Sandhu, the No 11, was at the crease – with eight needed off two. Pakistan, after having put up a strong show in the run chase, knew the game had slipped from their hands.

But Nashra felt that the scenario freed her; she had nothing to lose. As Klass delivered the penultimate ball, Nashra caught

215

it flush on her bat and it sailed beyond the boundary fence. The equations had suddenly changed, and with two needed off the last ball, Nashra's next shot held consequences unlike any before in her life.

The South Africans, meanwhile, were caught in a dilemma – whether to stop the single or try not to lose. Nashra also had a choice to make – to go for the boundary again to try to win the match outright or go for the single that would tie the game. She chose to touch the ball and sprinted across for a single. 'It was unbelievable,' Mark recalls. 'The great thing for me as a coach was that they made the decision themselves. They had to decide – "Are we going to take the risk of going for the win? Or what will it do if we take a point from here moving into the ICC championship?" And we knew that point was pretty valuable.'

For as unwilling as everyone in the team was to come to terms with Nashra hitting a massive six, it was a situation which the coaches had prepared for. 'I know a lot of teams don't really spend much time on the 10s and 11s, but I was insistent. Some of the top-order batters would get very frustrated. Sana was one of them who would say, "I want more practice." But I needed the lower-order batters to improve,' said Richards.

The several hours invested in working on Nashra's batting paid off at a critical time and drew them closer to World Cup qualification. Even though South Africa were fourth in the table, Pakistan, at fifth, had a better chance, with three more wins expected to be awarded as walkovers by India.

The tourists continued their dominant run in the T20Is as 50s by Nida Dar and Bismah Maroof helped Pakistan overhaul South Africa's total of 119 with two overs to spare in the first T20I, in Pretoria. Sana Mir had led the way with the ball, returning figures of 3 for 14 before Nida Dar's all-round display (2 for 30 and 53) downed the hosts by seven wickets.

Bismah, who had scored an unbeaten 53 in the first match, followed up with another half-century in the second (47-ball 63*), in Pietermaritzburg, as Pakistan scored 128 for 5. In response, Marizanne Kapp and Lizelle Lee stroked half-centuries, but dragged the match into the last over, needing seven to win off Nida Dar. They managed to overhaul the target off the penultimate delivery, but not without hiccups.

In a tour where the fortunes had see-sawed, Pakistan took an edge again. The hard-hitting 26-year-old Iram Javed made her first major impression in international cricket with a 45-ball 55 to lead Pakistan to a four-wicket win. Her innings helped the side chase down the 139-run target with two balls to spare.

But it wasn't a lead they could hold for long. The bowling attack, which South African captain Sune Luus had hailed as the 'best in the world', was torn apart in the fourth match of the series, in Benoni. Nida Dar led the way with an aggressive 37-ball 75 and was aided by Aliya Riaz's unbeaten 17-ball 35, as Pakistan smashed 172 for 5 – its second highest total in T20Is. Nida followed up on her batting performance with a return of 2 for 20 with the ball. But Lizelle Lee's 31-ball 60 put paid to her efforts as South Africa levelled the series again.

For a tour which Pakistan had competed so well in, whether in victory or defeat, the deciding T20I proved to be anti-climactic. Lee's unbeaten 48-ball 71 helped South Africa make light work of the 126-run chase. They won the match in the 16th over by nine wickets and took the series 3–2.

Despite the results in both limited overs formats, it remained one of Pakistan's most satisfying performances. Barring the last game of the series, they had matched extremely strong opponents away from home in conditions that had been better suited to the hosts.

'When we went to South Africa, I honestly didn't expect that result,' Bismah admits. 'I knew we were improving as a team but didn't know that we would be able to compete so strongly against them. The early momentum that we got made us believe that we could beat them.'

For Coles and Richards, the series marked a culmination of all that they had worked towards in terms of player improvement and team building. The leadership had also passed on seamlessly, not only to Bismah but also to Javeria, who often filled in for her. The results were a clear indication that the team was on the rise again and had taken some significant strides forward. The end of the series, however, brought an abrupt end to their coaching tenure. Mark had to head back to New Zealand to be with his ailing grandmother and uncle, and he left his job.

Their departure from the set-up also coincided with several dramatic changes taking place in Pakistan cricket – one that was sure to have a long-term impact, for better or for worse.

13

GOING DOWN, STRIKING BACK, RISING UP

AFTER SEVERAL DECADES of national rule, in which power shifted hands between the triumvirate of the Bhuttos, Nawaz Sharif and military dictators, political control of Pakistan went outside the traditional strongholds. Imran Khan – the chief of Pakistan Tehreek-e Insaf – was sworn in as prime minister on 18 August 2018.

For most of his two decades in politics, Imran was viewed as an outsider. Even though he had long been a vocal Taliban sympathiser, he still basked in the image of a charismatic, globe-trotting, world-beating cricketer. His gregarious lifestyle was well documented and, for many, his clean and ultra-modern image was a draw as they brought his political party to power at the national level.

Few men in Pakistan's history could match his popularity. Voters understood that he could live the rest of his life in comfort with the money he had earned and the fame that he had garnered from cricket. The sole reason that he was stepping out on to the streets and begging for votes – so he said – was to give the people of his country a better life, health and prosperity. It was a siren call.

After he assumed power, however, Pakistan's gross domestic product witnessed a sharp decline, Taliban forces were empowered and media control was tightened. It should, perhaps, have been predicted; those who had witnessed Imran's reluctance to challenge the Zia-ul-Haq tyranny weren't surprised to find that he didn't stand up to regressive and orthodox traditions. Even as late as June 2021, his response to Axios journalist Jonathan Swan regarding the 'rape epidemic' in Pakistan during his tenure was rather obvious. 'If a woman is wearing very few clothes it will have an impact on the man unless they are robots. It's common sense.'

In the outrage that followed, he defended his statement by claiming that his words had been taken out of context, but it was a flimsy defence. As was happening all around the world, Pakistan's politics were slipping towards conservatism.

His early days as the leader of the country had been quite different, however. They bristled with action and the promise of a positive future. He gave up several luxuries enjoyed by previous prime ministers and even proposed peaceful relations with estranged neighbour India.

In cricket, he brought in Ehsan Mani, the former president of the ICC, to chair the PCB. Mani, in turn, appointed Wasim Khan as the chief executive officer. Wasim was a British-born Pakistani who had played first-class cricket in England and served as the head of Leicestershire County Cricket Club. Even as two highly educated men, who had largely been away from the inner politics of Pakistan cricket, were brought in to make the cricketing system in Pakistan more organised and robust, it was obvious they would have to fulfil the ambitions of the patron-in-chief.

Much of Imran's popularity stems from cricket. Not only is he the best player ever produced by the country, and one of the finest all-rounders in the world, but his success in leading Pakistan to its only 50-over World Cup title, in 1992, made him one of the nation's most iconic figures. His achievement shot the sport to such popularity, and inspired so many to take up the game, that endless controversies since then haven't been enough to kill the love for cricket in Pakistan. He exhibited leadership skills of the most traditional order in one of the toughest jobs in the country. His ways were authoritarian; an appealing trait in a Pakistani leader. The fact that he found success and made his authority unquestionable ensured his methods were palatable. His word on the game since then has been hard to challenge.

One of the earliest decisions Imran took as the PCB's patron-in-chief was to controversially get rid of departments (teams represented by corporations and government bodies) from the men's domestic structure. To improve the quality of cricket and serve as a better bridge for those players making it to the international level, he allowed the sport to be run instead by six provincial teams. Departments had till then been the backbone of Pakistan's domestic cricket. Not only did they bring in sponsorship for the board but they also provided permanent employment and contracts to nearly 600 players every year. They were scouting and feeding the system with cricketers and money.

The side effect of dismantling the system was that more than 400 men were taken out of the domestic structure – which eventually led to the loss of jobs and contracts. The move also had a trickle-down effect on women's cricket. Those who were contracted with ZTBL were fortunate to retain their jobs, but those who were with State Bank of Pakistan, one of the chief employers of women cricketers (paying anywhere in the range of PKR 35,000–95,000 per month), didn't get a contract extension.

The women's domestic structure was reduced from 16 teams to a pool of 45 players, who were divided into three representational teams. Sana Mir wasn't impressed by the decision of the women's wing. 'There are a lot of players who want to play but we have shrunk the system so much that they have no place to go and express their talent,' she said. 'The choice of the top 45 players is made by three national selectors. If you're a 25-year-old and they don't think you're in their future plans, you have no place to play cricket. In such a scenario, the pressure of marriage and other issues build up. That's what is going to hurt Pakistan cricket. Three selectors might have a vision, which is fair, but the structure shouldn't stop a player from playing cricket.'

Of those who got a chance to play, only ten were offered central contracts by the board, and only two of those were allocated in the top grade (captain Bismah Maroof wasn't one of them). The rationale of Urooj Mumtaz, the newly appointed general manager of the PCB women's wing, was that 'contracts should be earned and not seen as a privilege'. While the pay for the contracted cricketers increased, ranging from PKR 80,000–150,000 per month (based on grades) to go with higher match fees, daily allowances and improved travel and accommodation facilities, it also meant that in most cases not every player in the playing 11 was financially secure.

Sana further questioned the decision: 'Most of the cricketers come from middle- or lower-middle-class background. How are their parents going to afford their girls going for practice so regularly?'

While Imran hasn't stated his position on the impact on women's cricket, for their male counterparts he claimed that the job losses would only be teething problems for the larger financial and cricketing betterment of Pakistan.

The change was brought about with a long-term view to not only make provincial cricket financially independent but also to improve the cream of the crop. Was it really making cricket a more appealing sport for parents to send their daughters to play? Or did it prove detrimental?

For all the disinterest that Imran Khan has historically shown towards women's cricket, it may be safe to argue that his desire to revamp men's cricket possibly didn't fully take into account the collateral damage to the women's game. The complexities of the challenges that women cricketers had to face to be a part of the system were different from those faced by their male counterparts. To begin with, earning opportunities weren't equal – with fewer matches there was less exposure and, as a result, less interest from brands in being associated with them. In the face of social constraints that held back families from sending their daughters to play cricket, the financial rewards weren't lucrative enough to tempt them to try.

At least as late as the 2018 T20 World Cup, several players were skipping one or more meals on cricket tours to save money. It wasn't because the board wasn't paying them for their food, but so poor was their financial health that every rupee saved went a long way in helping their families back home.

Thus, while allowing the top 45 cricketers to play against each other would have enabled higher-quality cricket, the reduced number of players who were getting a chance to stake their claim was a natural demotivator. The move to rid the domestic system of the departments led many to question the unquestionable Imran Khan's decision – despite its good intention.

Some approached the prime minister to bring departments back, some wrote letters arguing for the expansion of the domestic structure. But Imran, who viewed the change purely through the lens of men's cricket, stuck by his ideas, just as he had successfully done with so many of his beliefs through the course of his captaincy.

Wasim Khan was crucial to the board's long-held plans to bring international cricket back to Pakistan. Thanks to both his credibility and his experience working in the Western world, he was able to open a dialogue with the cricket boards in England, Australia, South Africa and New Zealand – who hadn't toured the country for at least 15 years – and was able to convince them to return.

With the cricket boards of the West Indies, Zimbabwe and Sri Lanka – who have traditionally maintained good relations with the PCB – playing their part by sending their men's teams to Pakistan, Bangladesh soon followed suit. In October 2019, the Bangladesh Cricket Board's women's team toured for three T20Is and two ODIs. Iqbal Imam, who had previously served as the team's batting coach, was brought back into the set-up as an interim head coach for the home series in Lahore.

The series played out much as Pakistan would have hoped. In what served as a useful preparation for the upcoming T20 World Cup, set to be played in Australia in early 2020, it clean swept Bangladesh's challenge in the 20-over series.

It was the first time since the 2005 Asia Cup that Pakistan were playing an international match at one of their premier stadiums. In the first T20I, at the Gaddafi Stadium, Bangladesh pace bowler Jahanara Alam picked up four wickets, while Rumana Ahmed scored a half-century, but Pakistan won by 14 runs after scoring 126.

Bangladesh challenged the hosts again in the second T20I, but once again came up short. Bismah Maroof, who was named player of the match in the first game, carried on her good form and stroked her career-best 70*. Javeria Khan also scored a half-century, and the 95-run partnership between the duo helped them to 167 for 3 before they limited the visitors to 152 for 7, courtesy of Sadia Iqbal's three wickets.

Javeria continued her dominance and stroked another half-century in the third match to aid Pakistan's victory in the low-scoring thriller. Sana Mir played only one match in the series, the second T20I, in which she returned underwhelming figures of 1 for 35. Having skipped the first match due to personal reasons, she surprisingly missed the third match.

However, the veteran all-rounder put on a better show in the ODIs, in which Bangladesh put up a much stronger fight. In the first game, Nahida Khan's 68 helped Pakistan to 215, before Sana's triple strike became a key factor in them falling 29 runs short.

In the second game, Nahida stroked another half-century – a 79-ball 63 – to help her side to 210, but they were outplayed by the visitors. Despite a late collapse, Fargana Hoque's 67 proved handy as the tourists finished level in the 50-over contest, winning the last match with one wicket and one ball to spare.

It was a well-contested series even though the eventual result may not look like it on paper. For, although it reflected Bangladesh's growing stature in international cricket, two of their most experienced cricketers – Rumana Ahmed and Salma Khatun – were quick to note that Pakistan had played better cricket in the past. They were also among the first to predict the slide that was to follow. What they weren't aware of was that old wounds had started to open through the course of the five-match series. Sana was realising that in the absence of Mark, her support system was crumbling.

When Wasim Khan took over as chief on 6 December 2018, he was quick to admit that the attitude towards women's cricket needed a change. An all-women's selection committee was formed for the first time.

Urooj Mumtaz was appointed as chief of the panel, alongside Asmavia Iqbal and Marina Iqbal. The decision may have stemmed from good intentions, but the appointed selectors were recently retired cricketers who were on friendly and not-so-friendly terms with those who were still playing.

It was part of the PCB's larger vision to bring former cricketers back into the fold. Ehsan Mani had approached Shaiza Khan to head the women's wing, but she turned the offer down. With limited options to choose from, the hunt for an able candidate ended with Urooj Mumtaz. Inexplicably, not just for one role, but for multiple leadership positions – GM of the women's wing, chair of the selection panel and a member of the cricket committee. There were multiple flaws in such an arrangement, none more obvious than the fact that too much power had been concentrated in the hands of one individual who was appointed to oversee her own responsibilities.

Much as in her playing days, she was juggling too many jobs at one time, including her role as a commentator and her profession as a dentist. She had become all-powerful in Pakistan women's cricket.

The decision to give all the positions of authority to one person came in for criticism but was always brushed aside by the board with a generic response of not having enough qualified candidates for these roles. An almost identical situation played out in men's cricket at the same time, with Misbah-ul-Haq being appointed as head coach, chief selector and head of the cricket committee. But the reason for his appointment in three key roles was different – the PCB wanted a singular vision for the team.

Even as Urooj and Sana had maintained a peaceful stand in public, the acrimonious relationship the two shared from their playing days wasn't a secret. Not surprisingly, it didn't matter that Sana had risen to become the first Pakistani woman cricketer to be ranked No 1; her place in the team was under pressure.

Two weeks after the series against Bangladesh, Sana announced that she wanted to take a break from cricket and would not be available for the next tour, which was to be played in Kuala

Lumpur against England. Without specifying the reason or the time frame for her absence, she stated, 'I will utilise this time to plan and reset my future objectives and targets.'

The three ODIs and three T20Is against England were not only critical for Pakistan's 50-over World Cup qualification, but were also a much-needed warm-up for the forthcoming T20 World Cup. With a change in the coaching set-up already putting the team out of sorts, an absent leader only added to the unrest.

Shedding light upon her decision, Sana reveals, 'The same set of people who had given me a tough time in 2016/17 were back. It wasn't a pleasant situation to be in. It was difficult for me to continue once Mark [Coles] left, and there was the same instability within the team.

'With Mark going away, the new coach struggled to give any clarity to the players, failing to tell the players what they wanted from them. All this with only three months left for the World Cup. I wanted to take time out to think.'

Pakistan left for Kuala Lumpur without Sana and struggled badly in both the ODIs and the T20Is.

Bismah Maroof's successive 50s in the first two ODIs were of little significance as England won comfortably by 75 and 127 runs respectively. In the third game, rain helped Pakistan make a lucky escape and bag some much-needed championship points. The contest at the Kinrara Academy Oval was washed out after only 37.4 overs of play, in which they scored 145 for 8.

The Pakistan team weren't granted such mercies in the T20Is, although they fought valiantly at least twice in three games. Bismah Maroof's 58-ball 60 took Pakistan to 125 in a 155-run chase.

After being swatted aside in the second contest, Javeria put on an impressive display with the bat in the last match of the series. Despite her 46-ball 57, though, Pakistan fell 26 runs short of England's 170-run total.

It was an expected scoreline in the end, but it was also obvious that Sana's inclusion could be the spur that the team needed going into the blue riband tournament. The board urged her to return to the team, and, after initially resisting, she eventually agreed.

'I knew that my concerns were right, and things weren't happening the way they should've been. But I put aside all those concerns because I still wanted to be remembered as someone who was serving the team.'

Bismah Maroof was a pale version of herself on 20 January 2020, staring blankly at the piece of paper in Urooj Mumtaz's hands as she listed the players selected for the T20 World Cup. The captain and the chief selector were aware of the uproar that would follow. Bismah didn't look up as Urooj announced that the players had been primarily selected on the form they had shown in the last two international series Pakistan had played and the recently concluded domestic competition.

As Urooj read out the names in alphabetical order, Bismah took a heavy breath and raised her eyes to the media men gathered in the room between the announcement of two names – Sadia Iqbal and Sidra Nawaz. It was a disclosure that Sana Mir, her cricketing mentor, had been left out after being called up for a training camp. Questions over Sana's exclusion were expected and, even before the journalists could ask them, Urooj explained the rationale and hailed Sana's contribution to the game.

Sana had played only one T20I and four domestic matches during the period that Urooj claimed was key to the team's selection. She had been overlooked in favour of the 16-year-old leg-spinner Syeda Aroob Shah, who had played just three T20Is in her career up to that point. The difference between the two had been their performances in the National T20 triangular women's cricket championship, in which Sana had picked up four wickets at an economy rate of 8.07, while Aroob had taken five at a miserly 5.53.

Sana's rise in the years under Mark, not to mention a career that had recently seen her reach the top of the ODI rankings, was dismissed. Under the New Zealander, she had picked up 31 wickets in 16 ODIs at a stunning average of 13.54 with 22 per innings with the bat. In T20Is, she hadn't been able to replicate the same success, picking up only 22 wickets in 30 matches, but had conceded runs at a fairly restrictive economy rate of 6.23. She was still the highest-ranked Pakistani cricketer in the bowlers and all-rounders global rankings, placed at ninth and tenth, respectively. Her experience on the big stage was also disregarded.

By then, it wasn't really about form, numbers or performances in a domestic tournament. The power struggle between such a prominent player and the administration had reached ugly levels.

Breaking from her usually diplomatic public persona, Sana took to Twitter soon after her omission: 'Don't blame a clown for acting like a clown. Ask yourself why you keep going to the circus.'

Bismah, who was caught in the crossfire, made her position public. 'It was a tough decision to leave out Sana Mir,' she said at the press conference. 'I wanted to have her in the squad over which I, along with the selection committee, had deep deliberations. We had to decide between her and the emerging players who had been impressing on all the stages.'

Sana, under whose captaincy Urooj quit her playing career, was ousted. On 25 April 2020, she announced her retirement from the game, two years earlier than she had originally intended. 'I wanted to play cricket in an environment where I was happy. Playing cricket like this was frustrating me. As a player, that you could not be vocal about anything was going against my core self. I thought it was better for me as well as the team to move on.'

What Sana foresaw in her battle with the administrators was something which Andy Richards also picked up on when he visited the team during their preparation in Australia before the most high-profile women's World Cup in history. The team looked out of sorts to him.

'It was painful to see all our work undone, all in a matter of months,' Richards notes. 'We'd got them to a stage where they were doing really well. But at the World Cup, they had no clear plans or guidelines of what they were doing.'

Pakistan had a horror show at the tournament, worse than any had predicted.

Placed in Group B with England, the West Indies, South Africa and Thailand, they had a shot to finish in the top two and qualify for the semi-finals. South Africa defeating England, one of the favourites, in their opening encounter did complicate matters a bit, but they still stood a chance.

The tournament started well for Pakistan as they dominated the West Indies with an eight-wicket win. It was a clinical victory in every sense. All the bowlers played their part in restricting the West Indies to 124; so did each of the four batters, who chased down the score with ten balls to spare. The eight-wicket victory was a sign that they meant business and could possibly lock horns in a three-way battle for the title with England and South Africa.

In the next match against England, at the Manuka Oval in Canberra, they weren't expected to win, but after keeping the opposition to a fairly competitive 158 for 7, their batting failed them. Barring Aliya Riaz's 33-ball 41, there was no credible performance, which eventually led to them falling 42 runs short of the total.

With two must-win games to play, the biggest blow from the England match was an injury to Bismah Maroof. The captain had fractured her right thumb and required surgery. She was ruled out of the tournament, and the mantle of captaincy at a World Cup once again fell on Javeria Khan's shoulders.

Up against a South African team on a roll, Pakistan started well after they were asked to field. Diana Baig's double blow up front reduced them to 17 for 2 and, at the halfway mark, South Africa stood at 54 for 3. However, Laura Wolvaardt's counter-attack – an unbeaten 36-ball 53 – helped her side to 136 for 6.

It was a fairly tough chase on a slowish wicket at the Sydney Showground Stadium, and the Pakistan players' early struggles with the bat put them on the back foot, reduced to 26 for 3 in the seventh over. Javeria Khan and Aliya Riaz revived the chase, with Iram Javed also making a late charge, but they couldn't quite provide the flourish the team needed in the final overs. They tottered to 119 for 5 and had to rely on the West Indies to clinch an unlikely victory over England later in the day if they were to stand a chance of qualifying out of the group.

As expected, however, that didn't happen. England crushed the Stafanie Taylor-led side by 46 runs, and that result ended Pakistan's hopes.

The last match against Thailand counted for little. And if pride was at stake, even that was flattened. The Thailand team, in their first World Cup, were inspired. Thailand are amongst the fastest-improving teams in women's cricket, and their spirited performances on the biggest stage, despite losses, earned many admirers. In the final match of their World Cup, Thailand's players tore into the deflated Pakistani attack. Natthakan Chantham scored a 50-ball 56 to help her side amass 150 for 3.

The contest was abandoned due to rain, and the points were shared. Had Pakistan's players come out to bat, maybe it would have been too stiff a chase for them in the prevailing conditions. That they finished fourth among five teams, which included an out-of-form and misfiring West Indies above them, showed just how poorly they had performed. That even Thailand was in the process of beating them added further ignominy to a forgettable campaign.

To make their March 2020 worse, the outbreak of the COVID-19 pandemic brought a premature end to the IWC cycle. With the matches between India and Pakistan yet to be played, and the BCCI yet to offer a walkover, the series was abandoned and the points between the two teams were split equally. The six points from the three ODIs that had seemed to be coming their way, and which would have ensured Pakistan's direct qualification to the 2021 50-over World Cup (which was later postponed to 2022) never materialised. And in turn, with the split points, India qualified directly for the tournament, leaving Pakistan to make its way through the qualifiers.

The year 2020 tested sports bodies in a way that hadn't been seen since the Second World War.

Globally, the sports industry was one of the worst hit. No matches meant no revenue, and job losses and pay cuts inevitably followed. But as unorganised as the PCB had historically been, it managed to navigate through the tricky challenges with both skill and empathy. It is possible that the PCB sensed an opportunity to solve another issue while dealing with the problems posed by the health crisis.

The rising death toll made people apprehensive about congregating, let alone travelling to play. For cricket boards to revive their economies in the midst of the raging pandemic, they needed allies. In these tragic times, the PCB were among the earliest to offer help to other cricket boards and agreed to send their team abroad to play under strict health and safety guidelines.

This decision gave the PCB an opportunity to revive their own cricketing economy. At a time when terrorism wasn't perceived as the most feared threat to life, and despite the hassles and insecurities brought on by living in a bubble, by agreeing to tour other countries the PCB earned themselves a huge amount of goodwill which would help bring international cricket back to Pakistan on a full-time basis. Scheduled talks with the boards of New Zealand, Australia and England were fast-tracked, and each agreed to send their men's team to Pakistan for the first time in nearly two decades. Before that, the Babar Azam-led team travelled to England, New Zealand and South Africa in the space of one year.

Despite uncertainties everywhere, the PCB were able to revive cricket. While the financial crunch had forced most boards to seek profitability and, as a result, cut down on several women's matches, domestic cricket and the junior men's team, the PCB kept their cricket calendars busy. Even in these difficult times, they went ahead with most of their domestic tournaments and even sent their 'A' team for a tour to New Zealand.

During the months of no cricket in the mid-2020s, Pakistani women players, who were without contracts, faced the consequences of the economic meltdown – as did people in most parts of the world. The players who were contracted by the board or ZTBL were fortunate, but those who had lost contracts following the removal of departments from the game suffered financially. Following several rounds of requests, the PCB bailed out unemployed Pakistani women cricketers – who didn't have any means of financial sustenance – with a three-month retainer of PKR 25,000. They also agreed to send their women's team to play in South Africa and Zimbabwe in January 2021.

In October 2020, a national camp was organised, and a new head coach was hired. David Hemp, a former English domestic cricketer who had played 24 internationals for Bermuda and had coaching experience with Melbourne Stars in the WBBL was entrusted to take Pakistan cricket further. It was a brief glance at Pakistan's matches during the 2020 World Cup that convinced him there was potential talent to work with.

'I'd seen some of the players and I knew that the skill levels were there. There was obvious talent. The challenge was around consistency in performance, like a lot of teams that aren't ranked highly.'

Following the success of Mark's tenure, the PCB were less hesitant in appointing another foreign coach. It was a novel welcome for Hemp, who had never travelled to the country. 'You get on the roads, you see a lot of traffic, and you see a lot of bikes – from the left lane and right, going at 90 miles an hour. And the next thing you see is a bike with four or five people and two kids on the handlebars.

'It was a bit different, but from the first moment I felt very welcome, as if I'd been there longer than I actually was. Everybody was very accommodating, very open.'

Most cricket tours are usually filled with new experiences – places discovered, cuisines tried and friendships forged – but the tour to South Africa was unlike any other. For as novel as the experience was, of playing in a bio-bubble, it wasn't what the players were looking forward to. Apart from matches and practice sessions, they were stuck in their rooms and a common area in the team hotel, spending a good part of their time bingeing on TV shows and playing online mobile games.

The safety protocols also forced the 17-member contingent to practise in small pods. The teams were split into four groups and were trained by different members of the support staff, including the strength and conditioning coach and the analyst. Hemp tried to look on the bright side. 'Because there were small groups, you were able to get some quality work done, and we did. A lot more time goes into planning it out, but it worked well with the restrictions that we had.'

When the matches began, Pakistan looked like a jaded version of themselves. Against a South African side that was without the injured captain Dane van Niekerk and vice-captain Chloe Tryon, they lost 3–0 in the ODIs and 2–1 in the T20Is.

For most of the ODIs, Pakistan were chasing, and it was primarily due to the efforts of Nida Dar and Aliya Riaz in the middle order – the two most improved cricketers under Mark's tenure – that they could go as far as they did in giving the hosts a scare. Although Nida was an experienced cricketer and Aliya was an upcoming talent, both of them were late bloomers in the game – by Pakistani standards.

For a long time, Nida's cricketing philosophy was an extension of her personality: jovial and carefree. Growing up, she enjoyed Salman Khan movies and 'fan-girled' over Shahid Afridi's style of play. Her cricket reflected that style. Even though she had remained a part of the core that had been forged under Sana Mir since making her debut as a 23-year-old in 2010, she often misfired. At her best, she was instrumental in Pakistan bagging both the Asian Games gold medals and had also scored a century in an unofficial ODI. Despite evident talent, however, her batting philosophy of swiping everything out of sight often proved costly.

The exclusion from the 2017 World Cup side was the turning

point, and under Mark she realigned her thought process and approach to the game.

Her earlier attitude had possibly been misplaced. As a loud prankster with funky hair-dos most people found funny, she wasn't always viewed as a serious cricketer by outsiders. Soon after taking over, Mark received similar feedback on her personality. 'When I first asked the selectors about Nida, they would reply, "Not very good, a troublemaker. You won't get anything from her, a bits and pieces cricketer." So, she wasn't selected. I remember telling all the cricketers who weren't selected that I would be willing to give them my thoughts.'

Nida's serious version turned up to question Coles. 'Is the door closed on me?'

Coles, still unsure of where her chances stood, responded, 'I don't know what is going to happen to me. But if I'm around, you need to get a bit fitter, and then we can work on a few other things.'

Over the next few months, he noticed that Nida was willing to work on the feedback and showed the coach that she was willing to put in the hard yards expected of her. 'Every domestic tournament that she was involved in, I could see her running in the field after the game, getting fitter. Her body shape changed tremendously, working in the gym, doing extras.'

The transformation was so significant that in the two years under him, she became the team's best T20 cricketer. A sign of that improvement was a contract with Sydney Thunder to play in the 2019 WBBL season – making her the first Pakistani woman to get interest from a foreign league.

The journey was a bit different for Aliya, who made her debut in 2014 as a 22-year-old. Tall and strong, she was a natural athlete from Rawalpindi, who had played several sports growing up. Even though her cricketing talent was evident early on, it took her some time to find a permanent place in the team. A batting all-rounder who could bowl medium pace, her utility came best in the lower order – a spot no player had been able to adequately fill before her. Her ability to control play as well as attack with the bat was a rarity.

That Aliya and Nida could be consistently good together in the middle order, a long-time weak link of the team, enabled the side to play the quality of cricket they did on the 2019 tour of South Africa.

' They were at it again, in the same country, in 2021 – but with a different coach.

Hemp had entered the Pakistan set-up with several plans, but at an uncertain time. With women's international cricket cut down and barely any domestic matches to give them some action, much of his assessment of the team was made in training camps. He had expressed his desire to push the team to the top four in the world – a spot where they could have found themselves in the ODI rankings had the pandemic not abruptly ended the IWC season. But in real terms, they were still not there, and Hemp had limited opportunities to take the team higher with the cricketing calendar so badly affected.

In his first international assignment, there were three specific players who stood out – Nida Dar, Aliya Riaz and Diana Baig. Yet again, Javeria Khan was leading the side in the absence of Bismah Maroof, who had pulled out for personal reasons.

The first ODI, which also happened to be the first international match they had played in nearly a year, was enough to deflate their spirits. After restricting South Africa to 200 for 9 at Kingsmead in Durban, their batting was found wanting on a slowish pitch. By the 41st over, they were reduced to 137 for 8, with only Nida Dar left to marshal the tail. She did that expertly in the company of Diana Baig, who threw her bat around for a breezy 34-ball 35. They brought the match down to the last ball, with Baig needing to hit a four off Nadine de Klerk. She couldn't, and the hosts went one up.

'That loss shattered our confidence massively,' admits Hemp. 'Getting so close and not getting over the line whacks you a bit. It takes it out of you mentally, not just physically.'

If there was any opportunity to recover from that situation, it was downed by a similar script in the next game, where they were reduced to 73 for 5 in a 253-run chase. Nida Dar and Aliya Riaz resurrected the innings with a 111-run partnership (at that time the highest for the sixth wicket by Pakistan but bettered by the same duo later in the year). The former fell soon after scoring her second consecutive half-century, but Riaz's counter-attack kept Pakistan in the chase. Fatima Sana, in the lower order, played her part with a run-a-ball 22, but her team eventually fell 13 runs short of South Africa's total.

'We got close again, and then we panicked a bit,' said Hemp. 'And then we got away from what we were doing so well for so long. That's got a lot to do with the history of not winning enough. Once winning becomes a habit, you learn to win from different situations. That was the challenge.'

After having given Pakistan two opportunities to make a comeback, South Africa left nothing to chance in the third ODI. Despite getting a 79-run start by openers Lizelle Lee and Laura Wolvaardt, the hosts were bowled out for 201, courtesy of Diana Baig's 4-fer. All the Pakistani batters got starts but were undone by the pace duo of Shabnim Ismail and Ayabonga Khaka and leggie Sune Luus, who combined to bag nine wickets as Pakistan's innings was shut out on 169.

As the tour wore on, the fight began to fade in the Pakistan players. In the first T20I, their 124 was chased down in 19 overs. The 16-year-old Ayesha Naseem provided glimpses of her hard-hitting powers. Kainat Imtiaz, who had transformed from a medium-pacer with a slinging action to a batter who could bowl, scored a useful 24, but there wasn't much else to take away – and it was a similar story in the second match of the series.

Aliya Riaz, leading in the absence of the injured Javeria Khan, held the fortunes of her team's batting yet again. Chasing 134, Pakistan ended on 115. The manner of the defeats, coupled with the experience of being stuck in a bubble, had made it a tour they all wanted to finish as soon as possible.

'The challenge with COVID is that you can't leave the hotel, you can't get away from cricket,' Hemp explains. 'You can't walk on the beach, see different faces or go to the cinema. You're waking up, going for breakfast, having meetings, going to training, coming back, having your dinner and going to sleep. You do that over and over again. It's important to clear your head at times, switch off from cricket. We tried to do movie nights, have game nights, but you're around the same set of people all the time. It can be mind-numbing.'

The tour wrapped up on a sweet note, though, with a victory in the final, albeit inconsequential, T20I. Javeria Khan had returned to the side and notched up an unbeaten 56 to lead Pakistan to 127 for 6. Anam Amin's miserly spell and double blow early on had kept South Africa to 68 for 4 in 12.3 overs when rain stopped play. As per the DLS method, the visitors were eight runs ahead. Even as the target looked close, with rain reducing the equation, Pakistan had played out their perfect game, according to their coach.

There was little time for them to celebrate that win, however, as a series was announced against Zimbabwe mid-tour. Unfortunately, it had to be abandoned after a solitary one-dayer, as Emirates Airlines cancelled its operations from Harare to Dubai for 15 days – bringing a sudden end to the challenge.

Even though the players, who were eager to return home, weren't complaining, Hemp believes playing more cricket against Zimbabwe would have served them well. 'The South Africa series was frustrating. Across all those games we had opportunities, some better opportunities than others. That series against Zimbabwe would have boosted the confidence of our girls massively. We missed out on that.'

✧✧✧

Cricket, by itself, was hard to come by during the first year of the pandemic. Even training had taken such a hit that, only a few months earlier, with COVID-19 raging at its peak, Diana Baig had to travel nearly 850 kilometres to train.

Brought up in conservative Gilgit-Baltistan, in the hilly northern parts of Kashmir, she had defied her family's order to concentrate on academics, and the neighbourhood's disapproval of women playing in the open. Cricket wasn't a sport she could pursue in school, where she played football, basketball and athletics. But at home, along with her cousins, there were competitive battles. 'I really liked Abdul Razzaq,' admits Diana. 'He could bat as well as bowl. He was a complete all-rounder. I used to believe that my elder brother was also like Abdul Razzaq, because he would play really well against his friends. I idolised him, and since he only made me bowl at him, I was always fired up to get him out. There was only a small space inside the house to run in and bowl, so I learned to put spin on the ball, do whatever I could to get him out.'

Picked as an 18-year-old in 2013, it took her nearly four years to get a consistent run in the team. She was a standout athlete – the best fielder Pakistan has produced by a distance and also a footballer with international caps. However, the COVID-19 pandemic brought a halt to cricket and training.

'After playing non-stop cricket for nearly two years, the COVID-19 break allowed us time to spend with our families. But the moment we had to resume cricket, it was a bit of struggle. In order to have a certain rhythm, you have to be playing regularly. When I went home, there were no facilities to train.

'It was also a tough time, but we all tried to stay in touch with cricket. Most of the players live in Lahore or Karachi – where there are other facilities to train. But not much has changed in Gilgit over the last ten years. There were no net facilities back then, there are no net facilities now. No girls were going out to play then, no girls are going out to play now. I was stuck at home all the time.

'After a while, even though COVID-19 was at its peak, I came to Lahore and stayed at the university hostel to resume my practice. Since cricket training wasn't allowed back then, I would go early in the morning for practice, when there was no one around.'

When cricket resumed and the PCB managed to hold camps, Hemp's concerns were different. His long-term plans of taking the team higher up the rankings – and helping the players go up as well – had taken a massive beating with the uncertainties of the cricket calendar.

'It was a frustrating year. We were trying to get together with Sri Lanka on a number of occasions, but it kept getting cancelled due to COVID. Even the qualifiers in Zimbabwe got postponed. We didn't know how we were going to go.'

All they could do within their limitations was organise training camps and play inter-squad games, or at times play against the Under-16 boys' team. 'There isn't a large pool of players,' continues Hemp. 'After a point, the players get to know each other, and you need reasonable competition. There are ways in which you can do it, but it can get really frustrating when you plan for something and it gets knocked back.'

The alterations of the schedules and the challenges he noticed with the players unable to close out games encouraged the design of his training methods – with a similar vision to that which Mohtashim had: back a few players and work on them to come good.

Net sessions were reduced, and the emphasis fell on putting players in match scenarios, forcing them to make more decisions while practising. It didn't necessarily bring immediate results for the team but showed up in the improved performance of individual players – especially batting all-rounder Omaima Sohail, Muneeba Ali and pace bowler Fatima Sana.

It was also reflected in their next series, which was played in July 2021, when Pakistan visited the Caribbean with a squad of 26 players. It was an interesting decision by the board to send two teams to play international matches as well as 'A' games, providing greater exposure to a larger pool.

The West Indies players were pleasant hosts, though not on the field. Pakistan took time to warm up to the conditions, but by then, both the ODI and T20I series had been lost. But fans, even if few, were back in the stadium and were witness to Nida Dar becoming the first Pakistan cricketer to bag 100 T20I wickets when she dismissed Deandra Dottin in the tenth over of the first match. She bowled a tidy four-over spell, returning 2 for 15, but West Indian pace bowler Shamilia Connell's three wickets ensured that Pakistan remained ten runs short in their 137-run chase.

In the rain-affected second T20I, Pakistan were left to chase 111 in 18 overs after the West Indies had scored 125 for 6. However, the visitors brought about their own downfall with five out of six players being run out. Even as Nida Dar and Aliya Riaz braved their way through in tricky conditions, they could only manage 103.

The hosts completed a clean sweep with a more dominant display in the third match. Veteran off-spinner Anisa Mohammed and skipper Stafanie Taylor shared seven wickets to bowl out Pakistan for 102. Diana Baig and Anam Amin had put the West Indies in trouble early on in the chase, but Taylor's unbeaten 43 helped them cruise to a six-wicket win.

Taylor's all-round dominance continued in the ODI leg as well as they thumped Pakistan in the first three of the five-match series before Fatima Sana's combined nine wickets over the next two games gave the visitors consolatory wins.

The lack of matches and the barren run of victories had a damning effect on the spirits of the team. Irrespective of the individual improvements, there wasn't much encouragement coming through on the cricketing front.

Pakistan cricket, which was reviving itself, received another massive blow on 17 September 2021, when the New Zealand men's team decided to walk out of the tour before even playing a match.

Ramiz Raja, a former international skipper and one of the leading voices of Pakistan cricket, had been recently appointed as chair, returning to the PCB administration after nearly 17 years. His desperate pleas could do little to stop the visitors from leaving once they believed there was a security threat. (A New Zealand player's wife had received a message from the email address hamzaafridi7899@gmail.com.) Even before the New Zealand cricket officials could share details about the issue, the team – which was set to play its first match in Pakistan since 2002 – had left the country.

Information minister Fawad Chaudhry and interior minister Sheikh Rashid claimed that it was a hoax email sent by a person living in India. Cricketers, administrators and celebrities expressed their anguish over New Zealand's decision and, possibly aware of its larger repercussions, even tried to hail Pakistan's security record. With England set to tour next, the British High Commissioner was also requested to testify to the safety arrangements made by the cricket board.

None of it worked. England, set to travel to Pakistan for the first time since 2005, also backed out. 'There is the added complexity for our men's T20 squad,' the English Cricket Board stated. 'We believe that touring under these conditions will not be ideal preparation for the T20 World Cup, where performing well remains a top priority for 2021.'

Beyond this, no rationale was offered as to why the women's team didn't travel for their scheduled three one-dayers either. It would have been their first-ever series in Pakistan.

Once again, the PCB had to depend on the West Indies Cricket Board. Former skipper Merissa Aguilleira supported Pakistan's efforts in bringing back cricket, and the board sent its team for a three-match one-day series, which was to serve as a preparation for the World Cup qualifiers.

But Pakistan's preparations were disrupted yet again – this time by several players testing positive for COVID-19, shortening the training camp. Even as the hosts were whitewashed, a few positive signs emerged. Anam Amin, the fine left-arm spinner whose fitness standards were a concern, shone through with nine wickets at a economical rate. Similarly, the tall, bespectacled, left-handed opener Muneeba Ali, who had been persisted with for four years without many performances to justify her inclusion, scored her maiden half-century.

With Sana Mir retired, Bismah absent for over a year due to injuries and childbirth, and Javeria not in the best form, Pakistan's results weren't impressive in the post-Coles era. And as intense as Javeria could be with her preparations, she would retreat into her shell if things were not going the way she had hoped. A lot of the pressure during this period was soaked up by Nida Dar, Aliya Riaz and Diana Baig, and the situation also forced the younger players to put themselves in positions of responsibility.

In the World Cup qualifiers that followed, they were handed a loss by Bangladesh despite Aliya Riaz and Nida Dar scoring a record 137-run partnership. The tournament was called off after rising COVID-19 cases in the country, and Pakistan qualified on the basis of its pre-tournament ranking.

Even though Pakistan's cricketing performances slipped after 2019, beyond the field, several key changes took place.

✧✧✧

While women's cricket continues to get foster-parent treatment, the outlook of the board itself has come a long way: from being indifferent, to being unsupportive, to causing hindrances, to letting them play. On many occasions, the PCB has used women's cricket as a front to enhance its global image or to bring international cricket back to the country. Whatever the reason, these efforts have served to help the sport and the players.

On 4 May 2021, triggered by Bismah Maroof's decision to take a break from the game due to her pregnancy, the PCB rolled out a last-minute parental policy. This not only offered women cricketers paid leave but also a contract extension and support programme to reintegrate them into the game – a decision far ahead of other Asian nations.

Had it been in place a few years earlier, the likes of Nain Abidi could have benefited enormously from it. Having last played for Pakistan in 2018, she moved to the USA and became a mother the following year. Even though women would usually retire from playing cricket after marriage, Nain Abidi felt she had a few more years of cricket left in her and wanted to pursue her ambitions in her adopted homeland.

The road back to playing professional sport wasn't easy; she had to wade through a series of physical, emotional and financial strains. For several months after giving birth, she suffered from severe back and wrist pain. With her husband out at work for nearly two weeks every month, she spent several days in isolation with a baby in a distant land when she tested positive for COVID-19 – having to take care of herself as well as the child. 'It was a period of incredible lows,' she reflects. 'I wanted to cry and scream. There were times when I would think, "Should I be doing all this?" Mentally, I was exhausted. When your hormonal levels drop, it feels like you've lost everything. There were a lot of people around trying to tell me how a child should be raised. That just added to the stress.'

After several months of working on her fitness, she juggled the demands of motherhood and professional sport to make a return. However, a few days before the start of a national championship, which could have helped her return to international cricket, her husband sprained his ankle and she had to skip the event to be by his side.

She couldn't achieve what she desired but gave hope and a new outlook to many others.

Bismah had it easier. For as unlucky as she has been to miss out on centuries and on opportunities to lead the side in World Cups, and battling numerous injuries, there are also reasons to believe that she is possibly the most fortunate of them all.

For girls not from financial and politically influential sections of society or from army backgrounds, support to play cricket is often tough to find. For Bismah, it was a seamless process, with parents, relatives, neighbours, partner and in-laws being supportive of her interest and encouraging her to pursue her passion regardless of the stage of life she was in. She isn't the rebellious kind and probably would have come to terms with social limitations had they been imposed on her. In turn, she set new benchmarks and aspirations for the coming generation of women cricketers.

In her post-cricket career, Qanita Jalil is working as a fitness trainer in Australia, while Kainat Imtiaz's mother and Nazia Nazir, along with nine other women, are officiating as umpires in Pakistan. Sana Mir, Marina Iqbal and Urooj Mumtaz have regular commentary stints on cricket broadcasts, while Batool Fatima is coaching kids. Asmavia Iqbal is serving as a selector, and Ayesha Jalil is handling cricket operations. Many other women have entered the cricket space and gained prominence by talking about the game as presenters, journalists and YouTubers.

In a country with a population of more than ten million women and girls, 86 have succeeded in representing Pakistan in its most popular sport, defying odds and achieving honours despite the system rather than because of it. There isn't a lot of cricketing success to show over the 25 years, yet within the few moments of glory – Kiran Baluch and Shaiza Khan's efforts in the 2004 Karachi Test, the two Asian Games gold medals, the two World Cup victories against India, Sana Mir's rise to the No 1 ranking, and a few odd wins against England and South Africa – Pakistan players have managed to bring about several important changes, some at the national level, but mostly locally.

Ayesha Naseem and Qanita Jalil in Abbottabad, Nida Dar in Gujranwala, Saba Nazir in Muridke, Nazia Nazir in Haveli Lakha, Sajjida Shah in Kotri, Diana Baig in Gilgit, Nahida Khan in Chaman and many others have opened doors for women in conservative towns and villages to step outside and play.

The cricket itself is extending beyond big cities. Even as Karachi and Lahore continue to be the hub for women's cricket, the top three players in the current national team are Nida Dar, Aliya Riaz and Diana Baig, who hail from the small towns of Gujranwala, Rawalpindi and Gilgit, respectively.

One of Pakistan's most promising talents is the 16-year-old Ayesha Naseem from Abbottabad. She is big and strong and can muscle the ball as very few can in world cricket. Even though she was exposed to cricket in Karachi, where her father worked for a few years, her professional career began in 2015 when she represented Abbottabad. Her talent was evident early on, and she was soon selected for the national squad. Several colleges from Lahore and Karachi invited her to join, knowing that she wouldn't be able to pursue her cricket in the orthodox town of Bagan in Abbottabad. Tempting as the offers were, however, she passed them up. She has greater motivations in life.

'The village from where I come, people don't even let their daughters step out of their homes, let alone play cricket,' Ayesha says. 'My family received complaints from people in the neighbourhood for letting me play cricket. It's that criticism that's driving me to greater heights. A lot of my friends are incredibly talented but are unable to play because they don't have the support of their family. I'm playing from Abbottabad so that parents can see for themselves what their daughters can achieve if they are given the freedom to play.'

Playing cricket, and the accompanying fame, have also had a significant effect on the social lives of those from the metropolitan cities of Lahore and Karachi. Nain's act of returning to cricket after motherhood opened doors for many others who believed it wouldn't have been socially acceptable. That Nain could reach such an inspirational position was thanks to her discovery that a women's team even existed after Kiran Baluch's record double ton. That Kiran could achieve what she did was because Shaiza fought against convention and put a team together against all odds.

Cricketers have become role models. With Bismah making a career after marriage and motherhood, she has set a new norm for women.

For decades, politics has acted on society, and society on cricket. Now, there is hope that cricket will start acting on society. At least there are signs of a start.

The rogue elements are still out on the streets, threatening women who play cricket, much as they did to Shaiza more than three decades ago. But they cannot influence the minds of parents who want to see their daughters follow in the footsteps of those women they see representing Pakistan on TV, in newspapers and on billboards. The theory that women playing cricket is an unholy act doesn't find as much acceptance any more. Hadeel Obaid, who runs late-night tape-ball matches during the month of Ramadan for young girls in Karachi, continues to face threats from religious groups. She hasn't bothered to entertain their warnings and, over the five years of successfully running the events, she has seen the number of threats by extremists reduce. More parents come along with their daughters each year and stay back to watch them play until 3.00 a.m.

Shaiza and Sharmeen, in their pursuit of personal ambitions, allowed many others to aspire and achieve, and the achievements of each passing cricketer continue to spread the light of hope far and wide, to distant towns and villages. In treading a tough path, the 86 women who have so far represented Pakistan have left behind an easier trail for others to walk on – aspiring cricketers as well as those who simply wish to step outside. And that, without doubt, is one of the greatest legacies anyone in sport has ever created.

ACKNOWLEDGEMENTS

THE IDEA FOR this book occurred in 2019 when, relegated to a portion of the couch, my knee needed rest, but the rest of me wasn't ready for it. Over the next three years, I got an opportunity to deep dive into the story of Pakistan women's cricket, which remained my source of escape when the world around us was crumbling, minds numbed and spirits deflated.

Through the course of these months, more than a hundred hours of audio files were transcribed, rendering the late-night cups of chai ineffective and often exhausting me into sleep. But as tiring as the process of researching, interviewing and writing this story was, it wouldn't have been possible without the help and support of numerous people who joined me in this journey – a debt that I may not be able to repay.

At some point, for a few fleeting hours, this project was a shared dream with Ahsan Nagi, who unfortunately couldn't ultimately be a part of it. Nevertheless, he lived through the entire journey, making life easier for me – not only facilitating interviews but also helping me reach out to people from various walks of life who would aid my understanding of Pakistan far beyond the cricket field. He entertained my endless phone calls, messages and requests, becoming my go-to person for everything I needed for the book, and he took a considerable amount of time out from his already hectic schedule to ensure that everything was in order for the story. In simple terms, I couldn't have written this book without him.

To tell a story of Pakistan women's cricket, it was obvious that I needed many to trust a stranger from India. Afia Salam was the first one to do that. Not only did she provide me with an extensive understanding of cricket, history, politics, culture and society but also opened access to several other people.

Shaiza Khan was one of them, without whom the story of Pakistan women's cricket itself wouldn't have been told. It took a long time for her to agree to speak for this book, but when she did, it made my life so much easier.

Like her, many cricketers, coaches, administrators and journalists often spent several hours, sometimes over multiple sittings, sharing their journeys and understanding – some sharing personal experiences, some providing the ring-side view, some who could recollect details with great precision, some who could provide the unpopular perspective. Some great, descriptive storytellers of the cricket on the field, some who only seemed to remember the drama and the fun times off it. Some master readers of personalities and some who could expertly explain the big picture. Some who told the stories of cricket, some who gave me lessons on Pakistan's history and politics. Some who opened up their library of resources, some who directed me to a wealth of information elsewhere.

Ali Khan, Amita Sharma, Andy Richards, Aisha Jalil, Aliya Riaz, Anuradha Dutt, Asmavia Iqbal, Aroob Shah, Ayesha Naseem, Aun Jafri, Batool Fatima, Bismah Maroof, Chander Shekhar Luthra, David Hemp, Diana Baig, Faizan Lakhani, Fatima Sana, Gemaal Hussain, Hadeel Obaid, Isabelle Duncan, Javeria Khan, Kainat Imtiaz, Kiran Baluch, Lisa Sthalekar, Mahwash Rehman, Marina Iqbal, Mark Coles, Meher Minwalla, Mehmood Rasheed, Mohtashim Rashid, Munizae Jahangir, Nahida Khan, Nain Abidi, Nida Dar, Nikhila Natarajan, Nooshin Al Khadeer, Pramila Bhatt, Purnima Rau, Ramiz Raja, Rishad Mahmood, Roha Nadeem, Rumana Ahmed, Saba Nazir, Sadia Iqbal, Salma Khatun, Sana Mir, Shahid Hashmi, Shamsa Hashmi, Shoaib Ahmed, Shubhangi Kulkarni, Sidra Nawaz and Snehal Pradhan, in different ways, played a massive part in helping me with the research for the story. It helped immensely that Sami ul Hasan ensured that access to all of PCB's resources were made available without a second request.

There were few who shared my enthusiasm for this story as much as Jodie Davis did. Not only did she extensively detail her own experiences, she also shared her rich collection of photographs and newspaper clippings, which made the research on the early days of Pakistan cricket that much easier. Similarly, the efforts of many other journalists, writers and scorers, who have recorded bits and pieces of this story over the years, have proven to be of immense help.

Osman Samiuddin, Bharat Sundaresan and Shamya Dasgupta provided support at different stages of the process – research, writing and publishing. Karunya Keshav was around through it all and much more, often calming my insecurities about writing this story.

Samod Sarngan was one of the earliest to believe in this story and even tried to handhold me through the research and writing process before eventually giving up out of frustration. But in the process, he offered me direction and some invaluable advice.

Garima Srivastava was only a chai-bribe away from making her phone available for use as a recorder for several interviews and helping me get in touch with a few people for the book. Shoaib Kalsekar helped me understand various practices and writings of Islam relevant to the story, apart from being my unofficial Urdu translator.

As disinterested as Arka Banerjee and Rashmi Ramesh are in the subject of cricket, they were the first people to hear the stories from me. They offered their perspective and help at different times.

My colleagues at Cricbuzz remained ever-present. Ganesh Chandrasekaran, Purnima Malhotra and Shirshendu Roy were always only a phone call away. Atif Azam played the translator's role for the interviews of the Bangladesh cricketers. Kaushik Rangarajan, Prakash Govindasreenivasan, Pratyush Sinha and Tristan Holme read, edited and offered suggestions when I felt stuck through the writing process.

Although not entirely surprised, getting a book published on women's cricket was tough, tougher than I had initially anticipated. Kanishka Gupta took the story to publishers and Peter Burns of Polaris Publishing and Karthika V.K. of Westland Books put their trust in it.

Kamila Shamsie was generous enough to spare time from her busy schedule to write the foreword for this book at short notice, so were Raf Nicholson, Aatif Nawaz, Firdose Moonda, Lawrence Booth, Ebba Qureshi and Tim Wigmore, who read the final draft and sent in their reviews.

Most importantly, my family and friends, who have remained my constant source of love, encouragement and support through the tough and the good times, were there for me again, as always.

Shaiza Khan	Sharmeen Khan	Abida Khan
Aisha Jalil	Kiran Baluch	Maliha Hussain
Meher Minwalla	Najmunissa Ismail	Shabana Kausar
Shahnaz Sohail	Sultana Yousaf	Nazli Istiaq
Asma Farzand	Nazia Nazir	Nazia Sadiq
Ruksana Khan	Sadia Butt	Shazia Hassan
Deebah Sherazi	Kiran Ahtazaz	Mahewish Khan
Muqudas Khan	Khursheed Jabeen	Sajjida Shah
Uzma Gondal	Zehmarad Afzal	Batool Fatima
Huda Ziad	Rabiya Khan	Sabeen Rezvi
Mariam Butt	Maryam Butt	Shabana Latif
Mariam Agha	Urooj Mumtaz	Armaan Khan
Asmavia Iqbal	Qanita Jalil	Sabahat Rasheed
Sana Javed	Sana Mir	Tasqeen Qadeer
Shumaila Mushtaq	Humera Masroor	Bismah Maroof
Nain Abidi	Sumaiya Siddiqi	Sadia Yousuf
Almas Akram	Javeria Khan	Nahida Khan
Sania Khan	Naila Nazir	Sukhan Faiz
Marina Iqbal	Kanwal Naz	Nida Dar
Shumaila Qureshi	Mariam Hasan	Masooma Junaid
Sidra Ameen	Rabiya Shah	Kainat Imtiaz
Elizebath Khan	Iram Javed	Javeria Rauf
Anam Amin	Maham Tariq	Sidra Nawaz
Aliya Riaz	Diana Baig	Ayesha Zafar
Ghulam Fatima	Nashra Sandhu	Aiman Anwar
Muneeba Ali	Natalia Pervaiz	Omaima Sohail
Fareeha Mehmood	Fatima Sana	Sadia Iqbal
Rameeen Shamim	Syeda Aroob Shah	Saba Nazir
Kaynat Hafeez	Ayesha Naseem	

STATISTICAL HIGHLIGHTS

TEST RECORDS

Highest Score: Kiran Baluch (242) vs West Indies, 2004 **(world record)**

Highest Partnership: Kiran Baluch-Sajjida Shah (241) vs West Indies, 2004

Best bowling figures in a match: Shaiza Khan (13/226) vs West Indies, 2004 **(world record)**

Best bowling figures in an innings: Shaiza Khan (7/59) vs West Indies, 2004

Youngest debutant: Sajjida Shah made her Test debut at the age of 12, making her the youngest debutant in Test cricket

ODI RECORDS

MOST RUNS

Player	Matches	Runs	Average	Strike Rate	HS	100/50
Javeria Khan	116	2874	28.74	62.76	133	2/15
Bismah Maroof	108	2602	27.97	56.83	99*	0/14
Sana Mir	120	1630	17.91	43.23	52	0/3
Nain Abidi	87	1625	20.83	49.73	101*	1/9
Nahida Khan	62	1318	23.53	63.57	79	0/8

MOST WICKETS

Player	Matches	Wickets	Average	Economy Rate	Strike Rate	Best Bowling
Sana Mir	120	151	24.27	3.7	39.3	5-32
Sadia Yousuf	59	78	22.78	3.75	36.3	5-35
Nida Dar	84	74	31.01	3.99	46.5	4-15
Asmavia Iqbal	92	70	36.2	4.65	46.6	3-15
Shaiza Khan	40	63	23.95	4.36	32.9	5-35

MOST CATCHES

Player	Matches	Catches
Sana Mir	120	42
Javeria Khan	115	34
Bismah Maroof	108	34
Nain Abidi	87	27
Nida Dar	84	22

WICKETKEEPING RECORDS

Player	Catches	Stumpings
Batool Fatima	51	46
Sidra Nawaz	32	12

HIGHEST PARTNERSHIP (FOR EACH WICKET)

Wicket	Players	Runs	Opposition	Venue	Year
1	Nahida Khan, Javeria Khan	96	England	Kuala Lumpur	2019
2	Nahida Khan, Javeria Khan	133*	Ireland	Colombo	2017
3	Javeria Khan, Bismah Maroof	117	New Zealand	Lincoln	2016
4	Bismah Maroof, Nida Dar	181	Ireland	Dublin	2013
5	Bismah Maroof, Nida Dar	91	Sri Lanka	Dambulla	2018
6	Nida Dar, Aliya Riaz	137	Bangladesh	Harare	2021
7	Sana Mir, Asmavia Iqbal	66	Sri Lanka	Karachi	2005
8	Shaiza Khan, Batool Fatima	49	Netherlands	Karachi	2001
9	Nida Dar, Diana Baig	60*	South Africa	Durban	2021
10	Sana Mir, Sadia Yousuf	23	India	Derby	2017

HIGHEST INDIVIDUAL SCORES

Players	Runs	Opposition	Venue	Year
Javeria Khan	133*	Sri Lanka	Sharjah	2015
Javeria Khan	113*	Sri Lanka	Dambulla	2018
Nain Abidi	101*	Ireland	Dublin	2012

WICKETKEEPING RECORDS

Player	Catches	Stumpings
Batool Fatima	51	46
Sidra Nawaz	32	12

HIGHEST PARTNERSHIP (FOR EACH WICKET)

Wicket	Players	Runs	Opposition	Venue	Year
1	Nahida Khan, Javeria Khan	96	England	Kuala Lumpur	2019
2	Nahida Khan, Javeria Khan	133*	Ireland	Colombo	2017
3	Javeria Khan, Bismah Maroof	117	New Zealand	Lincoln	2016
4	Bismah Maroof, Nida Dar	181	Ireland	Dublin	2013
5	Bismah Maroof, Nida Dar	91	Sri Lanka	Dambulla	2018
6	Nida Dar, Aliya Riaz	137	Bangladesh	Harare	2021
7	Sana Mir, Asmavia Iqbal	66	Sri Lanka	Karachi	2005
8	Shaiza Khan, Batool Fatima	49	Netherlands	Karachi	2001
9	Nida Dar, Diana Baig	60*	South Africa	Durban	2021
10	Sana Mir, Sadia Yousuf	23	India	Derby	2017

HIGHEST INDIVIDUAL SCORES

Players	Runs	Opposition	Venue	Year
Javeria Khan	133*	Sri Lanka	Sharjah	2015
Javeria Khan	113*	Sri Lanka	Dambulla	2018
Nain Abidi	101*	Ireland	Dublin	2012

BEST BOWLING FIGURES

Players	Bowling figures	Opposition	Venue	Year
Sajjida Shah	7-4	Japan	Amsterdam	2003
Sana Mir	5-32	Netherlands	Potchefstroom	2010
Urooj Mumtaz	5-33	West Indies	Karachi	2004

HIGHEST TEAM SCORES

Score	Opposition	Venue	Year
280/7	Ireland	Dublin	2013
277/4	Netherlands	Fatullah	2011
271/5	Ireland	Colombo	2017

BIGGEST VICTORY MARGIN (BY RUNS)

Victory margin	Opposition	Venue	Year
193	Netherlands	Fatullah	2011
157	Ireland	Dublin	2013
153	Japan	Amsterdam	2003

BIGGEST VICTORY MARGIN (BY WICKETS)

Victory margin	Opposition	Venue	Year
9	Ireland	Colombo	2011

SMALLEST VICTORY MARGIN (BY RUNS)

Victory margin	Opposition	Venue	Year
4	West Indies	Karachi	2004
12	Sri Lanka	Sharjah	2015
20	West Indies	Karachi	2004

SMALLEST VICTORY MARGIN (BY WICKETS)

Victory margin	Opposition	Venue	Year
1	Netherlands	Karachi	2001

MOST WINS (OPPOSITION WISE)

Opposition	Matches	Won	Lost	NR
Ireland	18	12	6	
West Indies	33	9	24	
Sri Lanka	30	9	21	
Netherlands	12	7	4	1
Bangladesh	11	6	5	
South Africa	24	4	19	1
Japan	1	1	0	
Scotland	1	1	0	
Zimbabwe	1	1	0	
New Zealand	13	1	12	
Denmark	1	0	1	
England	11	0	10	1
India	10	0	10	
Australia	12	0	12	

NOTEABLE RECORDS

BEST BOWLING: Sajjida Shah picked 7 for 4 against Japan - the best figures in women's ODIs

MOST DISMISSALS IN AN INNINGS BY A WICKETKEEPER: Batool Fatima has effected six dismissals in an innings twice in her career - vs West Indies in 2004 and vs Sri Lanka in 2011. Only New Zealand's Sarah Illingworth and India's V Kalpana have effected six dismissals in an innings, but only once.

MOST RUNS AGAINST AN OPPOSITION: Javeria Khan's 472 runs in 11 innings is the most by any player against Ireland Women

MOST WICKETS AGAINST AN OPPOSITION: Sadia Yousuf's 24 wickets in 10 matches is the most by any player against Ireland Women

YOUNGEST DEBUTANT: Sajjida Shah made her ODI debut at the age of 12, making her the youngest debutant in international cricket

LONGEST INTERVAL BETWEEN APPEARANCES: Nazia Sadiq, who made her debut for Pakistan in the 1997 world cup and was also a part of the first-ever Test match, didn't play an international game for 11 years and 41 days before becoming a part of the national team for the 2009 tour of Ireland, where she also featured in the first-ever T20I played by Pakistan

MOST RUNS WITHOUT A CENTURY: Bismah Maroof sits on top of that pile with 2602 runs, closely followed by South Africa's Trisha Chetty

T20I RECORDS

MOST RUNS

Player	Matches	Runs	Average	Strike Rate	HS	50s
Bismah Maroof	108	2225	27.46	92.82	70*	11
Javeria Khan	105	1895	22.03	93.76	74*	9
Nida Dar	108	1207	15.08	96.02	75	4
Nain Abidi	68	972	18	79.21	56	3
Sana Mir	106	802	14.07	70.66	48*	0

MOST WICKETS

Player	Matches	Wickets	Average	Economy Rate	Strike Rate	Best Bowling
Nida Dar	108	103	18.16	5.38	20.2	5-21
Sana Mir	106	89	23.42	5.51	25.5	4-13
Sadia Yousuf	51	57	17.82	5.81	18.3	4-9
Anam Amin	57	57	20.01	5.42	22.1	4-16
Asmavia Iqbal	68	44	22.75	5.97	22.8	4-16

MOST CATCHES

Player	Matches	Catches
Nida Dar	108	34
Bismah Maroof	108	30
Sana Mir	106	26
Nain Abidi	68	22
Asmavia Iqbal	68	18

WICKETKEEPING RECORDS

Player	Catches	Stumpings
Batool Fatima	11	39
Sidra Nawaz	18	27

HIGHEST PARTNERSHIP (FOR EACH WICKET)

Wicket	Players	Runs	Opposition	Venue	Year
1	Javeria Khan, Javeria Rauf	123*	Ireland	Solihull	2013
2	Sidra Ameen, Bismah Maroof	99*	Bangladesh	Delhi	2016
3	Javeria Khan, Bismah Maroof	109	Bangladesh	Cox's Bazar	2014
4	Bismah Maroof, Nida Dar	93	India	Providence	2018
5	Bismah Maroof, Javeria Khan	83	West Indies	Providence	2011
6	Aliya Riaz, Ayesha Naseem	65	South Africa	Durban	2021
7	Ayesha Naseem, Fatima Sana	69*	West Indies	North Sound	2021
8	Sana Mir, Sidra Nawaz	35	Australia	Providence	2018
9	Sana Mir, Aliya Riaz	30	New Zealand	Nelson	2016
10	Almas Akram, Batool Fatima	20	India	Taunton	2009

HIGHEST INDIVIDUAL SCORES

Players	Runs	Opposition	Venue	Year
Nida Dar	75	South Africa	Benoni	2019
Javeria Khan	74*	Ireland	Providence	2018
Bismah Maroof	70	Bangladesh	Lahore	2019

BEST BOWLING FIGURES

Players	Bowling figures	Opposition	Venue	Year
Nida Dar	5-21	Sri Lanka	Kuala Lumpur	2018
Nida Dar	4-5	Malaysia	Kuala Lumpur	2018
Sadia Yousuf	4-9	Ireland	Dublin	2013

HIGHEST TEAM SCORES

Score	Opposition	Venue	Year
177/5	Malaysia	Kuala Lumpur	2018
172/5	South Africa	Benoni	2019
167/3	Bangladesh	Lahore	2019

BIGGEST VICTORY MARGIN (BY RUNS)

Victory margin	Opposition	Venue	Year
147	Malaysia	Kuala Lumpur	2018
58	Bangladesh	Cox's Bazar	2018
55	Sri Lanka	Sharjah	2015

BIGGEST VICTORY MARGIN (BY WICKETS)

Victory margin	Opposition	Venue	Year
10	Ireland	Solihull	2013
9	Ireland	Dublin	2013
9	Bangladesh	Bangkok	2016

SMALLEST VICTORY MARGIN (BY RUNS)

Victory margin	Opposition	Venue	Year
1	India	Galle	2012
1	England	Loughborough	2013
2	India	Delhi	2016

SMALLEST VICTORY MARGIN (BY BALLS)

Victory margin	Opposition	Venue	Year
1	Sri Lanka	Colombo	2018
2	South Africa	Pietermaritzburg	2019

SMALLEST VICTORY MARGIN (BY WICKETS)

Victory margin	Opposition	Venue	Year
1	Sri Lanka	Colombo	2018

MOST WINS (OPPOSITION WISE)

Opposition	Matches	Won	Lost	Tied	NR
Bangladesh	15	14	1		
Ireland	14	12	2		
South Africa	18	7	11		
Sri Lanka	13	6	6		1
West Indies	16	3	10	3	
India	11	2	9		
Malaysia	1	1	0		
Netherlands	1	1	0		
Thailand	2	1	0		1
England	14	1	13		
New Zealand	8	0	8		
Australia	10	0	10		

To be noted: Pakistan have lost all the three tied games in the Super Over.

MOST RUNS AGAINST AN OPPOSITION: Javeria Khan's 381 runs in 14 innings is the most by any player against Bangladesh Women, followed by Bismah Maroof's 367 runs in 11 innings

CAPTAINCY RECORDS

Captain	Matches	Won	Lost	Drawn
Shaiza Khan	3	0	2	1

ODIs

Captain	Matches	Won	Lost	Tied	No Result
Shaiza Khan	40	8	32	0	0
Sana Javed	4	0	4	0	0
Urooj Mumtaz	26	4	21	0	1
Sana Mir	72	26	45	0	1
Bismah Maroof	18	10	6	1	1
Javeria Khan	17	3	14	0	0
Sidra Nawaz	1	0	1	0	0

T20Is

Captain	Matches	Won	Lost	Tied	No Result
Sana Mir	67	27	37	2	1
Bismah Maroof	38	16	21	1	0
Javeria Khan	16	5	10	0	1
Aliya Riaz	2	0	2	0	0

SELECT BIBLIOGRAPHY

Wounded Tiger: A History of Cricket in Pakistan, Peter Oborne, Simon & Schuster UK Ltd.

The Unquiet Ones: A History of Pakistan Cricket, Osman Samiuddin, Harper Sport

The Fire Burns Blue: A History of Women's Cricket in India, Karunya Keshav and Sidhanta Patnaik, Westland Sport

Skirting the Boundary: A History of Women's Cricket, Isabelle Duncan, The Robson Press

Insha'Allah Democracy, Mohammed Ali Naqvi

'Strong Arms: the story of Pakistan women's cricket', Kamila Shamsie, *The Cricket Monthly*, 16-10-2019

'Darkness Descends: 1977-1988', S Akbar Zaidi, *The Dawn*, 17-10-2017

Pakistan Women Cricket Association, Letter by Tahira Hameed to President, Board of Control for Cricket in Pakistan, 15-10-1978

Pakistan Women Cricket Association, Letter by Tahira Hameed to Lt Col Rafi Naseem (Secretary, Board of Control for Cricket in Pakistan), 29-09-1979

Pakistan Women Cricket Association, Letter by Lt Col (Retd) Rafi Naseem (Secretary, Board of Control for Cricket in Pakistan) to Iqbal Dar (President, PWCA), 26-01-1980

2nd Open Women Cricket Tournament, Letter by Tahira Hameed to President, Board of Control for Cricket in Pakistan, 03-03-1981

Affiliation of Pakistan Women Cricket Association with BCCP, Letter by Tahira Hameed to Air Marshall M. Noor Khan, (President, Board of Control for Cricket in Pakistan), 04-05-1981

Letter by Tahira Hameed to Chief Justice (Retd) A.R.Cornelius, 18-10-1981

'The song remains the same', Nadeem F Paracha, *The Dawn*, 06-05-2013

'Man behind PPP's anthem passes away as "Dila Teer Bija" lives on', Rafay Mahmood, *The Express Tribune*, 04-01-2019

'37 named for women's cricket camp', *The Dawn*, 01-05-1997

'PWCCA an officially recognised body', APP, 13-11-1997

'Blonde Aussie guru on Qadir, cricket and girls in Pakistan', Nikhila Natarajan, *The Indian Express*, 21-12-1997

'Pakistan women cricketers may never play again', *The Dawn*, 06-01-1998

'Noareen, S., & Naz, A. (2021). Women's Emancipation during Musharraf Era (1999-2008)'. *Global Political Review*, VI(I)

'In Memorium: A valuable innings cut short', Shazia Hasan, *The Dawn*, 23-12-2018

Veteran Journalist Najam Sethi Arrested, letter by Ann Cooper (Executive Director, The Committee to Protect Journalists) to Nawaz Sharif, 10-05-1999

'Remember when Ireland played their first Test?', Raf Nicholson, *The Cricket Monthly*, 09-05-2018

'Pakistan Women defeat MCC', Rick Eyre, ESPNCricinfo, 13-08-2000

'Meet Shaiza Khan, the Pakistan women's captain', Tanya Aldred, *The Guardian*, 29-08-2000

'Platinum-Gold', Ardeshir Cowasjee, *The Dawn*, 15-10-2000

'Well begun... half done', Afia Salam, *Women's Cricket International*, 2000

'They came, they saw, they conquered', Afia Salam, *Women's Cricket International*, 2001

'PCB Scrutiny Committee Meeting on Women Cricket', PCB, 18-07-2002

'Scrutiny of Women's Cricket in Pakistan', PWCCA, 17-10-2002

'Scrutiny of Lahore based Women Cricket Associations conducted', PCB, 29-10-2002

'PCB to take over women's cricket affairs in Pakistan', PCB, 11-1-2003

'Shaiza, Sharmeen and Kiran elected MCC members', ESPNCricinfo, 24-01-2003

'PCB files petition against PWCCA', *The Dawn*, 23-07-2003

'PWCCA gets IWCC recognition', *The Dawn*, 16-08-2003

'Ramiz trying to sabotage tour', PWCCA, 12-02-2004

'ICC saves Women's World Cup', Scott Heinrich, BBC, 27-06-2004

'Women Cricketers accuse Shahryar of favouritism', *The Dawn*, 22-12-2004

'Women cricket championship from March 1', *The Dawn*, 19-02-2005

'ICC takes over running women's game', ESPNCricinfo, 03-04-2005

'HR activists beaten as police foil marathon bid', Amjad Mahmood, *The Dawn*, 15-05-2005

'Pakistan cricket set for shake-up', Jenny Thompson, ESPNCricinfo, 03-08-2005

'Boost to women's cricket', *IRIN News*, 23-08-2005

'PWCA critical of PCB women wing', *The Dawn*, 28-10-2005

'Shaiza to lead Karachi', *The Dawn*, 18-02-2006

'Cricket to make Asian Games debut in 2010', Asian Cricket Council, 20-04-2007

'Uphill battle in the search for a level-playing field for Pakistan's women cricketers', Isaam Ahmed, *The Guardian*, 29-10-2007

'Still in the nets', Amber Rahim Shamsi, *Himal Mag*, 09-12-2008

'The World Cup beckons', Urooj Mumtaz, ESPNCricinfo

'A good beginning', Urooj Mumtaz, ESPNCricinfo

'Pakistan's women struggle for recognition', Reuters, 03-03-2009

'Under the aunties' wing', *The Dawn*, 05-04-2009

'Sana replaces Urooj as Pakistan women's skipper', *The Nation*, 05-05-2009

'Azra Parveen serves notice to PCB chief', *The Dawn*, 14-05-2009

'Pakistan's women issue writ against PCB', ESPNCricinfo, 27-05-2009

'Prolific Urooj to resume cricket after studies in UK', *The Dawn*, 11-08-2010

'The Golden Girls', *The Dawn*, 05-10-2010

'I dealt with PWCCA in PCB's interest: Zakir', Shazia Hasan, *The Dawn*, 15-11-2009

'Efforts for women's cricket to go on despite ill health: Shirin Javed', Shazia Hasan, *The Dawn*, 23-12-2009

'PCB women's wing holds first-ever meeting', *Business Recorder*, 05-01-2010

'BCCI not to send cricket teams to Asian Games', PTI, 01-06-2010

'Bushra Aitzaz to replace seasoned official: Shirin Javed quits as women wing's head at PCB', *The Dawn*, 04-11-2010

'Pakistan women break taboos in winning Asian gold', Reuters, 21-11-2010

'Sana Mir warned by PCB over remarks', *The Dawn*, 10-06-2011

'Shiv Sena protests against Pakistani players in HIL', Reuters, 14-01-2013

'Pakistan women's matches shifted to Cuttack', Amol Karhadkar, ESPNCricinfo, 18-01-2013

'Bajrang Dal slams Pakistan's cricket matches in Cuttack', IANS, 22-04-2013

'A chance for Pakistan's women to grow in stature', Raf Nicholson, 03-07-2013

'Female Pakistani cricketers in sexual harassment row', M Ilyas Khan, BBC News, 11-07-2013

'PCB bids farewell to Bushra Aitzaz', 22-11-2014

'Sana Mir - Trailblazer, Captain, Icon, Purnima Malhotra', Cricbuzz, 18-02-2017

'India v Pakistan, women's edition', Snehal Pradhan, *The Cricket Monthly*, 19-04-2018

'All "cool" in Nida Dar's world', Cricbuzz, 03-10-2019

'And the maidens started swinging it', Cricbuzz, 19-02-2020

'Cricket coach Mark Coles moved to Pakistan for a job that paid nothing - it changed his life', Jehan Casinader, stuff.co.nz, 09-08-2020

'Life in a bubble - the Nida Dar diary', Cricbuzz

'Juggling cricket with a toddler in tow', Cricbuzz, 28-07-2021

'When Iqbal Bano Defied Zia's Dictatorship To Sing "Hum Dekhenge" At Alhamra', Ali Madeeh Hashmi, Naya Daur Media, Medium.com, 04-09-2019